A PROSPECT OF RICHMOND
Janet Dunbar

The people and events—famous and infamous, great and small—that have shaped Richmond's unique character over 900 years are here brought vividly to life. Only fifteen minutes by train from the hustle and bustle of London, Richmond has retained its picturesque charm as the author most clearly shows.

JANET DUNBAR

A Prospect of Richmond

REVISED EDITION

WHITE LION PUBLISHERS LIMITED
London, Sydney and Toronto

This White Lion Edition 1973
Reprinted 1977

ISBN 85617 995 7

Made and printed in Great Britain
for White Lion Publishers Limited,
138 Park Lane, London W1Y 3DD
by Hendington Limited,
Lion House, North Town, Aldershot, Hampshire.

For
My Grandchildren

Acknowledgments

I wish to express my thanks to the following for valued assistance in the preparation of this book: Mr Gilbert Turner, Librarian of Richmond-upon-Thames Public Libraries, Mrs Christine Blyth, the Reference Librarian, and her colleagues; Mr Edward Croft-Murray, Mr S. O. Ellis, Mrs Rosemary Burton, Mr John Gloag, Mr R. Alpe, Mr R. S. S. Allen; the officials of the Manuscript Room, British Museum, and the Controller, H.M. Stationery Office. Mr James Pope-Hennessy kindly gave permission to quote from his *Queen Mary*, and the Rev. R. S. Mills allowed me to use material from his talks on Petersham. I also thank the Controller, H.M. Stationery Office, for permission to quote from the *Greater London Plan*, 1944.

I am indebted to Mr Gilbert Turner for bringing the fine Hilditch painting to my notice; and to Mr Edward Croft-Murray, Lady Hesketh, Mrs Hélène Winslow, Mrs Marion Ward, the Directors of the Richmond Royal Horse Show, the Manager of the Richmond Ice Rink, the Trustees of the British Museum, the Director of the Royal Botanic Gardens, and the Richmond-upon-Thames Libraries Committee for permission to reproduce prints, paintings, and photographs; and to the Duke of Northumberland for permission to reproduce the rear endpaper.

The index has been compiled by Lysbeth Merrifield.

Contents

Illustrations

PLATES IN HALF-TONE

A PROSPECT OF RICHMOND

Illustrations

MAPS AND PLANS

COLOUR PLATES

Introduction

RICHMOND, in Surrey, famous for the wonderful view from its Hill over the "Matchless Vale", is not a suburb of London: that is perhaps one of the astonishing things about it. Only fifteen minutes by fast train from Waterloo Station, it remains recognisably what it was in the eighteenth century—a self-contained little town that is still mainly Queen Anne and Georgian in its centre.

The story of Richmond is a right royal one. The pageant of kings and queens begins in early medieval times, and it has continued up to the present age. The history of England can be traced through the history of Richmond, and the day-to-day existence of the common people everywhere in the realm quickens into vivid life in the records of this riverside resort.

Richmond is an ancient town, but it is not a museum. Change and decay are inevitable, renewal and growth a condition of nature. From the sixteenth century onward, inhabitants of the town cried Woe and behold! when familiar buildings came down to make way for a newer look: from the eighteenth century onward, householders held Indignation Meetings when there was a danger of the Rates Going Up. Patterns of thought and behaviour repeat themselves in fascinating variations. Disapproving Richmond fingers pointed at the dissolute nobles of the 1500s, the outlandish Carolean fashions of the 1600s, the uninhibited raffishness of the 1700s, the Sabbath-breakers of the 1800s—just as they point to the gaudy goings-on in our own day. But Richmond has always been a place to come to, if you want to enjoy yourself, disapproving fingers or no.

The Prospect changes—and remains essentially the same. To the Reader, I offer the lines of Aubrey, a great lover of this beautiful town:

> I have [herein] mixed Antiquities and natural things together; they will be of some use to those who love Antiquities, and on that account I expose them to the Candid Reader, wishing him as much pleasure in the reading of them as I have had in the writing of them.

CHAPTER ONE

———◆◆◆◆◆———

Beginnings

TRADITION has it that Edward the Confessor, "delighting in the fair scenery", called the tiny hamlet on the banks of the Thames by the name of Syenes, the expressive Saxon word which signified everything that was bright and beautiful. Perhaps the prospect was enhanced by the sparkling river, winding through the water meadows below a hillside crowned with trees. The settlement was, in fact, not much more than a collection of fishermen's huts with a few cultivated strips behind, but Syenes—bright and beautiful— Edward found it and Syenes it became, until another king re-named it Rychemond nearly five centuries later.

There are no records of the first house of any size to be built by the side of the Thames at this place, but it is probable that there was a simple manor-house in 1066; the usual structure of wood, roofed with thatch, containing a central hall, or 'houseplace', a lean-to at the back for a kitchen, and a loft over the hall. It is possible, too, that the lady of the manor did what she could to keep out the draughts with embroidered hangings; after all, Matilda of Flanders was stitching away at the Bayeux Tapestry, and the Norman ladies who followed their lords over to England in the wake of the conquering William were accustomed to a more comfortable standard than the rude Saxons.

The first manor-house at Shene of which there are records belonged to Henry I. A manor was a unit of measurement. The counties were divided into 'hundreds' and the hundreds into manors; the manor contained a large house and the demesne (or domain) which belonged to the local lord; the villeins, the peasants, had primitive cottages and a few roods of land. Round the hamlet of Shene, the land was divided into two Fields: Upper Field and Lower Field, the line of demarcation being approximately where

[1]

Sheen Road and Paradise Road are now. These fields were further sub-divided into 'shots', a Saxon measurement of land: a shot, or 'furlong', was the length of the furrow before the plough was turned. The approximate boundaries of the local shots, related to present-day streets, are given in an appendix. Parkshot is the only name to survive from those far-off days.

The manor-house which came into the possession of Henry I in the twelfth century would have been a country house of the period, still with a large central hall, but with a few rooms built out of it. The manor was self-supporting, the peasants tilling the fields and being allowed a few strips of their own for wages. All land was on lease from the lord of the manor, the names of the holders being inscribed in the Court Rolls. Henry had a turbulent people to govern and foreign enemies to circumvent, and he was an absentee landlord as far as Shene was concerned. The manor next appears in the records as belonging to one Belet, who held it by virtue of his service as cup-bearer to King Henry—an important office, and one much coveted by the nobles. The original Belet—or Belot, as it was sometimes spelt—had come over from Normandy with the Conqueror, and fought at Hastings. His name appears in the Roll of Battle Abbey, as printed in Holinshed. He was rewarded with a grant of serjeantry: lands in Surrey which he held by personal service to the King, this office to descend to his heirs.

The last male Belet, Michael, held the office in the reign of King John, but he offended that dictatorial sovereign, and was deprived of his lands. After allowing time to cool the King's anger, Belet sued for pardon, and got himself reinstated, after paying King John a fine of 500 marks—a huge sum. The manor then descended through the distaff side, Belet's daughter, Emma Oliver, leasing some of the land to Master William Kilkenni, Archdeacon of Coventry, for five years, "with all the fruits of the said land now there, and with demesnes, homages, rents, villeinages, fisheries, meadows, feedings, pastures."

By the time of Henry III, a number of houses for the courtiers and royal household had been built near the manor-house, which was now too small for the accommodation of the Court. It was probably a structure of wood and masonry, containing a large hall with a minstrels' gallery and an open timber roof, covered with wooden shingles on the outside. There was an upper chamber, a solar, or

[2]

Anno Ros ze oktaus awage henrich vii taurerez regie illustrissimi
ordinata y hervgani zuvek So regie ... ...iditislan : ...

Henry VII, Builder of Richmond Palace

Richmond Palace from the Green, 1680

F. Gasselin.

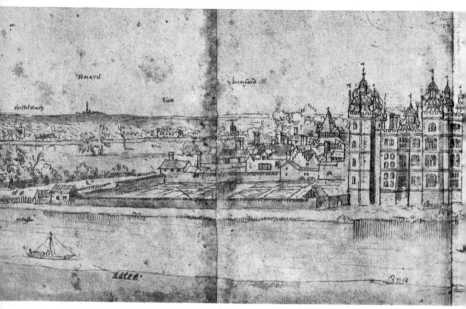

Richmond Palace, 1562

A. v. d. Wyngaerde.

Richmond Palace, 1638

F. Hollar.

MONT

RICHMOND

J. Siberechts.

A Prospect of Richmond

withdrawing-room, a chapel, a room for dresses called the ward-robe, kitchens, pantries, and a buttery. The interior of the hall was plastered, painted, and gilded. At one end was a daïs, with a bay window behind, and there were probably many fine decorative features along the walls of the great hall, for Henry III was noted for his patronage of painters and gilders, and possessed fine taste himself.

The manor had reverted to the Crown by the reign of Edward I, and though he and his queen, Eleanor of Castile, sometimes came to Shene, they did not live there for any length of time. When they visited the manor there was generally a tourney—a combat between equal parties of knights. Each knight had to swear that he entered the tourney solely as an exercise in arms, and not to satisfy any private quarrel, but this vow was often honoured in the breach rather than in the observance: tourneys became bloody affrays, in which the combatants were only too ready to pay off old and new scores. The tourneys were held on the field before the manor-house (now the Green) and were begun with considerable pomp and ceremony, the knights riding round the place of tourney preceded by pages bearing aloft their personal standards, while the king and queen, surrounded by the Court, sat on a raised platform outside the gates of the manor-house. This platform was a gorgeous sight, draped with hangings of brilliant colours picked out with gold.

The manor-house was now finely furnished. Queen Eleanor had brought with her from her native Spain the idea of using carpets as floor-coverings. It had long been an Eastern and Moorish custom to hang fine carpets on the walls of houses; knights returning from the Crusades were familiar with this fashion. In Spain, thicker carpets were laid on the floors, and the Queen introduced them at Shene, together with tapestries for the great hall and her own chamber. It was an era of exquisite embroidery. The ladies of the Court had little else to do but ply their needles, and they copied Norman and Spanish designs, embroidered hangings and covers for their beds, and borders for their best garments. In the evenings they played at chess, or draughts, with ivory draughtsmen, and some of them would sing to a lute accompaniment. It was pleasant to sing in unison, or divide for a round; that new song, *Sumer is icumen in*, was becoming known through travelling minstrels, and the charming melody was easily learnt.

[3]

The Court did not come often enough to make much difference to the few hundred people who lived in the small village of Shene. Their way of life followed the pattern of the seasons, as it had done since time out of mind. The men worked on the land for the lord of the manor from dawn until mid-afternoon, then cultivated their own strips. The women, helped by the children, spun thread on distaff and spindle; that new-fangled invention, the hand-turned spinning-wheel, was coming into use, but no villein's wife could afford such a labour-saving contrivance. She had plenty to do; besides helping her husband on his strip of land, she brewed the small ale, baked the bread, and cooked the coneys which he snared in the woods, or the fish he caught in the near-by Thames.

It was a hard life, but not an unduly oppressive one. The peasant, as well as his betters, had acquired valuable rights through Magna Carta, which the hated King John had been forced to sign. One of its provisions ran:

> No Freeman, Merchant, or Villein shall be excessively fined for a small offence; the first shall not be deprived of his means of livelihood; the second, of his merchandise; the third, of his implements of husbandry.

There were simple amusements. Children played at Hoodman Blind, a form of Blind Man's Buff, in which the 'he' had a sack slipped over his head as he tried to catch the others. A band of strolling-players would pass through Shene on their way to Windsor, and set up a stage at the end of the village street; or a minstrel would stop for the night, sitting in one of the cottages while everyone crowded in to hear the newest songs from London, which few of them had seen. Jugglers were especial favourites; there was often competition to give them bed and board in return for an extra sight of their marvellous feats.

It was in the fourteenth century that Shene became a regular royal residence. Edward II was away fighting wars or quelling rebellions for much of his unhappy reign, and did not often come to the manor, but his terrible consort, Isabella of France, "the she-wolf queen", had her eye on the perquisites to be got from Crown property. In 1327, "in furtherance of a resolution of Parliament", her creatures there were able to get her a handsome number of gratuities which included "the Manor of Shene, in the county of Surrey, of the value of £30 a year," for her services in the matter of the treaty with France. She constantly meddled in affairs of State, bedevilled the proceedings of government, appropriated to herself vast amounts from the treasury, took her husband's enemy, Mortimer, as paramour, plotted the King's death, and still managed to die in her bed years later: an achievement, considering the bitter enemies she made·all through her life.

Men were quick to draw sword or dagger in those dangerous times. If the aggressor was a peasant he might, if not caught and summarily executed, quietly disappear into another county; the villeins stuck by each other, and an extra pair of hands to help with the work was always welcome. A man of rank or position could not efface himself so easily. He generally sued for pardon, and there are many entries in the Court Rolls of items like this one: "Pardon to Simon son of Maurice de Petresham for the death of John son of Walter Paroles of Shene." Servants took advantage of a master's death. The heirs of John de Bereurco, of the manor of Shene, laid a suit against Hubert de Swyneford, his yeoman, who,

> immediately after the death of the said John, with the assent of others of the servants, asserting that he had a charter of feoffment of the said John, which the jury said was made by fraud, intruded himself into the said manor and still holds the same.

The local records have curious items of suits at law brought during the reign of the next king, Edward III. Benedict de Fulsham applied to the Barons of the Exchequer for his rights. He told them, through a counsel whom he had prudently retained, "that he, when he was the late King's butler, caused by the King's order by word of mouth without any other warrant, seven tuns of wine to be placed in the manor of Shene." He was being refused payment because he had no written warrant for the delivery of the said wine. Surely the new king would discharge the debt? There is no record of the result of this plea.

Edward III was always prodigal of money; the continual wars with France ate into the exchequer, and there was one time when his queen, Philippa of Hainault, gave up her crown and all her jewels, which her lord pawned to the Flemish merchants. He went even further—"he pawned the person of his valiant kinsman, the earl of Derby, who actually gave himself up to personal restraint, while Edward stole away with his queen, and the child she nourished [John of Gaunt], to Zealand." Edward was only able later to redeem his long-suffering kinsman by threatening the Commons that "he himself would go to Flanders and surrender his royal person to his creditors." Coin was scarce, and the Commons granted the King the fleece of the ninth sheep and the ninth lamb throughout England.

The King was not one to learn by experience. The royal establishment at Shene was on a scale of magnificence hitherto unknown. A great many chambers had been added, together with courtyards and extra kitchen quarters. A manuscript in the Harleian Collection gives a list of Edward III's household at Shene. It included many knights, esquires, clerks of the pantry, buttery, spicery, cellars, kitchens, and other domestic offices. There were chaplains, a physician, an apothecary, several butlers, tailors, master-bakers and their underlings, standard-bearers, ushers, carpenters, coopers, smiths, engineers, hundreds of archers and men-at-arms, artificers and workmen attached to the armoury, falconers, horse-servants. The chamberlains and great officers of the household had numerous servants of their own—all paid from the royal purse.

It was a brilliant Court, destined to be described by one of the greatest of early English poets, who was there in person. Geoffrey Chaucer held various official positions at Court, but he spent a good part of his time writing poetry and reciting it at gatherings of the nobility. He came under the patronage of the Queen, and has left a charming picture of a bevy of ladies at Shene, going to see jousting in front of the manor-house:

> The surcoats white of velvet, well sitting
> They were iclad, and the seams each one
> As it were [in] a manner garnishing,
> Was set with emeralds one and one . . .
>
> . . . and each on her head
> A rich fret of gold, which, without dread,
> Was full of stately rich stones set;
> And every lady had a chaplet.

A banquet at Shene must have been a magnificent spectacle. The King and Queen and the royal family sat under a canopy on the daïs at the end of the hall—the "high table"—waited on by the King's carver, server, and cup-bearer. The table glittered with gold plate, the wine-goblets were studded with precious stones, the knives and spoons had ivory and silver hafts. The nobles and their dames sat at long trestle tables covered with fine linen, eating from silver plates, drinking from silver tankards or wine-cups. Servants hurried from the buttery and the cellars, carrying trays of food, superintended by the Lord High Steward, wearing his chain of office. In the gallery, musicians heralded the arrival of every dish at the high table with a flourish on their stringed instruments, and a young esquire carried in the wassail bowl, with its embossed cover of silver gilt. The whole scene glowed with splendour: the richly hued silks and velvets, the vermilion and azure of the armorial shields painted on the walls, the glittering gold furnishings at the royal table on the daïs.

Edward III and Philippa of Hainault had a long married life, which ended when the Queen died of a dropsy at Shene, after an illness which lasted for two years. Edward had not been a notably faithful husband—there had been an episode of the attempted seduction of the Countess of Salisbury which had set the tongues whispering—and after the Queen's death he scandalised the Court and infuriated his relations by giving a share of her jewels and wardrobe to one of Philippa's maids, Alice Perrers. Contemporary accounts of this woman vary widely. One chronicler refers to her roundly as "the King's mistress", another uses plainer language, and Stow calls her "a certaine proud woman, called Alice Pierce, who by overmuch familiaritie that she had with the King, was cause of much mischiefe to the realme." Later historians seem to have taken sides to a surprising degree over what was, after all, a common state of affairs throughout history. The Victorian Agnes Strickland, usually so precise, reluctantly "feared that the King's attachment to this woman had begun during Philippa's lingering illness", but quickly adds: "We will not pursue the subject." Folkestone Williams, equally Victorian but more partisan, applies whitewash very thickly and does not find it at all surprising that Edward III should have a fatherly interest in this accomplished

[7]

woman, and that she "was regarded as a daughter and . . . as a daughter she behaved, probably amusing his leisure by reading romances and playing chess."

The ascertainable facts are that Alice Perrers (or Piers, or Pierce) was a native of Henney in Essex, was of mean birth, and had been a common drudge. "She had not even beauty to recommend her, and owed her advancement solely to a persuasive tongue." How she first came into the Queen's service is not quite clear, but she seems to have had a strong personality, and there is evidence to show that she ingratiated herself with the royal family to such an extent that she shared in all their amusements: "The King caused twelve ladies, including his daughters and Alice Perrers, to be clothed in handsome hunting suits, with ornamented bows and arrows, to shoot at the King's deer."

The King made Alice some very handsome presents, including the manor of Ardington, in Berkshire, which belonged to his aunt; a house and shop in the parish of All Saints, London, the manor of Bramford Specke, and the cancellation of her many debts. These gifts were ostensibly to show the King's thanks for Alice Perrers's kindness to the Queen during her illness; it was the munificence of the presents which caused the disapproving chroniclers of the period to put Alice's enrichment down to a deal more than gratitude. She continued to live in the manor-house of Shene, and she would pass out of the story now if it were not for the further exploits of this remarkable woman. She had such power that she was actually able to interfere in the administration of justice; according to Stow,

> she exceeding the manner of women, sate by the King's justices, and sometimes by the Doctors in the Consistories, persuading and dissuading in defence of matters, and requesting things contrary to lawe and honestie, to the great dishonour of the King.

It was natural to ascribe the King's infatuation to witchcraft, and it was put about that she kept in her pay a friar who used waxen images to get rid of her enemies. There was, in the end, such an outcry against her—she would do anything for money and was responsible for many abuses against the common people— that some of the high officers of State managed to get her banished for a time. But Alice was a woman of resource. There came a day when William of Wykeham needed her help. He was not the kind of man normally to seek assistance from a woman like Alice Perrers, but she possessed information which he needed. Alice said she would assist him on condition that he used his influence to have her re-admitted to Court. William of Wykeham had no choice but to agree, and Alice returned to Shene—and to the King's favour.

The recorded history of Alice Perrers by no means stops there. After the King's death, her enemies in high places were quick to strike again. The Steward of the Household, Sir Richard Scrope, charged her with undue influence over the late King, and interference with the course of justice. Once again she was banished from Court life, and her goods forfeited. However, according to Folkestone Williams, a stalwart partisan of the lady: "This severity defeated its own purpose. One of the most distinguished knights of the Court, Sir William de Windsor, married her." The de Windsor family was connected with Shene, and it was there that Alice had first met the knight. He had been Lord Deputy Lieutenant of Ireland, an important position, "and was the last man in that chivalrous age to ally himself with an infamous woman." No mention is made of the fact that William de Windsor had long been her lover, the liaison starting during the time Alice had been on terms of close intimacy with the King.

Alice had been married before, though there is hardly any mention in the records of her first husband, by whom she had several children—probably two sons and a daughter. Her second marriage silenced her enemies, and established her as a respectable member of society; she had her confiscated lands restored, and ended her days with an honoured title and a solid establishment.

After the death of Edward III, his grandson, Richard, succeeded to the throne. The first heir, the Black Prince, was dead, and Richard, his sole surviving child, had been brought up by his mother in France. A naturally extravagant and pleasure-loving young man, he soon increased the Court, and set a standard of magnificent dress and luxurious living which the nobles were not slow to follow. Agnes Strickland considered that Richard had been reared "with the most ruinous personal extravagance and unconstitutional ideas of his own infallibility." It is clear that he had been spoilt from birth, had an imperious will, and was not a man to be crossed.

Richard married the fifteen-year-old Anne of Bohemia, the eldest daughter of the Emperor Charles IV, born in Prague. It was the usual political, arranged royal marriage, but it turned out to be unexpectedly and unmistakably happy. Anne possessed such a sweet and gentle disposition that Richard quickly became devoted to her. She also had similar extravagant tastes to his own, and was fond of finery; she introduced a new fashion, the horned cap which was the headgear of the ladies of Bohemia and Hungary:

> Two feet in height, and as many in width, its fabric was built of wire and pasteboard, like a very wide-spreading mitre, and over those horns was extended glittering tissue or gauze. Monstrous and outrageous were the horned caps that reared their heads in England directly the royal bride appeared in one . . . at church or procession, the diminished heads of lords and knights were eclipsed by their ambitious partners.

The royal couple liked Shene better than any of the royal manors, and it became their favourite summer residence. The Queen had her own hall, in which she received the wives of important nobles. She also had her bower, opening into a garden where she walked with her ladies—a sweet-scented garden, full of gillyflowers and hollyhocks, pansies and roses. Richard sometimes accompanied her in strolling through this pleasaunce, and there is a charming account of them both walking hand in hand, the King reading aloud from one of the romances which had been translated from the French, and which were beginning to appear in England.

Court entertainments were on a vast scale; Stow states in his *Annales* that ten thousand persons are said to have sat down to the King's hospitable board every day. Even allowing for some exaggeration, there is plenty of evidence to show that both Richard and Anne dipped their hands deeply into the treasury for their banquets and entertainments, always on the most lavish scale. The manor-house must have been an animated sight on these occasions. In the great kitchens, the master cooks directed their assistants to turn the enormous haunches of venison on the spits before the fires; the bakers in the bakehouse made bread and pasties; dozens of scullions ran about at the behest of their superiors, collecting provisions stored in the larder, cider and beer from the huge butts in the buttery, cheese from the pantry. In the cellar, wine was kept in casks, to be broached only by the butler. Everything, except the wine, was home-grown. The orchard at Shene was renowned; here grew pippins and pears, figs, peaches, cherries, mulberries, grapes, medlars, and quinces. The royal cooks had not far to go to gather fruit for their pies. The kitchen garden yielded salads and green vegetables, as well as the many herbs which were used to season food.

The existence of a very large Court at Shene led to the establishment of many more inns to take the overflow of people. There had also been many taverns in the village in earlier centuries, and now they were enlarged, and rooms provided for officials, bishops' chaplains, and other minor dignitaries in attendance on personages at the Court. The inns could not in any sense be described as clean or comfortable, by twentieth-century standards. Their chief business was to sell ale, and they did a thriving trade.

The brewers of ale were mostly women. The ale-wife would put out an 'ale-stake' after every brew—a pole with a bush of leaves at the end. The village ale-conner, or ale-taster, on seeing the stake would go into the tavern and taste the ale; if he did not think it was good enough he had powers to confiscate the whole brew. Ale which came up to standard was allowed to be sold—and after the ale-conner had departed, many an ale-wife promptly doctored her brew with a generous measure of water. There were no general shops; the peasant's wife made rye bread, and cooked food in a primitive oven set on bricks and filled with burning faggots. When these had burned out she raked the ashes to one side and put in the bread, pasties, and perhaps a jointed coney which her husband had caught. When the oven had cooled down the food was cooked. In an iron cauldron supported on a tripod she simmered soup made from peas and beans, and she also had an iron frying-pan for cooking the fish which had been caught—lawfully or unlawfully—in the Thames.

The peasants who lived in their small cottages dotted over the manor lands at Shene were well above the hunger line, but the fantastic scenes of wasteful extravagance which they saw going on at the manor-house roused much sullen anger. Dislike of the King had been growing in London for a long time. His reckless spending was impoverishing the exchequer, his arrogant temper antagonised everyone who attempted to persuade him to pay more attention to the needs of his people and less to the gaudy pleasures in which he indulged at Shene. It was well known that he would not even listen to his Ministers of State, when their advice conflicted with his own obstinate determination to enjoy himself to the utmost. The more sober and experienced Ministers knew that the mutterings of the London citizens were bound to surface at some time.

The fact that open rebellion did not break out was due to the Queen. Anne was extravagant, but she lacked the haughtiness and overweening pride that made Richard so detested. She had a natural nobility which impressed everyone who saw her, and she was as gay as she was warm-hearted and charitable. Anne was always trying to present Richard in a favourable light to his subjects. This was not an easy task. The King's uncles and other powerful nobles had joined a confederacy designed to overrule the authority of the King and virtually rule the country themselves, retaining Richard as a puppet. This underground revolutionary movement met with considerable success; Richard was aware of it, but he was not strong enough to stand up against them. It suited the confederacy to have him at Shene, "enjoying with his customary zest the pleasures by which he took care to be surrounded." There was a war on with Scotland, but the nobles preferred to fight that without interference from their liege lord: they were going to make their own terms when it was over. Richard would be satisfied enough with the mock warfare of his numerous martial tourneys at Shene, where the knights in the King's party had their armour and apparel garnished with white harts and crowns of gold about their necks, while ladies, wearing robes to match, led their gallants' horses by golden chains.

In the circumstances, Richard preferred to keep away from London, and he was seldom seen there. He found it necessary, however, to keep on good terms with its citizens. He was, not surprisingly, often short of ready money, and his transactions with the London bankers were known to everybody. In the year 1392, he asked the citizens, through their bankers, to grant him a loan of a thousand pounds, a request that was peremptorily refused. An Italian merchant offered to advance the loan, whereupon there was uproar, rioting, and bloodshed. The citizens set on. the unfortunate merchant and almost tore him to pieces. If they thought fit to deny the King a loan, who was a foreigner to presume? Richard was exceedingly angry, and retaliated. As the city did not keep the King's peace, he said, he would take back her charters, and remove the courts of law to York. This was a serious prospect for the citizens, who cooled down, and asked the Queen to mediate for them and turn the King's wrath.

Anne now had more influence than anyone else over her husband, and she was able to persuade him to 'forgive' the London citizens. The King consented to go on a progress through the city, and so on August 29th, 1392, a splendid cavalcade set out from Shene for London, the King riding on a fine horse with gilded trappings. They were followed by practically the whole Court, decked out in their richest attire, with a small army of servants in attendance. At London Bridge the Lord Mayor, Venner, presented the Queen with a white palfrey, and the King with two white horses, their trappings of gold cloth embroidered with red and white, and hung with silver bells. To these were added a rich crown of gold, garnished with pearls and gems.

The city was packed with people, and there was an unfortunate incident when the crowds rushed forward to catch a sight of the King and Queen on London Bridge, which was encumbered by fortifications and barricades guarding the drawbridge towers in the centre and the gate towers at each end. The Queen's maids of honour were in a *charrette*, a benched wagon lined with scarlet cloth, and as the throng pressed forward, this conveyance was overturned:

> Lady rolled upon lady, one or two were forced to stand for some moments on their heads, to the infinite injury of their horned caps, all were much discomposed by the upset, and, what was worse, nothing could restrain the laughter of the rude, plebeian artificers; such a reverse of horned caps did not happen without serious inconvenience to the wearers. At last the equipage was righted, the discomfited damsels replaced, and their charrette resumed its place in the procession.

King Richard duly addressed the citizens, pointing out the error of their ways, gave back the city key and sword to the Lord Mayor, and restored their ancient privileges. The citizens were grateful, and further presented the King with two gilt basins containing two thousand gold nobles, and a silver-gilt engraved and enamelled table, valued at a thousand marks.

It would have been cheaper to have lent him the thousand pounds in the first place.

The glittering progress through London was an occasion never to be forgotten by those taking part, and it was destined never to be repeated. In 1394, plague was raging in London, and many people fled the city, some of them coming to Shene. It is probable that Anne caught the infection from one of these: she was taken ill at Whitsuntide, and died within a matter of hours. At first Richard could not grasp the fact that she was really dead. She was the one human being he had cared for with a deep and enduring love, and it seemed impossible that she should no longer be at his side. When at last he had to face his loss he became half crazed with grief and rage. His wrath turned itself on the place where he had been so happy: he cursed Shene, every stick and stone of it, and gave orders that the manor-house should be pulled down. Then he took his place in the great cortège which accompanied the coffin of Anne of Bohemia to London, the nobles and their dames clad in black, with black hoods over their heads, and carrying lighted flambeaux, following behind. The citizens of London, sombrely clad, met the sad procession, and "looked wonderingly at the King, all distraught and disordered."

In Shene, workmen had already begun to hack at the walls of the manor-house, in accordance with the King's orders. . . .

CHAPTER TWO

The Manor

THE village was growing. The manor on the banks of the Thames had long attracted some of the noble families from London, and they had begun to build themselves houses at Shene, leasing the land from the Crown. One of the reasons why they wanted a second home was a practical one: plagues and fevers might break out in the city at any time, and it was desirable to have a place in the country to which they could fly at the first dread warning of the pestilence. The terrible Black Death of 1348–49, and the later scourges, had ravaged the entire country, and almost half the population of the kingdom had perished. The people did not, of course, realise that insanitary conditions of living, and the toleration of enormous numbers of flea-carrying rats, led to epidemics; but they knew from experience that plague was contagious, and therefore the farther they got away from centres of population the more chance they had of escaping the plague when it broke out.

There were as yet no roads or streets in Shene, in the modern sense of the term, but there was the bony structure of the village which remains to this day—the main highway from London, which led to the manor-house and the river, and a thoroughfare up the Hill, which passed through the neighbouring hamlet of Patriceham and eventually led to Kingston. The houses which the gentry and rich merchants from London built were of lath and plaster, and usually had an upper storey with a window, glazed or unglazed. The one-roomed peasants' cottages were of timber, rubble, and clay, with thatched roofs and beaten earth floors. Shops as such did not exist in villages. The local craftsmen— coopers, wheelwrights, potters, and the rest—supplied the needs of their neighbours, against payment in kind, or, more unusually, coin. Travelling fairs brought booths which were set up at the end

[15]

of the village, displaying an enticing variety of merchandise from London: wines and spices, ribbons and fancy pieces of cloth, new conceits "from France" which were homely copies of what the grand folk wore or used.

Every family grew its own corn, and there was a water-mill for grinding it, though some used hand-grinders in their own homes. The villagers paid the miller in kind; he kept back a proportion of the corn for himself. The medieval records of towns are full of complaints about dishonest millers, taking more than their fair share, and no doubt the miller at Shene was not any less sharp; but in a close-knit community like a small village a flagrantly dishonest miller would soon have found it difficult to get a pair of shoes made, or his mill-wheel mended when it needed repair. One had to be circumspect in cheating, as in everything else.

The next important crop to corn was barley, used for making malt for the ale which was the chief drink of the common people. Hemp and flax were also grown, to supply the goodwives' spindles. Most families had a few sheep which they pastured on common land, a cow or two, and hens and geese.

The peasant was no longer a serf, as he had been in the old days, depending entirely on the produce of a few strips of land in return for his work in the demesne. The great scarcity of labour after the Black Death had given him a new value, and he could now command wages, either in the form of more land for himself, or in coin. He could eat better than his grandfather had done: the fact that he complained of hard times indicates that he must have had reasonably good times, according to his position and the standards of the day.

The more energetic of the peasants were able to become employers themselves; they leased land from the steward of the manor and employed their fellow-villagers to work on it. The steward was glad enough to agree, as it was the only way of getting the land tilled and productive. In this way there began to grow up a new class—the middle man, the farmer. The peasants who worked for him remained labourers, and a really ambitious man soon became a tenant farmer on a large scale.

Dues of many kinds still had to be paid to the lord of the manor, through his steward, and the manor of Shene collected substantial revenues. The manor-house had not, in fact, been razed to the ground, as Richard II in his grief and rage had ordered. A small part of it had been pulled down, but a considerable portion had been left habitable and still furnished, as Froissart, who was in Richard's entourage, mentions in his "Chronicle" that King Richard stayed at Kingston, Shene, and Chertsey on his way to Windsor. There is no record of his ever having actually lived at Shene again; the manor-house was inhabited only by a few servants and soldiers. The timber and broken masonry left lying on the ground were a useful quarry for villagers who wanted to improve their homes; they could slip into the courtyards at night with their families and help themselves. Officials of the Crown came down to Shene at intervals to hold Court Leets and to collect revenues; beyond that, the people were concerned only to live their own lives.

Henry Bolingbroke, who ousted Richard II, and was implicated in that unhappy monarch's murder, ascended the throne as Henry IV. He did not often visit the manor of Shene, but his heir, Prince Henry, took a fancy to the place and liked staying there, especially as the hunting was good. Prince Hal was a lively young man and his high spirits and mischievous wit irritated his sombre-minded father. On one of the rare occasions when the Court was at Shene, Prince Hal appeared in a gown of blue satin, full of holes, with a needle suspended from a silk thread at each hole.[1] The explanation of the jape was a simple one. The Prince was receiving his education at Queen's College, Oxford, and it was the custom, on the Feast of the Circumcision, for the bursar to present to every member of the College a needle and thread in memory of the founder, Robert Egglesfield—*aiguile fil* being accepted as a punning version of his name. The royal undergraduate had decided to do honour to the founder of his college many times over, but there is no record that his royal father was amused.

Prince Henry had always been a wild young man. A fearless soldier, he fought in the Welsh campaigns against the redoubtable Glendower, and he returned to England full of the reckless spirit engendered by the rough life he had led in the mountains of the Principality. As Prince of Wales he possessed no revenues, and when his father died and he became Henry V he immediately

[1] Holinshed

[17]

began spending on a royal scale. One of the first things he did was to set about repairing and extending the manor-house at Shene. It is possible he wanted a good hunting-box within easy reach of London, but he restored the building so thoroughly that Thomas de Elmham, one of Henry's biographers, describes it as "a delightful mansion, of skilfull and costly architecture, and becoming to the royal dignity." No authentic detailed description has come down to us, except that the restored manor-house had a moat; but there is evidence that it must have been a substantial building, as there are records of many payments to stone-cutters, carpenters, and other craftsmen and labourers for their work on the manor-house at Shene.

Henry also founded two conventual houses at Shene, as some atonement for his father's part in the murder of Richard II. One was built on the north side of his manor (in what is now the Old Deer Park) for forty monks of the Carthusian order, the Prior being John Wydryngton. It was called The House of Jesus of Bethleem, and the dimensions were considerable, the Great Hall being over 130 feet long, the quadrangle 360 feet long, and the cloisters 600 feet long. The second foundation, Syon Nunnery, was for nuns and monks of the Order of St Bridget, and was built on the Middlesex side of the river. Both houses had large endowments, and the monks' and nuns' chief duty was to pray daily for the King's health, and, after his death, for his soul, and the souls of his kin.[1]

Henry often came down to hunt deer in his manor, bringing friends or entertaining foreign notabilities, on hunting and hawking expeditions. Shene was convenient to the King for more than sport. There were quarries in the district, and stone was often sent to London. In 1417, Thomas Frank, John Boreford, and John Snell were instructed by the King's steward to fill two boats with stone, and row them to London to repair the King's highway in Holborn, "which is so muddy and deep that great perils have happened to men with the King's carriage and others crossing there, and greater are feared."

The King's carriage was not, in fact, often seen in London. Henry V had been a soldier from the time he had first come to manhood, and he was soon turning his thoughts to war with France—

[1] The monastery still exists at S. Brent, in Devon.

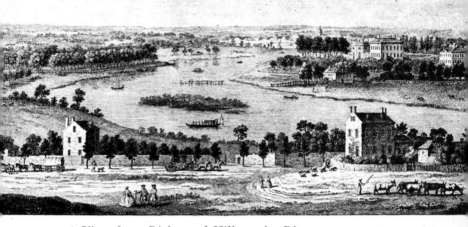

A View from Richmond Hill up the River, 1749

. Vivares, after Antonio Jolli.

Veue de la Maison Royal du Cote de la Tamise, 1736 (Richmond Lodge)

B. C. Chatelain, after Marco Ricci.

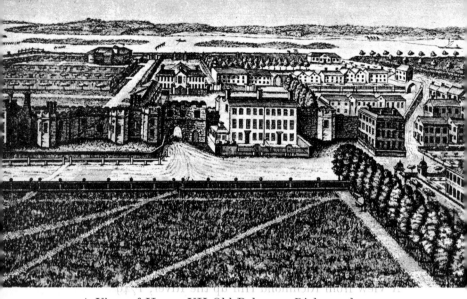

A View of Henry VII Old Palace at Richmond, 1742

N. Parr, after W. Shaftoe.

By courtesy of Mr Edward Croft-M

The Gateway, Richmond Palace, about 1795

By courtesy of Mr Edward Croft-M

the occupational disease of the Plantagenet kings. Henry set sail for France, fell in love with Katherine, the beautiful daughter of the French king, wooed her—and asked for a dowry of two million crowns. He was refused, and decided to win his bride at the point of the sword. After months of fighting and much negotiation, the match was agreed upon, and Katherine de Valois became Queen of England, though with a dower of a good deal less than two million crowns.

Henry V, like many another who had known straitened means in their youth, was almost as extravagant as Richard II had been. He loved display, and when he and his lovely young Queen were at Shene they had the costliest gold and silver table furnishings: one spice plate alone was valued at over £700. Their bed, with arras drapery and coverings of cloth of gold, was valued at £140. Henry was often in debt. He was once obliged to pawn one of the choicest of his swords, with a heavily jewelled hilt, to pay for his extravagant mode of living, and there is no record that he later redeemed it. He had a passion for hawking, and when he came to Shene his falconers had to see to it that only the best birds were obtained for his sport. The saddles of the King's horses were richly ornamented, the saddle-cloths thickly embroidered and bordered with silver bells.

Queen Katherine had equally luxurious tastes. Her bed was of azure, ornamented with true lovers' knots and crystal knobs, with

> Fair sheets of silk
> Chalk white as milk,

the hangings embroidered with green popinjays. There were Spanish carpets on the floors, and cloth of gold hangings in the royal bedchamber. The Queen's gowns were of velvet or satin, powdered with jewels, and often trimmed with expensive fur such as ermine or miniver; while her enormous head-dresses "elicited the severest censures."

Katherine travelled to Windsor to give birth to her child, a son who was destined to become Henry VI. Her husband was in France at the time, prosecuting the siege of Meaux; the fact that he was married to the French king's daughter had not prevented his renewing the war in France. After the fall of the town, Katherine joined him, leaving her infant son at home. She found Henry ill; the long rigours of warfare had undermined his constitution. He died shortly afterwards, leaving an heir eight months old; Katherine herself was not yet twenty-one.

Henry VI was crowned king in his eighth year. He was strictly brought up by his guardians who included a cardinal, and was guarded from the wiles of women all through his young manhood.

War with France was, as usual, going on, and when the King was twenty-four the politicians decided that it would be a good tactical stroke for him to marry the Queen of France's niece, Margaret of Anjou. Henry VI was, according to one chronicle,

> beautiful in person, of a highly cultivated and refined mind, holy and pure in thought and deed, resisting with virtuous indignation the attempts of the unprincipled females of his court to entangle him in the snares of illicit passion, yet pining for the sweet ties of conjugal love and sympathy.

He was undoubtedly a lonely young man, and his careful up-bringing had possibly made him rather a prig. It would have been interesting to see the faces of the young ladies who "presented themselves before him immodestly attired" when he turned away with the rebuke: "Fie, fie! forsooth, ye be much to blame."

Margaret of Anjou was very beautiful, and Henry was content. "King Henry," said a chronicler, "new to the delights of female society, was intoxicated with the charms, the wit, and graceful manners of his youthful bride." It was to be the case of a lamb married to a lioness; but the bride gave no hint of the forceful personality which lay behind her fair features; perhaps she was herself unaware of the ruthless qualities which the future would call out. It was gratifying to a fifteen-year-old girl to be Queen of England, and she was all sweetness, and grace, and pliancy.

It had been many years since a queen-consort had held her state in England, and the manor-house at Shene was in disrepair, especially that part known as the "queen's lodgings." Rebuilding soon began. Iron, timber, lead, stone, laths, lime, coal, and roofing tiles were ordered, and search was made in the district for suitable earth for making "brike"—tiles for decoration—as well as tilers to fashion them into intricate patterns. There was considerable additional building round the manor-house. The Keeper of the

Manor was given "a new little house, with a hall, divers chambers, a kitchen, and a little garden annexed." There was also fresh accommodation for the household, which had been considerably increased, and required local facilities. Henry had made a new park (now the Old Deer Park) and he paid John Bury "2*d*. a day wages to feed the King's fallow deer in winter within the same park, notwithstanding that he takes 6*d*. a day as Keeper of Shene manor." Plumbers were better paid: Richard Wolnothe received 12*d*. a day as "sergeant of the King's plumbery." John Young got 2*d*. a day for "keeping the ferry over the water of Thames at Shene manor", but he had to find his own boat.

Henry VI and Margaret often held their Court at Shene, where the river had a more rural setting than at Westminster or the Tower. Several of Henry V's old retainers were still there, and Henry VI did not forget good service. He gave a pension to John Benet, yeoman of the buttery, for thirty-one years of faithful service to Henry V and himself; and to Margaret, John's wife, for her good offices at the time of his own birth; they jointly received 100 shillings a year for the remainder of their lives.

Marriage had brought happiness to Henry VI, but it did not alter his fundamental nature. Deeply religious, a man of peace, his unmartial temperament unfitted him to deal effectively with the ambitious barons who constantly struggled against each other for personal power in the fifteenth century. It had always been difficult to keep the King's peace in England; in earlier centuries, the King himself, through his trusted officers, had generally been able to control earls and dukes who engaged in private wars. Henry VI did not wish to control anyone. He wanted to be left to pursue the contemplative life, to pray in peace, and enjoy a quiet life with his beautiful consort at one or other of their pleasant manor-houses. The barons and local overlords were quick to react to this weakness. They became a law unto themselves, attacking their neighbours when it suited them, and relying on having a strong arm, plenty of money for bribes, and the right allies. Formal law courts with all the appurtenances had been well established by Henry VI's reign; a contemporary picture of the King's Bench shows five robed justices sitting on a high bench; clerk with scrolls of parchment, pen-cases, and inkhorns at a bench below them;

attorneys, jurors being sworn by an usher, a prisoner, his jailer; and counsel for the prosecution and defence, wearing their gowns. The forms are all there—but for every case which came before the King's Bench and was properly pleaded, there were scores of misdemeanours and crimes committed which never reached a court of law.

It was an age of violence. Squires would arm their retainers and attack each other's castles. Impostors would lay claims to properties to which they had not a tittle of right—and seized the land if they could, until it was wrested from them again.

The King's officers who were supposed to enforce the law were themselves often worse than the malefactors they were expected to apprehend. With noble lords and rich barons escaping the consequences of great offences, lesser men committed crimes with impunity. Highwaymen infested the roads and made forays into towns and villages. An Italian traveller, describing a journey in southern England, wrote:

> There is no country in the world where there are so many thieves and robbers as in England; insomuch that few venture to go alone in the country, excepting in the middle of the day, and fewer still in the towns at night, and least of all in London.

The main route from London to Shene was well known as a dangerous one for men riding alone, or in too small groups. When messengers were required to go to London from Shene they went protected by a strong guard of trusted men. Outlying dwellings round the manor-house were constantly raided, often with the connivance of servants of the King. Members of religious establishments suffered as much as anyone. In 1443, Maud, the Abbess of St Bridget, Syon, "by Brayntford", complained to the King that she was being molested by the King's officers who were trying to take her stone and timber while she was building another conventual house, the Augustinian monastery of St Saviour and St Mary the Virgin. Henry issued an order that the Abbess and her nuns were not to be molested.

The happy years at Shene were destined to end. There were desperate events to come, leading up to the Wars of the Roses, and Shene no longer plays a part in the life of this royal couple.

CHAPTER THREE

The Palace is built

IN the reign of Edward IV, who wrested the throne from Henry VI in 1461, the manor-house at Shene knew royal state once more. Edward married Elizabeth Woodville, a knight's daughter who possessed extreme beauty, and made the most of it. She had been wooed by several men of her own rank, and might have married one of them, but "she was too slenderly gifted by fortune to venture on a mere love match."

It was a classic marriage of convenience. Edward had a queen who had done well for herself and was likely to be dutiful and complacent and turn a blind eye when required. Elizabeth had achieved the highest state in the land, and the opportunity to advance members of her family. She was well content.

Marriage was a business or political matter in the medieval world; this was taken for granted, hardly ever questioned. Love? A distemper of youth, which had nothing to do with serious things like the acquisition of good connections, land and money. Romantic passion was a subject for songs and poems, not a basis for marriage. Mutual affection, it was conceded, often grew out of a marriage, but the actual match was made by the parents, and children were brought up to expect nothing else.

Elizabeth Woodville had no fault to find with her loveless marriage. She liked Shene as much as did her royal husband. They both had exceedingly luxurious tastes, and the manor-house was new furnished with costly hangings and furniture. Building went on constantly; there were bowers, or summer houses, in shady nooks of the pleasaunce, "where the ladies of the Court were fond of retiring—not always alone." Besides hunting, Edward was particularly fond of jousts and tourneys, and he often held them at Shene. The large field in front of the manor-house

[23]

had always been an excellent venue for these knightly festivals. A large space was railed off, leaving openings for the entrances of the opposing parties, with gaily-pennoned tents for the combatants near by. The royal party and their friends sat on a daïs, while the onlookers crowded around. The knights fighting in the tourney wore heavy armour, their horses protected by chain armour and steel plates. The weapons were a blunt sword, the blows given on the flat, or a heavy wooden mace; the object was not to wound one's opponent but to unhorse him. If the combatants were not unhorsed at the first charge they could return to the end of the lists and make two more charges.

A joust was a fight between two knights, with lances for weapons. Again, the object was to unhorse the opposing knight, or to shiver his lance, which had two small projections at the end instead of sharp points.

The personal accounts of Edward IV and his queen give as long a list of velvets and "sattins" as any of the previous sovereigns, but there is a pleasing attention to modest items, such as this one in 1480:

> Paid to Alice Claver, sylkwoman, for an unce of sowing silk, xivd. . . . Shoon sengle soled and not lynede: blac j pair, iiijd. . . . Ostriche feders, xj.

Elizabeth bore her husband several daughters and two sons, who were often at Shene with their parents; both Elizabeth and Edward were at their best when their children were present. Apart from this interest, and their mutual love of display, there was little common ground between them. Edward was often unfaithful: his liaison with Jane Shore, wife of a goldsmith in the city, was notorious. Elizabeth had proved as complaisant as he had expected; any devotion she had left over from her children went to her brother, Anthony Woodville, and a row of sisters, all of whom she had helped to make good marriages.

Years of immoderate self-indulgence took their toll, and Edward IV died in 1483, at the age of forty-two.

> Where is now my conquest and royal array?
> Where be my coursers and my horses high?

Gone, all gone. Gone, too, was Elizabeth Woodville's peace of mind. From the day of her husband's death, she knew nothing but fear and sorrow. Richard of Gloucester, Edward IV's brother, he of the crooked back and the crookeder mind, was determined to get the throne, and he succeeded. The young King was deposed, and Richard Crookback was crowned as Richard III. Edward and his brother were shut up in the Tower. Their murder followed.

It was not until Bosworth Field, when Henry Tudor came from exile in France to challenge and conquer the usurper, that stable government became possible in England. He married Elizabeth of York, the "white and red roses were tied together", and the Tudor dynasty was founded.

The great days of the manor of Shene now began. Henry VII and his Queen, like several of their predecessors, preferred Shene to their other residences, and went there often. Arthur, their first son and Prince of Wales, was followed by a daughter, then by another son, Henry, "a boy remarkable for his great strength and robust health." Prophetic words. There were several more children, all of whom were sent to the manor of Shene to be nurtured, so as to be well away from the frequent outbreaks of sweating sickness in London.

Henry VII was a curious mixture of miser and prodigal spender. The economies he had been compelled to practise in his youth had an appreciable effect on him for the rest of his life. He would closely examine the itemised expenses of his household, then launch out into vast expenditure on banquets, tourneys, and other entertainments. The Queen was of a similar nature: fits of economy alternated with wildly extravagant sums spent on bed furnishings. Descriptions in the records tell of gowns "mended, turned, and new-bodied: freshly trimmed at an expense of 4d. to the tailor, newly hemmed when beaten out at the bottom, for which he was paid 2d. . . ." shoes which cost only 12d. "with latten or tin buckles." Then—

> The stuff for the Queen's bed consisted of two pairs of sheets of Rennes, four breadths, and five yards long . . . a pane [counterpane] of scarlet furred with ermine, and bordered with velvet or cloth of gold . . . a sperne of crimson satin, embroidered with crowns of gold, the Queen's arms, and other devices . . . garn-

ished with fringe of silk and gold, blue and russet . . . four cushions covered with silver damask on cloth of gold.

To these were added

a round mantle of crimson velvet, plain, furred with ermine, for the Queen to wear about her in her pallet.

The records are full of such descriptions, as well as of the large sums expended by the King. He raised money by the simple method of levying high taxes on the people. "It is good for them", was his ingenuous remark to the Spanish Ambassador. The people grumbled but paid, no doubt considering it a fair enough price for the peace which was such a relief after generations of violence and misrule. The Wars of the Roses had bled the country to the edge of ruin, and everyone was thankful that years of anarchy were at last giving place to some kind of order. There was a great longing everywhere for a settled way of life. Henry VII made it known that the lawlessness which had for so long disrupted the kingdom must come to an end. He was himself a man with a strong sense of order; he established new rules for the government of the royal household, which he directed should be kept "in most straightest wise." He was determined to pacify England; the laws would be kept, and men be unafraid to go about their business or keep their houses.

In the event he was successful. The old feudal system, in which strong-fisted barons divided the power of the country between them, finally disappeared during his reign; the King's Writ ran from the south to the north, and across to the Marches of Wales. Castles no longer needed to be fortified strongholds; commerce expanded, the arts were encouraged. Henry received poets and philosophical writers from all over Europe, he employed 'limners', and bought tapestries. The Queen was fond of music and often had musicians to entertain her.

With a royal Court again established at Shene, the village grew steadily. A middle class was emerging from the old feudal structure, and there were many houses, some built of timber, others of brick, each in its own garden. Craftsmen still worked at their trades in the village, but there were now shops as well as inns and taverns. Carts with iron-shod wheels rumbled daily from Shene to London and back, bringing merchandise from the city and food

and foreign fruits from the markets. The King's officers and local
justices were ready to apply the law impartially to rich and poor
alike. Serious crimes were dealt with by death or imprisonment,
usually under barbarous conditions. Minor offences were punished
by a spell in the stocks or pillory, which combined exposure to
ridicule with discomfort and the probability of being pelted with
refuse. Sometimes the punishment was made to fit the crime. A
baker who sold light-weight loaves was drawn along the main
street on a hurdle, with one of his dishonest loaves hung round
his neck. Justice was often rough, but it existed.

In 1499, Henry VII added to the conventual establishments in
Shene by building a convent of Observant Friars, of the order of
Franciscans, or Grey Friars, not far from the manor-house. [It
extended from the present Friars Lane to Water Lane.] At
the end of the same year, the manor-house itself was the scene
of calamity: it caught fire. Francis Bacon, in his life of Henry VII,
relates " . . . A great fire in the night-time suddenly began . . .
near unto the King's own lodgings, whereby a great part of the
building was consumed, with much costly household stuff." The
fire raged for over three hours, burning strongly, and the onlookers
were forced to let it burn itself out, for, in spite of the proximity of
the river, there was no fire-fighting apparatus. The royal family
and officers of the Court had been removed to a place of safety at
the first alarm; when the fire was over what remained of the
manor-house was uninhabitable. The Queen was deeply grieved.
She had spent much of her childhood at Shene, and her children
had become attached to the manor: they had all preferred it to the
royal residences at Greenwich, Eltham, or Windsor.

Henry promised to rebuild the house. He must have had a struggle
with his natural parsimonious instincts, but he, too, liked Shene,
and once he began discussing plans with the master-craftsmen, he
went to the other extreme, spending money without stint: "He
builded it up again sumptuously and costly, and changed the name
of Shene, and called it Richmond, because his father and hee were
Earls of Rychemonde [in Yorkshire]." The name is variously spelt
in the records: Rychemond in 1501, Richmonde in 1538, Riche-
mont in 1540, Rychemond in 1549, Richemonde in 1553, with
other variations in between. To avoid confusion, the familiar

spelling is used here. The name Shene remained in the east and west parts of the manor lands, but the area round the new building was called Richmond as soon as Henry made the proclamation.

It was rebuilt as a palace, totally different from the old manor-house. The moat which Henry V had made was filled in, and the level of the site raised. Henry VII's new palace was planned on a great scale, and grew into a complex of brick and timber buildings, covering an expanse of about ten acres. The Great Hall was 100 feet long and 40 feet wide, with a screen at the lower end and a daïs, paved with square tiles, raised 4 feet from the floor, at the other. Between the tall windows, the walls were painted with kings of England who had been renowned in battle, including William the Conqueror, Richard I, and Henry VII himself, the victor of Bosworth Field. There were statues below the windows, and hangings of tapestry and rich arras. The next important building was "a decent and pleasant chapel", nearly 100 feet long, with cathedral seats and pews; this had a jewel-encrusted altar, hangings of cloth of gold, and wall paintings of kings, like Edward the Confessor, who had also been saints.

The royal lodging was a freestone building, three storeys high, with fourteen turrets, covered with lead, "a very graceful ornament to the whole house and perspicuous to the country round about." The rooms here were splendidly furnished, the Queen's apartments being "gilded and damasked and in all a costly chamber." These large buildings constituted the main block; there was a maze of smaller buildings, towered and turreted, with courts and quadrangles, in one of which stood an elaborate stone fountain—

> ornamented with lions and red dragons and other goodly beasts, and in the midst certain branches of red roses, out of which flowers and roses is evermore running a course of clear and most purest water into the cistern beneath. This conduit profitably serves the chambers with water for the hands, and all other offices as they need to resort.

It is a little startling to find water laid on in the fifteenth century, but in this well-planned palace there were pipes leading to many of the rooms as well as to the numerous kitchens. The water was brought through three Conduit Heads, fed by lead pipes running from Richmond Hill, which abounds with springs. The White

Conduit, in Richmond Park, still exists; the Red Conduit was in Richmond Town Fields, and the third Conduit was situated on ground near the river, at the beginning of the Hill.

The main buildings were connected with a series of galleries, "paved, glazed and painted, beset with badges of gold, as roses, portcullises and such other." The most important of these galleries contained the Royal Library. Henry VII was always ready to spend money on books. He was a patron of philosophers and scholars, and his privy purse accounts show many entries itemising the purchase of books:

	£	s.	d.
To one Smerte for an English boke	1	0	0
To Frances Mareyn, for divers bokes, by bill	3	5	0
To Master Peter for certain bokes upon a Bille	11	3	4
To Hugh Dewes for printed bokes	0	13	4
To a boke bynder	0	6	8
Delivered to Quentin for bokes	20	0	0
To a Frenshman for certain bokes	56	4	0

Quentin Paolet, a Franco-Fleming from Lille, was the Librarian at the palace, and his name appears several times in the records. It is clear that Henry made provision for purchases of books and missals which he intended to buy, to replace those lost in the fire.[1]

There was a large orchard on the river side of the palace, a "place of herbs", and gardens planted "with many vines, seeds, and strange fruit right goodly beset." Among the gardens there were arbours and summer houses, with special tables for playing chess—a favourite game—and cards; there were bowling alleys, archery grounds, and tennis courts (these last for playing royal tennis, which is quite different from lawn tennis. One can still be seen, and played on, at Hampton Court).

When the palace was finished it extended along the river front from what is now Old Palace Lane to Water Lane, and was

girded and encompassed with a strong and mighty brick wall, barred and bent with towers in his each corner and angle and also in his midway. His openings be strong gates of double timber and heart of oak, stuck full of nails right thick, and crossed with bars of iron.

[1] The Library at Richmond Palace probably had most of the 'Royal MSS.' now at the British Museum.

The main gateway was on the northern side, flanked by the buildings of the wardrobe and the guard-house; these faced the old tourney field, which was now a level, well-turfed green of about 20 acres. The over-all effect of the palace, either from the north or from the river side, was of great splendour. Above the curtain wall rose a profusion of towers, turrets, and cupolas,

> upon each of them a vane of the King's arms painted and gilt with rich gold and azure, [which] as well as the pleasant sight of them, as the hearing in a windy day was right marvellous to know and understand.

Richmond was the largest of the many royal palaces, and, by all contemporary accounts, and from the drawings made while it was still whole, the most beautiful. Henry VII may have been close-fisted and a miser, but he built this "delightful mansion of curious and costly workmanship, befitting the character and condition of a king", this "splendid and magnificent house", as Aubrey called it, and for once in his life he did not pause first to count the cost.

The new Palace of Richmond was finished in time for the nuptials of Henry's eldest daughter, Margaret, to James, King of Scotland, for which negotiations had been going on for some time. The next royal event was the marriage of Arthur, Prince of Wales, to Katharine of Aragon. Prince Arthur was sixteen years old, the bride a little younger. It was a tragically short marriage, for the Prince caught the plague five months later, and died. It was noted that Henry VII took his loss philosophically, reminding his sorrowing wife that they had a second son, Henry.

Katharine showed the proper amount of public grief befitting a royal widow, but there were some who wondered what kind of marriage this could have been, short as was its duration. Prince Arthur and the Spanish princess could only converse through the stiff, formal medium of Latin, and there had never been the slightest pretence of affection between them. The Prince had had time, before his death, to make a will, and he bequeathed every-thing—jewels, plate, all his personal possessions—to his favourite sister, Margaret. There was nothing for the bride. Katharine was left without money; she was unable to pay her attendants, who nevertheless continued to serve her. The Queen gave her Croydon Palace as a lodging, but did not offer an allowance, only the cost of food. Katharine presently asked if she could remove to Richmond, and she was allotted a suite of rooms in the palace there.

Now began many arguments about money. Katharine's marriage portion had been agreed at 200,000 crowns, only half of which had been paid by her father, Ferdinand II of Aragon, at the time of the marriage. Prince Arthur having died, Ferdinand did not see why he should pay over the remaining half of the dowry, as his daughter had now no prospect of becoming Queen of England. Henry and his consort took this in very bad part, but they could not persuade the Spanish king to disgorge the other half of the agreed dowry.

With the palace built and furnished, Henry VII had become more grasping and tight-fisted than ever. He exacted enormous taxes from his subjects; no-one could guess at the size of the immense fortune he was accumulating and always scheming to augment. The Queen, too, saved money wherever she could. She kept careful personal accounts:

1502	£	s.	d.
To John Goose, my Lord of York's fool, for bringing a carp		1	0
To a poor man who brought a present of oranges and apples to the Queen at Richmond		1	0
To Louis Walter, bargeman, for conveying the Queen's Grace from Richmond to Greenwich with twenty-one rowers, each rower		2	0
To a servant of the Abbess for bringing a present of rabbits and quails to the Queen at Richmond		2	0
To Edmunt Calvert, for going from Richmond to London to Mistress Locke for Bonnets for the Queen			8
For milk at Richmond			3

It does not say whether Edmunt Calvert travelled to London by road or by water, but as there are many entries in the privy purse of payments to watermen, it is clear that the Thames was, as always, the main highway between Richmond and the metropolis. Vessels which required a large number of rowers were too expensive for domestic errands; the Queen used the services of the common watermen and paid them at the standard rate.

Elizabeth of York had been kind to Katharine, in spite of the difficulties of conversation where neither knew the other's language. It was a great blow to the young widow when her mother-in-law died early in 1503, after giving birth to a daughter. Katharine's own mother, Isabella of Spain, was also dead. Any question of Katharine's return to Spain was quickly settled by Ferdinand, her father, who wrote commanding her to remain in England. She was Princess of Wales, and it was the duty of her father-in-law, the King of England, to provide for her future. So reasoned Ferdinand. Henry VII was equally anxious to keep his daughter-in-law in England; so long as she was there, he still had a chance of laying his hands on the rest of her dowry.

Katharine was in desperate straits for money; she did not have sufficient to buy necessary clothes. She wrote pathetic letters to Ferdinand, pleading with him to send her an allowance. He wrote stiltedly affectionate letters back, and side-stepped the question of the allowance. King Henry also sent letters to Ferdinand, through his Ambassador, pressing for the rest of Katharine's dowry. The replies were formally friendly, the question of the money blandly ignored. The pressure continued, until a solution was at length found. Henry VII's second son, Henry, was now heir to the throne. The Pope would be asked for a dispensation, and a marriage arranged between Prince Henry and the young widow. What had Ferdinand to say to this plan? Ferdinand thought it was an excellent idea, and commended it, with his blessing—but still without an allowance—to his daughter.

Katharine was now eighteen, and Prince Henry was thirteen. She was not in the least enthusiastic about the proposed betrothal, writing to tell her father that she did not wish to marry another English prince. Again she begged him for money, telling him that she had been compelled to run into debt, and that the King of England even grudged her the food she ate:

> He said he is not bound to give me anything, and that even the food he gives me is of his goodwill, because your highness has not kept promise with him in the money of my marriage-portion.

She lacked linen and clothes.

> About my own person I have nothing for chemises; wherefore, by your highness's life, I have now sold some bracelets to get a dress of black velvet, for I was all but naked.

This was a satisfactory state of affairs for Ferdinand as well as for Henry. If the girl was in actual want she would be more ready to take the sensible course of marrying Prince Henry, and so assuring herself a more comfortable future. Katharine held out, but in the end she wrote resignedly to her father, saying that his Grace was not to study her inclinations, but to do what he thought best. The rest followed inevitably. Ferdinand wanted his daughter on the throne of England and Henry VII wanted the remaining portion of her dowry. Katharine was officially betrothed to the young Prince.

Henry VII died at Richmond in 1509, and his son became Henry VIII.

CHAPTER FOUR

Tudor Despot

HANDSOME, strongly built, obstinate, and passionately determined to have his own way in everything, Henry VIII began his reign with a question-mark in the minds of the Ministers of State. Would he honour his betrothal promise to his brother's widow? He could easily release himself from the engagement now that his father was dead. But there was the dowry. . . . Henry was not, in fact, much concerned with the unpaid portion of the dowry; Henry VII had left immense wealth, and Henry VIII intended to enjoy it. It is probable that he had long admired Katharine, who, according to a contemporary chronicler, was "pleasing in person. . . . There were few people who could compete with Queen Katharine when in her prime"—a woman's prime in those days being her early twenties. They were married with great pomp; and Katharine forgot her earlier objections to a marriage with a young man five years her junior, and exerted herself to please him. Ferdinand now sent the remainder of the dowry, as well as a substantial sum to his daughter, the new Queen of England, to pay her servants and attendants their arrears of wages. All promised to go as happily as the wedding bells which pealed out at the marriage and again at the Coronation.

At first everything indeed went excellently well. The royal pair resided at Whitehall, but they often came to Richmond, where they held many tourneys. There is an item in the State papers: "To Gibson, for velvets and silks, and for embroiders and saddlers provided for the jousts at Richmond . . . £446 10s. 9½d."

Henry engaged companies of players to perform masques at Richmond Palace; he was himself a talented actor, and sometimes took part in the performances for the amusement of the Queen and the appreciative Court. He was also an able musician, playing on the lute and other instruments, and composing airs. He was at Richmond at Christmastide in 1509, and gave 40s. to the Children of the Chapel for singing *Gloria in Excelsis*. On December 30th, the Players in the Hall performed a masque, for which he gave them 20s.

On New Year's Day, 1510, Katharine gave birth to a son at Richmond Palace, and there were elaborate rejoicings, both at Richmond and in London. The Revel Accounts for January 6th state that "the Queen's grace being delivered of a prince", there was a grand revel, "My Lord of Ely's barge being hired to bring the stuff to Richmond." Twelve pence was also paid on that day for strewing the house with rushes, and for extra cleaning, 8d. A grand indoor pageant was staged at Whitehall:

> Fair ladies in gowns of white and green satin sitting in an arbour made with posts and pillars covered with gold and twined with branches of roses, hawthorns and eglantine, [danced] before Katharine's throne, while a vast throng of the London populace watched the grand doings from a short distance away.

King Henry having himself danced stately pavannes and corantos,

> in high good humour bade the ladies come forward, and pluck the golden letters and devices from his dress and that of the company. Little did the young King imagine what pickers and stealers were within hearing, for scarcely had he given leave for this courtly scramble, when forward rushed the plebeian intruders, and seizing not only on him but his noble guests, plucked them bare of every glittering thing on their dresses, with inconceivable celerity; what was worse, the poor ladies were despoiled of their jewels, and the King was stripped to his doublet and drawers.

The rejoicings were premature. In February 1511 the infant prince died, the result, it was said, of a cold caught at his christening. Three years later, Katharine bore Henry another son, and had the terrible experience of losing yet another child, for the boy scarcely survived his birth.

In 1516, Queen Katharine bore a daughter, who was given the name of Mary. Henry was seized with the beginnings of that obsession which was to have such dire consequences—the determination to be father of a male heir to the throne. A third son was born, again lifeless, and the King did not hesitate to show his anger and disappointment.

Henry, in fact, had a son—a natural child, borne to him by the beautiful wife of Sir Gilbert Tailbois, with whom he had had a liaison a few years before. This boy, who was given the name of Henry Fitzroy, was now created Duke of Richmond, a gesture which disturbed Katharine more than the actual infidelity, as she saw in this illegitimate son of the King a threat to her own children's succession. She had not given up hope of producing an heir who would survive.

Plague was an ever-threatening hazard, as it had always been. In 1518, Sebastiano Giustiniani, the Venetian Ambassador, wrote to the Doge of Venice: "Rode to the King at Richmond, who is in some trouble, as three of his pages and an attendant have died of the plague." There was trouble of another kind a few months later. Years before, Henry VII, the King's father, had brought ordered government to the country, but the citizens of London had wills of their own, and were liable to break out into violence if they were incited. Henry VIII gave them short shrift when this happened. In 1518, Sebastiano Giustiniani wrote to the Doge, giving an account of some exciting happenings he had witnessed. A certain preacher, used to addressing the London crowd, began abusing strangers and foreigners in London, saying they disgraced their dwellings and took off the citizens' wives and daughters. He exhorted the rabble to attack all strangers and drive them forth from London. The preacher so worked on the populace that they began committing outrages on all foreigners they met.

Sebastiano Giustiniani, a foreigner himself, rode post-haste to Richmond, insisted on being admitted to the palace, though the hour was close to midnight, and told the King of the danger to strangers. Henry rose from his bed, and sent a messenger to tell the citizenry that he was on his way to London in person, "though in reality he never quitted Richmond," wrote Sebastiano in parenthesis. Henry did, however, issue a proclamation threatening death and loss of property to any who molested foreigners. A number of rioters were caught, and the King decided to make an example of them. Nicholas Sagudino takes up the story in a letter to Alvise Foscari in Venice. After saying that many of the rioters were executed out of hand:

The King came . . . with his Court in excellent array, the right reverend Cardinal being there likewise, with a number of lords, both spiritual and temporal, with their followers, in a very gallant trim. And his majesty being seated on a lofty platform surrounded by all those lords, who stood, he caused some four hundred of these delinquents, all in their shirts and barefoot, and each with a halter round his neck, to be brought before him. . . . The Cardinal implored him aloud to pardon them, which the King said he would not by any means do. . . . The criminals on hearing that the King chose them to be hanged, fell on their knees shouting "Mercy!" The Cardinal besought his majesty to grant them grace, some of the chief lords doing the like. So at length the King consented to pardon them . . . and the right reverend Cardinal with tears in his eyes made them a long discourse, urging them to lead good lives and comply with the royal will, which was that strangers should be well treated in this country. . . . It was a fine sight to see each man take the halter which hung from his neck and throw it in the air, and they jumped for extreme joy.

In another account, it is the Queen, not the Cardinal, who begged the rioters off. Katharine was on good terms with Cardinal Wolsey, and it is likely that she asked him to speak for the condemned men.

It was the year 1524, and Hampton Court was nearing completion. Thomas Wolsey, Cardinal, looked at the great palace he had built, and found it good. Men said that it was the finest building in the kingdom, far exceeding the royal palace at Richmond in spaciousness and dignity of architecture. There were those who made the same comparisons to the King, who had raised "the butcher's dogge" to great heights. They knew that Henry was becoming jealous of the Cardinal's power and influence. Wolsey had many enemies, ever ready to whisper in Henry's ear; but he also had spies who reported back on the King's moods and temper.

The time came when Wolsey found it politic to make a grand gesture. He presented Hampton Court with its paintings, its costly panelling, furniture, and fittings, its treasures of gold and silver, to Henry, explaining that he had intended from the first to build a palace worthy of the King's Majesty. Henry accepted the splendid gift, and invited the Cardinal, in return, to reside at his manor of

Richmond when he pleased. Wolsey accepted the exchange of residences with profuse thanks, and came to Richmond Palace. The Cardinal's extravagant tastes were soon apparent there; he kept a style of high living that most people thought unsuitable for a prelate. Wolsey, the son of an Ipswich butcher, had risen from obscurity to be a great prince of the Church, and he believed in surrounding himself with suitable state. In the winter of 1525, when the plague was raging in London, Henry learned that Cardinal Wolsey was spending Christmas at Richmond, "and kept household open to lords, ladies, and all that would come, with plays and disguisings, in most royal manner." Henry himself was at Eltham Palace, where the Court was leading a quiet life, befitting a time of visitation.

Wolsey's downfall was no longer a matter of speculation; he lost the King's favour and was stripped of his possessions. He left Richmond Palace, and lived in a lodge situated in what is now the Old Deer Park: "A very pretty house ... with a very proper garden, garnished with divers pleasant walks and alleys." This lodge was a part of the old Monastery of Shene, and it is on record that the Fathers of that House "persuaded him [Wolsey] from the vain glory of this world, and gave him divers shirts of hair, the which he often wore after."

When Henry VIII stayed at Hampton Court he often had fruit, vegetables, and flowers brought from the orchards and gardens at Richmond Palace. There are many references to disbursements for these in the privy purse accounts between 1529 and 1532:

	£	s.	d.
For a reward given to Lovell, the gardener at Richmond, for bringing sweet water and fruit		10	0
To the gardener at Richmond, in reward for bringing filberts and damsons to the King at Hampton Court		4	8
Paid to the same, in reward for bringing of grapes to the King's Grace		6	8
Paid to a fellow that brought flowers from Richmond to Hampton Court		1	8
Paid to the gardener at Richmond, in reward for bringing rose water and apples to the King		6	8

Paid to the same, in reward for bringing salad herbs
   to the King   5   0

Henry never knew the lack of money, as his predecessors had
done, and indulged his tastes to the full. Food cost several thousands
of pounds a year for the Court at Richmond. There was an enormous variety: beef, mutton, venison, veal, swan, goose, stork, coneys,
pheasant, heron, partridge, cocks, plovers, gulls, larks, sparrows,
quails, wild duck, mallard, snipe; with custards, jellies, fritters, and
a favourite sweet, cream of almonds, to follow. On fish days there
was a choice of ling, whiting, plaice, gurnet, haddock, pike, bream,
tench, conger eels, perch, cray-fish, and salmon or trout caught in
the Thames near by. The King and Queen dined at 11 A.M. and
supped at 6 P.M., when they were not entertaining guests, and the
noblemen were enjoined not to dine in corners: an intriguing
prohibition.

Henry found Richmond Palace useful in his matrimonial
ventures. The French Ambassador wrote to Charles V in 1530:
"The King absents himself from her [Queen Katharine] as much
as possible, and is always here [London] with the lady [Anne
Boleyn] while the Queen is at Richmond." Ten years later, another
French Ambassador was writing to his master, Francis I:

> There is a talk of some diminution of love and a new affection
> for another lady. The Queen has been sent to Richmond. This I
> know, that the King has promised in two days to follow her, has
> not done so, and does not seem likely to do so, for the road of his
> progress does not lie that way.

There had been two queens since Katharine of Aragon, and it
was a shrewd appraisal, based on the King's past conduct. Henry
had divorced Katharine of Aragon and married Anne Boleyn.
That marriage had ended on the scaffold for Anne, and Henry
had then married Jane Seymour, who had borne him a son,
Edward. She had died in childbirth, and Henry took Anne of
Cleves for his fourth wife. She was the queen who had been sent
to Richmond, according to Francis I's informant; his latest "other
lady", destined to be the next queen, was Katharine Howard.

Anne of Cleves stands out as a woman with a common-sensical
head on her shoulders, and one who intended to keep it there. She

made no fuss when Henry divorced her, but accepted Richmond Palace as her residence, and £3000 a year as her income, with amiability and grace. She had had no children, but was devoted to the Princess Elizabeth, the daughter of Anne Boleyn. The young princess was a solitary, self-possessed girl, mature beyond her years, with an older half-sister, Mary, and a young half-brother, the delicate Prince Edward, heir to the throne. In a Court full of whisperings and intrigues, these children of Henry VIII spent an uneasy existence, all three motherless, aware of currents and cross-currents without being able to understand them. Princess Elizabeth loved to go to Richmond to stay with the kind, affectionate ex-Queen, who had a passion for richly embroidered dresses and liked to have musicians and gay persons about her.

Henry himself was still fond of his lately divorced wife, and invited her to visit him and his new Queen at Hampton Court. Anne composedly accepted the invitation, and paid the visit, to the scandalised astonishment of the Court. There was more to come. Henry dined with her at Richmond Palace more than once, and it was noted that he was charmed afresh by her cheerfulness and good humour. The curious relationship continued, until rumours began to fly about that the Lady Anne had been delivered of a fair boy, and that the King was the putative father. Here was gossip indeed. The King had had Anne Boleyn committed to the Tower for alleged adultery. Now he was the centre of scandal himself, and a piquant one at that.

It was soon established that there was no truth in the gossip, but Henry, enraged, ordered an inquiry to trace the originator of the malicious report. It came out that one Taverner of the Signet had got it from his mother-in-law, who got it from old Lady Carew; and also from his own wife, who had it of Lilgrave's wife. Taverner and Frances Lilgrave were committed to the Tower, and there does not appear to be any record of what happened to them.

Henry's divorces, bringing him into conflict with the Pope, caused many ripples which were to lead to the great upsurge of the Reformation. Richmond did not escape the dissolution of the monasteries. The Convent of the Friars, by Richmond Palace, and the conventual houses which Henry V had founded at Syon and Shene, were closed.

Edward VI was ten years of age when he succeeded his father, Henry VIII. Gentle and thoughtful, the boy King often came to Richmond, and took great pleasure in entertaining his half-sisters there. Princess Elizabeth liked listening to the Court musicians, and dancing; Princess Mary had a passion for card-playing—the records of her domestic expenses show losses of seven or eight pounds a week, a considerable sum at that time. She had a naïve sense of humour; she maintained a woman jester, "Jane the Fool", who was one of her closest attendants. When Princess Mary was at Richmond with her half-brother and -sister she was at her best. The dark side of her nature, so like her father's, was held in restraint as she walked with them in the pleasant gardens of the palace by the Thames.

Edward and Elizabeth were Protestants; Mary had refused to change her faith, and, like her mother, was a Catholic. Edward's health had always been poor, and it was now precarious. Everyone knew it was unlikely that he would grow to man's estate. He died at the age of sixteen, after a reign of only six years. There being no male heir, Mary, the Catholic princess, ascended the throne. The Protestants in the kingdom knew fear. Religious persecution was habitual in Europe: the Inquisition in Spain was a terrifying example of what could happen to 'heretics'. Before Mary had been Queen for a week, there were secret meetings, the beginnings of plots. The great Catholic lords triumphantly anticipated high office. The Protestant lords watchfully waited on events.

Mary herself was intent on one thing—marriage. Her mother, Katharine of Aragon, had begun planning alliances for her when the Princess was six years old, the first choice being the Emperor Charles V of Spain. He was then twenty-six years old, and he solemnly undertook to marry the Princess Mary when she attained her twelfth year. In preparation for this high destiny, she was given a crushingly academic education. No idle books of chivalry or romance were to be allowed, these being considered corrupting to the morals of females. Cards, dice, and splendid dress were as pestiferous as romances. She was crammed with gobbets from the Gospels, the Old Testament, the works of Cyprian, Jerome, Augustine, Plato, Cicero, Seneca, Plutarch, Erasmus, topped off with the *Utopia* of Thomas More. Lessons in Greek and Latin must be committed to memory every day. Miss Strickland observes that Princess Mary was "an historical example of the noxious effect that over-education has at a very tender age. Her precocious studies probably laid the foundation for her melancholy temperament and delicate health." Known to posterity as Bloody Mary, it is, in fact, a wonder that she was not bloodier.

She had witnessed scenes as a young girl which had left terrible scars on her impressionable temperament. Catholic partisans of her mother, whom she had always loved as friends, were burnt at Smithfield or hacked to pieces—their crime being that they disapproved of Henry VIII's breaking away from the old faith and declaring his own spiritual supremacy, in defiance of the Pope. Mary was well inured to the idea of people being burnt at the stake for their beliefs. Then had come a personal humiliation which rankled long, though she made light of it at the time. She was not to be the Queen of Spain after all. The Emperor Charles V did not keep his troth to marry her: he allied himself instead to Isabella of Portugal.

There had been several attempts to find a husband for her, but Mary Tudor was still unmarried when she succeeded her half-brother. She did not mount the throne without opposition. There was a party, led by the Duke of Northumberland, which strove to exclude her from the succession, and to give the crown to Lady Jane Grey, who also had a title to it, but Mary had strong support in the Catholic nobility, and they were prepared to arm their tenantry and to fight on her behalf. This did not prove necessary: a show of force was enough, and Mary was proclaimed Queen Regnant. Northumberland, needless to say, was executed.

The Queen's marriage was desired for reasons of state by her Ministers, but by no-one more ardently than Mary herself. She was determined to marry a Catholic, and when it was suggested that she should marry Philip of Spain—son of that very Emperor Charles who had jilted her many years before—she eagerly acquiesced. In Spain, the suggested marriage was less well received by the proposed suitor. Philip was twenty-six, Mary thirty-seven. He told his father that he had no wish to marry a woman eleven years his senior. Charles V was set on a union with England, and the Prince's objections were set aside without ceremony. The Emperor told him he must go to England and woo her Queen.

The people of England did not want the marriage. The Protestants were sure that if the Queen married the Spanish prince he would bring the Inquisition with him to England. There were renewed riots, danger of civil war. Princess Elizabeth became involved: there were malicious tongues only too ready to accuse her of complicity in one or more of the plots to dethrone her Catholic sister, and Mary had her confined in the Tower. Nothing could be proved against her, however, and she asked to be released. The Queen's advisers were against the Princess being set at liberty, and Mary compromised by sending her half-sister, closely guarded, to Woodstock. The party spent the first night of the journey at Richmond, where her servants were dismissed by Sir Henry Bedingfield, her gaoler. This act gave her a great shock. "I think I must die this night," she told them despairingly as she bade them goodbye, and asked for their prayers. No harm came to her, and the next morning her disbanded servants, lingering on the banks of the Thames, were able to catch a glimpse of her between the files of soldiers as she was rowed across the river to continue the journey to Windsor, and thence to Woodstock.

Mary Tudor married Philip II of Spain in 1554, and spent part of her honeymoon at Richmond Palace. It was fated to be an unhappy union from the beginning, though Mary did all she could to win her husband's favour. There were masques and tournaments and all kinds of entertainments at Richmond; Mary spent money with great lavishness in order to impress her husband's retinue. The Spaniards were certainly impressed, but not quite in the way the Queen had intended. One of Philip's attendants wrote home from Richmond Palace:

> All entertainment here is eating and drinking, for they have no notion of any other. The Queen spends more than three hundred thousand ducats a year on victual; and all the thirteen Lords of Council, and the officers of the Queen's household, all the King's household officers (who are English), and the wives of all these, have their meals in the palace; and so have the ladies-in-waiting, and everybody else's servants, and two hundred guards. All these ladies and gentlemen sleep and have their apartments in the palace. . . .

After describing the vast quantity of food consumed, the Spanish gentleman turns to drink. "They drink more beer than there comes down water at Valladolid in a spring flood. The ladies and some of the gentlemen put sugar in their wine." Not surprisingly,

> There is a very great racket and rumpus in the palace. . . . There are so many thieves among them that these go about in twenties. They have no justice, and no fear of God. Mass is seldom said, and those who attend it do so against their will, except where the Queen is, for she is a holy woman and fears God. . . . We are admonished from His Majesty to raise no question about anything, but to put up with everything so long as we are in the country.

Philip himself found it difficult to put up with life in England for long. The following year, the Queen let it be known that she would shortly produce an heir, but a 'wise woman', who had attended Mary from childhood, bluntly told one of Philip's entourage that the Queen's supposed state "was by no means of the hopeful kind generally supposed, but rather a woful malady, for she sat whole days on the ground crouched together, with her knees higher than her head." Philip, realist that he was, knew that there was probably little possibility of an heir. The Spanish occupation of the Low Countries gave him a good reason for "returning to his duty", and he left England, promising to return in a short time. The weeks grew into months, and he did not come back. Mary, unhappy and deeply humiliated, was in a constant state of wretched ill-health. Her Catholic advisers saw their opportunities. The fires of Smithfield burned with renewed fury, and the toll of Protestant martyrs began.

Henry VIII's decree dissolving the religious foundations was rescinded, and many monks and nuns returned to their houses, including those at Richmond and Syon.

In 1557, the Queen's "truant spouse" came unexpectedly to England, and Mary was overjoyed. She immediately gave orders for great entertainment to be made. At Richmond, a great fête was given in Philip's honour, and the Princess Elizabeth—now undisputed heiress to the throne—was invited. Elizabeth was in London, staying at Somerset House, and the Queen sent the State barge to convey her half-sister up the Thames. Mary had long ago released Elizabeth from close surveillance; her spies could be relied upon to report on the Princess's movements and friends. Elizabeth herself had been carefully circumspect, trimming her

sails whenever necessary, and she was on good terms with the
Queen.

This invitation was designed to show the people that the heiress
to the throne was being treated with proper dignity, and the
royal barge was splendidly decorated with garlands of flowers, and
covered with an awning of green silk embroidered with golden
blossoms. Under this awning sat the gorgeously attired Princess,
now twenty-four years of age. She sat composed and smiling,
amid her maids of honour. "Six boats followed, with the gentlemen of Elizabeth's retinue, who were dressed in russet damask and
blue satin, with caps of silver cloth and green plumes." One
would give much to know what her thoughts were as the gorgeous barge sailed up the river to Richmond. Philip of Spain
had come back, but for how long? It was known that Mary
suffered from an incurable malady, and could not bear a child.
The people had been sickened by the appalling burning of 'heretics'—they longed for a Protestant sovereign.

The Queen received Elizabeth in the gardens of Richmond
Palace, and led her to the banqueting pavilion, which was decorated
with cloth of gold and violet velvet, the latter—subtle compli-
ment—embroidered in Anne Boleyn's device of a golden pome-
granate. Philip of Spain was friendly, the splendidly dressed
courtiers and their ladies respectful; the sun shone brightly and
the flowers were in bloom. A concert succeeded the banquet "at
which the best minstrels in the kingdom gratified the high musical
tastes of the royal sisters."

During the evening the Queen tried to discuss with her sister a
proposal made by the King of Sweden that Elizabeth should marry
his heir. This was a subject which the Princess had long experience
in parrying. She had had several offers of alliances, and while
dutifully considering them all had managed, with great skill, to
avoid marrying anybody. (Mary was outmanœuvred, and was
driven later to send Sir Thomas Pope to find out if Elizabeth's
constant refusal of suitors proceeded from any objection to the
married state in general. Sir Thomas returned as wise as he went.)

Elizabeth and her retinue left Richmond in the evening, and
returned in the royal barge to London. People living on the banks
of the river long remembered the beautiful sight of the procession
of boats gliding downstream in the evening light, while musicians

plucked at their lutes in the stern of the royal barge, and sweet singing voices echoed over the water.

Elizabeth, the heiress of England, became Queen the following year. In the raw, damp days of an exceptionally severe late autumn, Mary had caught a cold and died in November. Philip II had gone back to Spain long ago: there had been no real reunion between them. A gloomy, ailing woman, Mary's morbid obsession with her religion had not compensated for her failed marriage and barrenness. She had been hated and feared by most of her subjects, and the outward show of conventional grief at her funeral hardly went skin-deep.

On her death, there were many who felt that a black page of history had been turned over, and a fairer era was beginning. The new reign opened to the joyful clash of bells as the long-patient heiress of England, now Queen, rode to her Coronation royally attired, seated in a chariot covered with crimson velvet. All the houses in Cheapside were dressed with banners and streamers; the richest carpets and cloth of gold tapestried the streets. She smiled with equal grace on a poor woman who gave her a branch of rosemary at the Fleet bridge, and on the recorder of the city, in his gala dress, who presented her with a purse of crimson satin, containing a thousand marks of gold.

"I will be as good unto ye as ever queen was to a people," she said, and meant it.

CHAPTER FIVE

Queen Elizabeth lived here

THAT charming retreat, the village of Richmond, was still extending its boundaries. It was not yet a town—it would not be that for another two centuries or more—but many houses and shops had been built in the main street. A contemporary traveller notes that in country towns

> the houses are commonly of two stories, except in London, where they are three and sometimes four . . . they are built of wood, those of the richer sort with bricks, their roofs are low, and where the owner has money, covered with lead.

The wood-framed houses had white plastered walls between the timbering, and the doors and window-frames were of stout oak or elm.

"A row of good houses", Duke's Lane (now Duke Street) led to the large expanse of green which had once been the tourney and jousting-ground. Tourneys were but rarely held now, and the green expanse was used for pageants and other spectacles when the Queen was in residence in the great palace which dominated the scene at the river end. It was more often used for bull and bear baiting, favourite sports with the ordinary people as well as with the nobility. Frederick, Duke of Würtemberg, visiting "the far famed Kingdom of England" in 1602, described the baiting in the daily journal which he dictated to his secretary, Jacob Rathgeb:

> At such times you can perceive the breed and mettle of the dogs, for although they receive serious injuries from the bears, are caught by the horns of the bull, and tossed in the air so as frequently to fall down again upon the horns, they do not give in but fasten on the bull so firmly that one is obliged to pull them back by the tails, and force open their jaws. Four dogs at once were set on by the bull; they, however, could not gain any advantage over him, for he so artfully contrived to ward off their

[47]

attacks that they could not well get at him; on the contrary, the bull served them very scurvily by striking and butting at them.

During the day, when there were no animal baitings or spectacles, sheep were pastured on this piece of common land. The numbers were strictly limited by the steward of the manor, but his orders were often defied the moment his officers' backs were turned. Sheep meant wool and wool meant money. England had long been the European centre of the cloth trade; the raw wool was collected all over the country, not only from the farmers who had turned their arable land into more profitable pastures, but from individuals in the villages. Even a few sheep could produce an appreciable amount of extra money to supplement a villager's earnings at his craft or trade.

There were no manufactories in the village of Richmond, but the inhabitants were reasonably prosperous; wherever there was a palace and a court, there was money to be earned: embroiderers, saddlers, blacksmiths, sempstresses, extra cooks, perruquiers, mercers, pastrycooks, bakers—all could make a good living. Richmond was often full of rich folk, and fine houses that would need servants continued to go up—"Many fair and comely buildings of brick and squared stone" were built near the choicest parts of the river, for "the merchants of London plant their houses of recreation not in the meanest places."

As yet there was no outright freehold of houses. The manorial system, whereby the lord of the manor owned all the land, allowing strips of it to be cultivated by the labourers instead of being paid wages, had been modified through the centuries. In Richmond, by Elizabeth's time, there were several classes of tenantry. Freeholders were able virtually to own land and a messuage—the house standing on it; but they had to make regular payments to the lady of the manor, the Queen. Leaseholders, who were usually farmers, held their land and messuage for a fixed term of years, and for a fixed rental. In the Court Rolls, there are continual references to leases coming to an end, and either being renewed, usually at a higher rent, or changing hands. Copyholders were tenants of small holdings who paid rent instead of giving their labour, as their forefathers, the villeins, had done. Their land passed by inheritance from father to son by right of ancient custom, and when a copyholder died and his son

took over, the latter paid a small fine, the transaction being
entered in the manorial roll. Finally, there were the landless men
who no longer had a share in the common fields, or who had
had their share filched from them by ruthless neighbours. They
were compelled to hire themselves out as labourers, shepherds,
hedgers and ditchers, or harvesters, while their wives became
indoor servants or milkmaids.

Farm workers laboured long hours, but they knew how to
enjoy themselves, too. Paulus Hentzner, travelling from Windsor
to Hampton Court, saw a Harvest Home which impressed him as
a foreigner:

> As we were returning to our inn, we happened to meet some
> country people celebrating their Harvest Home; their last load of
> corn they crown with flowers, having besides an image richly
> dressed, by which perhaps they would signify Ceres, this they
> keep moving about, while men and women, men and maid-
> servants, riding through the streets in the cart, shout as loud as
> they can till they arrive at the barn. The farmers do not bind up
> their corn in sheaves . . . but directly as they have reaped and
> mowed it, put it into carts, and convey it into their barns.

In 1561, three years after Queen Elizabeth's accession, it
happened that Sir William Cecil wanted some herbs for his
garden. He was a high Minister of State—and was to become a
higher, as Lord Burleigh, one of Elizabeth's most trusted advisers—
and he did not think it out of place to ask for plants from the
royal gardens. His request was duly granted; the gardener at
Greenwich Palace would provide him with what he desired:
lavender, spile, hyssop, thyme, rosemary, and sage were recommended. If he wanted more he should send to the gardener at
Hampton Court or Richmond, where there were large herb
gardens.

The Queen did not often come to Richmond Palace in the first
years of her reign: she stayed at her palaces at Whitehall or
Greenwich, so as to be at the centre of state. Elizabeth had grown
up in a hard school, and she did not intend to make any mistakes
if she could help it. She had many enemies, who would rejoice to
see her thrown down from her high eminence. But she was adept
at hiding her thoughts. As courtier after courtier who had been

hostile to her during Mary's reign now came forward to make humble submission, she received them with "a graciousness of demeanour which proved that the Queen had the magnanimity to forgive the injuries, and even the insults", that had been offered to her as princess. One wonders what went on behind that enigmatic face as each flattering suppliant got down to his knees and asked pardon. The only time she ever allowed her feelings to show was when a member of the late queen's household, who had gone out of his way to offer petty affronts to Elizabeth when she was under Mary's displeasure, begged her not to punish him for his impertinence. "Fear not," replied the Queen. "We are of the nature of the lion, and cannot descend to the destruction of mice and such small beasts!" To Bedingfield, on the other hand, she became and remained a friend; he had been her gaoler at Richmond and Woodstock, but he had only done the duty enjoined on him, and she respected loyalty.

A more intriguing *volte-face* than that of time-serving courtiers was the move made by Philip II of Spain. His Catholic Majesty had once urged Queen Mary to visit the extreme penalty on her Protestant sister, a fact that Elizabeth well knew. Now he sent his Ambassador with a proposal of marriage. He would get a dispensation from the Pope to be allowed to marry his dearly-beloved sister-in-law. Elizabeth was sufficiently flattered to show his eloquent letters to her Ministers and courtiers, but she had also sufficient common sense to know that such an alliance would be detested by her subjects, and crack England into chaos. She was slowly pulling the country on to its feet, away from the yawning chasm of threatened bankruptcy. Henry VIII had debased the coinage, and the economy was still at a low ebb. A Catholic marriage would shake the slowly rising confidence of her people.

There was another strong reason against such an alliance: her title to the throne had already been impugned. The King of France had compelled his daughter-in-law, Mary, the sixteen-year-old wife of the Dauphin, to assume the arms and royal style of England. Mary was already Queen of Scots. Elizabeth had a contender for the throne. Marrying Philip of Spain was not the way to remain Queen of England. Elizabeth knew she must stand on her own feet, meet danger in her own way. She sent a courteous

Richmond Hill from near Cholmondeley House, about 1752

By courtesy of Mr Edward Croft-Murray

The Thames at Kew, Early Eighteenth Century

By courtesy of the Director, Royal Botanic Gardens

The Thames at Richmond, 1748

By courtesy of Mr Hermon Courlander

The Black Horse Inn, Eighteenth Century

By courtesy of Richmond upon Thames Libraries Com

Richmond Horse Ferry, about 1780

Robert Marris.

By courtesy of Mr Edward Croft-M

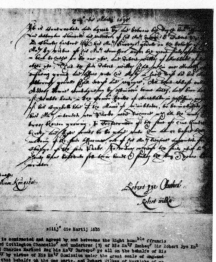

Deed of Purchase of Land in Mortlake
for the New Park,
Seventeenth Century

*By courtesy of Richmond upon Thames
Libraries Committee*

...mission Card to the New Park,
Eighteenth Century

*By courtesy of Richmond upon Thames
Libraries Committee*

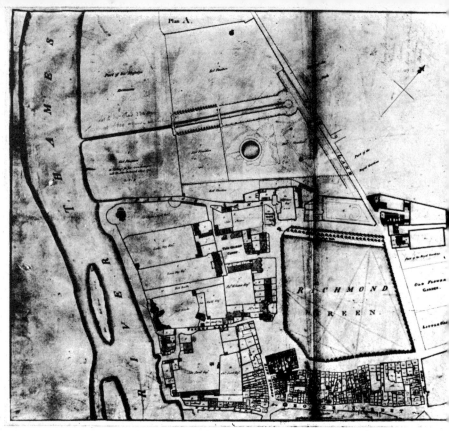

Royal Manor of Richmond, 1771 (Part of Plan)

Thomas Richardson.   *By permission of the Controller, H.M. Stationery Offi*

"The Prospect of Richmond in Surry, 1726"

Published by Henry Overton and J. Hook.   *By courtesy of Richmond upon Thames Libraries Comm*

but unmistakable refusal of marriage, and made an enemy for life.

It was restful at Richmond Palace. The air was soft and sweet, the gardens were ablow with flowers the year round, there was a pleasant sound of doves cooing in the courtyards. Elizabeth began to come regularly, sometimes arriving in spring and remaining until summer. The journey up the Thames with the Court was always a stately pageant. The royal barge with its gilt prow usually lay up on the bank of the river near the Globe Theatre, and was on show to visitors. Paulus Hentzner describes it as having "two splendid cabins, beautifully ornamented with glass windows, painting and gilding". When the Queen sailed in it the cabins were strewn with sweet herbs, and Elizabeth reclined on a cushion of cloth of gold, with a crimson velvet wrap about her feet. Twenty-one watermen rowed the barge, and it must have been a fine sight to see it, followed by the flotilla of attendant barges conveying the Court, as it sailed past the wherries and hoys on its way to Richmond. Cecil, "who, having succeeded in maintaining his head on his shoulders during the critical period of Queen Mary's reign, held it higher than ever as the confidential adviser and chief minister to her successor", had a house at Richmond, and Sir Francis Walsingham, the Earl of Leicester, the elegant Christopher Hatton, Walter Raleigh and Sir Philip Sidney, her favoured courtiers, were often at the palace. Leicester, who was Lord Steward of the Household, had to attend to the victualling of the palace when the Queen was in residence. Elizabeth was very fond of hawking and hunting, keeping packs of hounds at Richmond and energetically following the chase when she felt so inclined.

There were often concerts of music, and theatrical performances in the Great Hall of the palace. The Queen, who was a skilled performer herself on the lute and virginals, kept her own orchestra; a serjeant-trumpeter at £40 a year, sixteen trumpeters at £24 6s. 8d., two players on the lute at £19 5s. 0d. each, eight singers at £16 13s. 4d., as well as harpers, minstrels, players on the rebec, sackbut, viols, flutes, and drums. She also had her own dramatic troupe, the Queen's Men, the most renowned of all the London companies, being recruited from the best actors of the time, including the famous clown, Richard Tarleton. And the rising dramatist, Shakespeare, was invited to bring his plays to be performed at Richmond Palace.

One of Queen Elizabeth's most esoteric interests was fortune-telling. Peter Eisenberg, a Danish traveller to the English Court, tells of a book from the library of Henry VII which Elizabeth found in the palace, a work on "magic or the black art" called *Modus et Ratio Divinae Contemplationis*. In spite of the hard common sense which characterised many of her decisions and judgments, she had a weakness for astrologers, and often went to consult one of the most famous—or notorious—of them, John Dee, at his house at Mortlake.

Dee was born in London in 1527, the son of a vintner, and as he early showed an inclination towards learning, his father gave him the best education he could afford. The young man was a good mathematician, and took a degree at Trinity College, Cambridge. He studied at Louvain University and was for a time a professor at Rheims. His reputation as a scholar brought him to the notice of Edward VI, who gave him a pension, and he probably met the young king's half-sisters at this time. If he had stuck to his academic studies all would have been well, but Dee was fascinated by astrology and crystal-gazing, and became obsessed by alchemy, necromancy and the "philosopher's stone", which was said to transmute base metals into gold. The Princess Mary disliked him, and when, after she succeeded to the throne, she found that Elizabeth was friendly with Dee, Mary had him arrested for "practising against her life by enchantment." This charge could not be sustained by evidence, and he was at length released. When Elizabeth became Queen, she remembered that Dee had endured imprisonment for her sake, and she remained his friend.

Dr Dee settled at Mortlake, in a house opposite the church, and was soon looked on with suspicion by the inhabitants there, who were sure that he practised the Black Art. They once formed a mob and attacked his house, destroying nearly all his manuscripts and collection of rare books. Elizabeth sent him abroad as her "intelligencer", with a brief to write an account of the countries which had been discovered by English subjects, and consequently to which she had a claim. He accomplished this work, though the Queen does not appear to have made any practical use of the information. On his return she appointed him Warden of Man-chester College, where he remained for several years, and then returned to live again at Mortlake.

When the Queen was at Richmond she visited her old friend to have the future foretold by means of the "black crystal", which was probably a highly polished piece of coal with what appeared to be mysterious veinings. Dee wrote in his Diary for October 18th, 1578: "The Queen's Majestie had conference with me at Richemond, inter 9 et 11." And for November 27th, 1590: "The Queen's being at Richemond graciously sent for me. I cam to her at three quarters of the clok. Afterwards she sayd she wold send me something to kepe Christmas with." One of Elizabeth's last visits to the astrologer, an unexpected one for him, happened on the day he buried his wife, Johanna, but it did not make any difference: the Queen had her "conference", just the same.

The letters and journals of travelling foreigners often give the most immediate and vivid pictures of what people were really like in past centuries; impressions were written down while they were still fresh, and all kinds of details were added which one never finds in the history books.

The German traveller Thomas Platter went to Richmond to attend a Court in October, 1585. A Swiss acquaintance, a student named Caspar Thoman, met him as they were both looking round the chapel of the palace, and asked Platter how he should present a supplication to the Queen for a scholarship to an English college. Platter spoke to the Queen's Secretary, who examined the youth's credentials, advised him not to hand his petition to the Queen as she passed, as he had intended, but to leave it with him: he would help if he could. "Which he did," relates Platter, "for although bursaries are mostly founded for the natives in special cases, yet he received a good grant, so that he is still studying in England free of costs today." Elizabeth well understood the art of making long-term friends on the Continent of Europe.

One of the most observant of foreign travellers was Paulus Hentzner, already mentioned. He was born in Brandenburg in 1558, and became a jurist, a lawyer. When he was in his thirties he took a post as tutor to a young Silesian nobleman, and they set out in 1597 on a three years' tour which included

England. Hentzner kept a travel journal that was later published, and it was translated into English, and edited in the eighteenth century by Horace Walpole, who says in the Introduction:

> The Author seems to have had that laborious and indiscriminate passion for SEEING, which is remarked in his countrymen; and as his translator observed, enjoyed as much the doubtful head of a more doubtful saint in pickle, as any upon the shoulders of the best Grecian statue. Fortunately so memorable a personage as queen Elizabeth happened to fall under his notice.

Fortunately, indeed. In an account of a day he passed at Court, Hentzner gives us an unsurpassed picture of the living Elizabeth: what she looked like, how she spoke, her manner to others, details of her dress so clearly described that one almost hears the silk rustle. He notices everything, down to the smallest point of etiquette; you feel as if you were actually there with him. Though this particular visit was to Greenwich Palace, the same formality and ceremonial would have been observed at Richmond Palace when the Queen was in residence there.

Hentzner obtained an order from the Lord Chamberlain to be admitted into the Presence Chamber, which was hung with rich tapestry, and the floor, "after the English fashion, strewed with hay." He probably meant rushes.

> At the door stood a gentleman dressed in velvet, in a gold chain, whose office was to introduce to the Queen any person of distinction that came to wait on her. It was Sunday, when there is usually the greatest attendance of nobility. In the same hall were the Archbishop of Canterbury, the Bishop of London, a great number of Counsellors of State, Officers of the Crown, and Gentlemen, who waited the Queen's coming out, which she did from her own apartments when it was time to go to prayers, attended in the following manner:
> First went Gentlemen, Barons, Earls, Knights of the Garter, all richly dressed and bareheaded; next came the Lord High Chancellor of England, bearing the seals in a red silk purse, between the two, one of whom carried the royal sceptre, the other the sword of state in a red scabbard, studded with golden fleur-de-lys, the point upwards; next came the Queen, in the 65th year of her age (as we are told), very majestic, her face oblong, fair but wrinkled, her eyes small, yet black and pleasant; her nose a little hooked,

and her teeth black (a defect the English seem subject to, from their too great use of sugar); she had in her ears two pearls with very rich drops; her hair was of auburn colour but false; upon her head she had a small crown . . . her bosom was uncovered, as all the English ladies have it till they marry; and she had on a necklace of exceeding fine jewels; her hands were slender, her fingers rather long, and her stature neither tall nor low; her air was stately, her manner of speaking mild and obliging. That day she was dressed in white silk, bordered with pearls of the size of beans, and over it a mantle of black silk shot with silver threads; her train was very long, the end of it borne by a marchioness; instead of a chain, she had an oblong collar of gold and jewels. As she went along in this state and magnificence, she spoke very graciously, first to one, then to another . . . in English, French and Italian; for besides being well skilled in Greek, Latin, and the languages I have mentioned, she is mistress of Spanish, Scotch and Dutch.

Whoever speaks to her, it is kneeling; now and then she raises someone with her hand. While we were there, William Slawata, a Bohemian baron, had letters to present to her; and she, after pulling off her glove, gave him her right hand to kiss, sparkling with rings and jewels—a mark of particular favour. Wherever she turned her face as she was going along, everybody fell down on their knees. The ladies of the court followed her, very handsome and well-shaped, and for the most part dressed in white. She was guarded on each side by the gentlemen pensioners, fifty in number, with gilt halberds. In the ante-chapel, next the hall where we were, petitions were presented to her, and she received them most graciously, which occasioned the acclamation of *God Save Queen Elizabeth!* She answered it with *I thank you my Good People.* In the chapel was excellent music; as soon as it and the service were over, which scarce exceeded half an hour, the Queen returned in the same state and order, and prepared to go to dinner.

Hentzner's description of the Queen's dyed false hair was not made as a criticism; wigs were often worn by Court ladies and the fashionable dames of the period, no doubt following Elizabeth's lead. There is a warrant in the British Museum, signed by Elizabeth, ordering payment to "Dorothy Speckarde, our silkewoman, for six heades of heare, twelve yeardes of heare curle, one hundred devises made of heare." Six heads of hair and twelve yards of hair curl would easily be accounted for by the elaborate erections in Elizabeth's portraits.

The Queen kept her age with remarkable vitality. She still went hunting at Richmond, and would keep the Court dancing galliards until a late hour. She herself danced as nimbly at sixty-five as she had done at thirty. When Roger Aston delivered letters to her from his master, James VI of Scotland—her heir—he would find her dancing to a little fiddle, "*affectedly* doing so", he wrote irritably, aware that the purpose of this exercise was that he should tell the King the Queen was still so youthful, it would be a long time before James VI of Scotland would become James I of England.

She was to have a few more years of majesty and might, but the end was approaching. Elizabeth suffered greatly with the gout in her hands, and some intestinal ailment made her rigid with pain; she never complained, and "continued to talk of progresses and festivities as though she expected her days to be prolonged through years to come." There was still gaiety in the palaces, still music, but the dancing was slowing down. Elizabeth had a recurring fever that developed into symptoms which, for a long time, she would not admit to her physicians. She was afflicted with an overpowering melancholy and refused to take medicines. At the beginning of 1603, she became seriously ill, but would not give in to what she considered to be weakness. She grew worse, yet she sat up for ten days and refused to rest, so that in the end her attendants had to undress her and put her to bed by force.

Lady Southwell, one of the ladies in closest attendance on the Queen, gives an illuminating instance of Elizabeth's still obsessive vanity, dissolving at last in the cold light of truth:

In the melancholy of her sickness, she desired to see a *true* looking-glass, which in twenty years before she had not seen, but only such a one as on purpose was made to deceive her sight; which true looking-glass being brought her, she presently fell exclaiming at all those flatterers which had so much commended her, and they durst not after come into her presence.

Her attendants had left off painting her face, and for once she saw her natural visage in the glass.

[56]

Dr Dee still had a great deal of influence over Elizabeth, and he told her to "beware of Whitehall." She removed to Richmond, which she had always looked upon as the "warm winter-box" to shelter her old age, but even then she would not go to bed and stay there. Robert Carey, one of her kinsmen, on visiting her, found her sitting on a heap of cushions on the floor in one of the withdrawing chambers. She was too weak to go to Divine Service on the Sunday, and insisted on having cushions laid on the floor of the privy-chamber near by, and heard the service from there. Returning to her own apartment, she sat again on the cushions. The Archbishop of Canterbury and her faithful Cecil begged her to have medical aid, but the indomitable old woman told them "that she knew her own constitution better than they did, and that she was not in so much danger as they imagined."

She died on March 24th, 1603, "and was most royally interred" in Westminster Abbey a month later. Only her kinsmen and counsellors and ladies had seen the pain-wracked shell of a woman who had fought off death for so long: her subjects and the courts of Europe remembered the glittering monarch in all her jewelled splendour. Let us take a last glimpse of her, not in the stiff, formal portraits, but in one of the rare miniatures painted of her, that in the Tollemache collection at Ham House. She must have been about twenty at the time, the Lady Elizabeth, and she wears a black dress trimmed with pearls and fastened down the front with bows of rose-coloured ribbon. Her point-lace ruffles are looped with pearls and ribbons, and her auburn hair is set off with a satin fillet, decorated in front with a jewel from which three pear-shaped pearls depend. It is not a pretty face, but it is one to remember.

CHAPTER SIX

Decline and Fall

AFTER the death of Queen Elizabeth I, the glory began to depart from Richmond Palace, though it had a final period as a royal residence. James VI of Scotland, the Queen's successor, spent much of his time in his northern kingdom, and his consort, Anne of Denmark, preferred Whitehall and the other palaces to Richmond.

The royal pair had seven children. Prince Henry, the heir to the throne, was much attached to Richmond, and was very popular there. From contemporary accounts he was "virtuous and just," without being in the least pompous or priggish, and distinguished by "a mild and gentle behaviour", and when, after trying several residences, he chose Richmond Palace as his home, the inhabitants were greatly pleased. His tutor and the governor of his household were both considerable scholars, and they had an apt pupil. Prince Henry did not need persuasion; he learnt readily and thoroughly, and became master of several languages. He also showed, at an early age, a taste for the fine arts. He began to collect pictures before he went to Richmond, and was a patron of artists in England and abroad. Sir Henry Wotton, who had been Ambassador in Venice, brought back a number of paintings of the Italian School for Prince Henry's collection, and Isaac Oliver, a French painter, who had made his name in England in Elizabeth's time, painted miniatures of the Prince. An even more famous miniaturist, Nicholas Hilliard, painted a miniature of Prince Henry, full length, with a gauntlet in one hand. The Prince had agents on the look-out for "purchases of old paintings at a reasonable rate."

Prince Henry commissioned the Gascon architect, Solomon de Cans, to build a gallery to house his collection of pictures, sculp-

tures, "and everything worth possessing"—bronze statuettes by
Fanelli, medallions, coins, cameos, intaglios. Inigo Jones has been
given the credit for this picture gallery; he is actually in the
records as estimating for "the piling, planking and brickwork, for
making three aits [river islands]", and for repairs to the library
and the new gallery. There was also a great deal of work done on
levelling the site of the friary, next to the palace, which had been
pulled down in Henry VIII's time and had been left in a neglected
state. Inigo Jones was employed by the Prince as surveyor of the
works.

Contemporary records all agree on the outstanding character
and many-sidedness of Prince Henry. He was as brave physically
as he was alert mentally; a daring rider and an excellent tennis-
player. Above all, he loved sailing. Phineas Pett, one of King
James's shipwrights, built the prince a small vessel with a keel of
28 feet and a breadth of 12 feet, "handsomely carved and painted."
The Prince launched her with a bowl of wine, christening the
boat *The Disdain*, and he used her to carry him from Richmond
to his town house at St James's, or to Whitehall. Prince Henry
often navigated the little vessel himself, and the watermen and
bargemen along the river between Richmond and London
formed a great affection for this splendidly endowed, fearless
young man.

In 1612, the Prince was suddenly stricken with a mysterious
illness. As he grew worse, the King summoned doctors from
Cambridge and London to go to Richmond; they gave him
purgatives compounded of senna, rhubarb, and syrup of roses, and
applied the barbarous remedies of the day—glysters, pigeons
cloven in two put against the soles of the feet, scarifications of the
shoulders "to lower the humour." They could do nothing to ease
his agonised sufferings, and he died. A report on the post-mortem
examination has been preserved; in it, the doctors' confused
counsels about the unfortunate Prince's illness is bluntly likened
to the confusion of tongues at the Tower of Babel. The writer of
the report, a physician, goes on to say that Prince Henry's extraordinary patience under his sufferings probably misled the doctors,
and attributes his death to malignant fever.

"Loving he was, and kind to strangers," wrote Sir Charles
Cornwallis, and it was the qualities of humanity and tolerance,

gentleness and inborn nobility, which set this young prince apart in the murky politics and intrigues of the period.

When he died the next heir to the throne was the King's second son, who was to become Charles I.

Prince Henry's brother, Charles, Duke of York, had been a sickly baby and a weakling as a child, with an impediment in his speech and misshapen walk. At the age of four he was put into the charge of Lady Carey, "a careful nurse and sensible woman." It was well for her charge that she was. The King, irritated by his second son's disabilities, directed that the string under the boy's tongue should be cut to improve his speech, and his legs put in iron supports. Lady Carey remonstrated so urgently against such an outlandish order that the King gave way. Insensitive, choleric, arrogant, and domineering, James I was not a pleasant character to have on the throne of England.

The young Duke was often taken by Lady Carey to Richmond for "the sweet air", and came to know the palace well; it was always associated in his mind with peacefulness and tranquil beauty. After Prince Henry's death, Charles, now Prince Charles the heir, was established at Richmond Palace. His health had greatly improved, and he began to make himself the master of many sports—vaulting, "riding the great horse", shooting with the cross-bow and with the musket.

In 1617, the manor of Richmond was formally made over to Prince Charles, together with Ham House and the royal estates at Petersham. He had to attend his father's Court, but was at Richmond as often as possible, chiefly to satisfy his inordinate passion for hunting. A chronicler says: "He was learning extravagance rapidly . . . [and] was often glad to return to Richmond, where he found himself more at liberty than with his father, by whom he was too much restrained in his sports and pleasures."

James I died, unlamented by his people, in 1625, and Prince Charles was now King. In the same year he married Henrietta Maria, a Catholic princess, sister of Louis XIII of France. The old foreboding woke in his subjects; again there was dread of domination by the powerful Catholic countries on the Continent. Charles I was, however, a Protestant, and there were no overt demonstrations; though Henrietta Maria was disliked from the beginning, not only on account of her religion, but because of her imperious haughtiness. The new reign began ominously. Plague had broken out in London, and the Court was removed from Whitehall to Richmond, together with the exchequer and records. Richmond being considered safer than the metropolis, large numbers of London citizens who could afford it followed the Court, in spite of proclamations forbidding people coming from infected places approaching any of the King's residences. River boats going to London were not allowed to return; no vessels at all were permitted to sail from Kingston to London. The large numbers of people crowding into Richmond brought fresh alarms, and presently Charles, his Queen, and the Court were riding to the palace at Woodstock, near Oxford.

When the plague had died down the Court returned to Richmond, the manor of which Charles now settled on his consort. Both Charles I and Henrietta Maria were extravagant, especially in dress, and the foppishness and vulgar display of the Court became a byword. "Prodigals, in consequence, mutiplied prodigiously, and rivalled each other in the rapidity with which they went the road to ruin." Richmond was inevitably affected. New taverns appeared, houses of call flourished. The pox took toll of many a gallant who had fled from London to Richmond a few years earlier, to escape the plague.

Charles I was a patron of art, like his brother, though not on the same scale. He extended special patronage to the Dutch painter Van Dyck, whose many portraits of Charles I and the royal family show posterity what they looked like—idealised, as all portraits were at that time, but with a feeling of authenticity which does not always apply to other royal portraits. Charles added considerably to Prince Henry's collection, and the picture gallery at Richmond became known on the Continent as well as at home.

The Queen had long antagonised her husband's Ministers. In spite of the King's undertaking that his children should be brought up as Protestants, Henrietta secretly had her children instructed in the Catholic faith, and the fact was known to many. The King was forced to act. Prince Charles, the heir, was given the manor of Richmond, and sent there in 1641, the Marquis of Hertford having charge of the Prince "at his own House at Richmond . . . that he might avoid dangerous persons, priests and Jesuits." His tutor was

Bishop Duppa, who had been chaplain to the King, and could be depended upon to teach the heir to the Protestant throne the tenets of the Church of England.

Prince Charles did not stay long at Richmond; he and the rest of his family were naturally involved in the fortunes of the King. The Civil War, and its outcome, meant the end of Richmond Palace either as a home or a palace. Charles I, captured by the rebels, was offered lodgings in Richmond Palace, but refused to go. He was executed in 1649, and his family lived in exile on the Continent. The victorious Parliament proceeded to sell his possessions, and sent commissioners to survey the palace and its contents. This survey, done with great thoroughness and attention to detail, is our main source today for the descriptions we have of the palace which Henry VII built and which succeeding sovereigns enlarged and embellished.

The magnificent gallery of pictures collected by Prince Henry, and added to by Charles I, was sold, "and those set down as superstitious, destroyed." The contents of the palace, the furniture, tapestries, statuary, and jewelled objects, were next sold—to settle the arrears of pay of some of the rebel regiments, one authority suggests. Then the palace itself, valued at over £10,000, was sold to Thomas Rookesby, William Goodwin, and Adam Baynes; they re-sold it to Sir Gregory Norton, one of the judges who had signed the death-warrant of Charles I. Norton died within a year or so, and the place seems to have been allowed to sink into a state of neglect.

The Commonwealth acted quickly in their determination to change the social order. William Murray, Gentleman of the Bedchamber to Charles I, and his wife Katherine, tried to avoid the sequestration of estates edict by transferring their lands in Ham, Petersham, and Kingston, to others, but they were not successful, for it was laid down that "the goods be seized, appraised, and sold by the candle, [and] the rents levied." Later, a permit was issued to "Mrs. Murray's servants to enjoy her estates at Ham, and sow the ground till further orders."

The spoliation of Richmond Palace and the severe measures which deprived the former Court officials of their lands and wealth had an immediate effect on the inhabitants of Richmond and the adjacent villages. The long association of royalty with the

village had brought many of the nobility and London merchants
to live there, and a flourishing community of tradesmen and
craftsmen had grown up. The change in the fortunes of their
clients and customers meant a serious diminution of trade. The
villagers' sons and daughters, instead of taking up the father's
craft or entering service locally, now had to go to London, the
youths to be bound apprentices to strange masters, the daughters
to take situations in houses of which the parents knew nothing,
exposed to dangers which every mother thought of with fearful
apprehension. The break-up of close-knit families was a real
tragedy, but it was often inevitable. There were no industries in
Richmond; no prosperous cloth trade, no crafts like pottery or
lace-making, no large farms which could support widening circles
of relations. The only exports were fruit and vegetables, which
employed a limited number of people. The Civil War meant much
hardship for Richmond, whatever the loyalties of the inhabitants.

After the Restoration, when the exiled Prince Charles returned
to England as Charles II, many thought that Richmond would
regain its former importance as a royal residence. Charles, however, did not care for Richmond; he preferred Windsor. He had
the palace repaired and gave it to his mother to live in, but
Henrietta Maria found it too bleak and lacking in comfort without
its former splendid furnishings. The next royal occupant of the
palace was the infant Prince of Wales, son of James II, the Catholic
successor to his brother Charles. James had married Mary Beatrice
of Modena, as zealous a Catholic as himself, and the country was
again seething with bigotry, hatred, suspicion. When the Queen
gave birth to a son and heir in 1688 preposterous reports were put
about that the baby was a changeling, or a substitute child, or that
he did not exist at all. Protestant extremists, fearing a long
Catholic succession, went so far as to say that the child might be
the Queen's, but was not the King's.

The baby was healthy and well when he was born, but his diet
of "watter gruell", a concoction of barley-flour, water and sugar,
with a few currants added, did not agree with him, and he was
soon ill. The Queen sent him to Richmond, where the air was
purer than in London, under the care of Lady Powis. The doctors
had insisted that their diet was the right one, and when the child
did not improve, gave him Canary wine and Dr Goddard's Drops,

described by a contemporary as "nothing less than liquid fire, for if one falls on a piece of cloth, it burns a hole through it in half an hour." Colic, dysentery, and other disorders attacked the child as a result of this unholy dosing. When Lady Powis suggested trying milk they declared that he would die within half an hour if given this natural fluid.

Lady Powis thought the infant Prince would more likely die of their ministrations, in spite of the good Richmond air, and took matters into her own hands. She found a wet-nurse at Richmond, a brick-maker's wife, and gave the baby to the woman to nurse. The Tuscan Envoy, Count Terriesi, writing to the Grand Duke of Tuscany in August, 1688, gave his master an account of how the infant fared:

> I hear from Richmond that the Prince, thanks to a natural diet, is doing well. The greedy doctors, seeing they were defeated, combined to try and sell his Majesty a dearer nurse; but the Marchioness of Powis, perceiving this stratagem, sent them all out of the room and took samples of the milk of all the candidates and took them to the doctors for examination without their knowing which was which; they decided in favour of the aforesaid woman, which cut the earth from under their feet . . . they did not get the commission from her which they would have got from the two gentlewomen whom they preferred.

CHAPTER SEVEN

Law and Order

HUMAN beings, by nature anarchic and "agin restraint", have always found it necessary to support some form of authority to save them from themselves, if not from their fellow-men. The forces of law and order in Richmond, as in other towns, were the Vestry and the Manor Courts. Court Leets, which dealt with minor offences, were held from very early times, the fines being paid to the lord of the manor.

The Parish Church, as in every town and village, was the centre of life for the inhabitants. There had been a chapel in the village of Shene in the reign of Henry I; it was one of the four chapels of Kingston, in the advowson of Merton Abbey. A new church was built in Henry VII's time, for in a book of his private expenses there appears: "Item. Given to ye Parish Clerke of Richmond towards ye building on his new Church, £5." In a will preserved in Doctors Commons, dated July 17th, 1487, there is a clause mentioning the chapel of "Marie Magdalene de Shene"; and in 1558, lands were given by Thomas Denys for repairing the church, and for other charities.

Early in the sixteenth century, the first effective church council, the Vestry, was formed, and the first Parish Registers began at about the same time. The first baptism noted in the registers is of Walter Charleton, in February 1583. Sometimes an occupation is given: "Joseph son of John Baylie, embroiderer", appears in 1625, and "Elizabeth Mason, Ass Tamer" in 1626. After 1700, it was usual to give the father's trade in practically every case, the most frequent being 'watterman', and after that baker, carpenter, saddler, 'taylour', gardener, chandler, 'groacer', vintner, victualer, 'cuyrgion' (surgeon—probably surgeon-barber), 'a pottecary', 'shoomaker'. There is a fair sprinkling of 'basterds' and baseborn children. Sometimes the father, if a Gent., contributed to the child's maintenance by sending a capital sum to the Vestry. In 1701 the death is recorded of "Mark Bostley son of Richard, living upon London Bridge, harbourd ashour of hatts"—a reminder of Old London Bridge, lined with shops on both sides. There is an interesting entry in 1755: "Eliz. Sharp, a black of riper years of Mr. Darbys."

Banns began to appear in the registers about 1730, but not consistently; it is evident from other records that there were many omissions at Richmond. Sometimes the officiating minister is mentioned, as in May 1737: "The honble. Mr. John Talbot and Mrs. Henrietta Decker were married by special licence on Monday May 30 by Mr. Browne." In the marriage register, the letter and bracket (M) appear from time to time, indicating that the person concerned was illiterate and made his or her mark.

To return to the formation of the Vestry in the 1500s, its importance then, and for a very long time to come, is apparent in the records which have come down to us of this lively body of public-spirited men. The Vestry was the earliest form of local government, and the Vestry records, together with the Court Rolls—the records of the manor courts—give, between them, many an interesting glimpse into everyday life in Richmond in those far-off days.

People were fined for digging and carrying away clay and taking furzes or bushes from the common land, especially tile-kiln owners, who needed a constant supply of fuel and preferred to take it rather than buy it. The Vestry kept a sharp eye on the cultivated Common Fields. In 1618, Henry Marr "depastured one Lamb in the Cornfields" and was fined 12*d.*, being warned that if he did the same with his poultry he would have to pay 10*s.* Mr Marr had also taken away "Turff of and from the Common of this Manor to order and after an Admonition given him, therefore fined 20*s.*" One Leaver left his cow unstaked for three days on the Common Fields, "eating other men's corn", and was fined 6*d.* for each day.

There were, of course, many watermen in Richmond, some with rented land by the river, but others with no settled places to keep their craft, and there are several items in the records of watermen being fined for "putting up boats" on unauthorised land.

In 1624, the Vestry met to consider the ruinous state of the steeple of the Parish Church, and the necessity of repairing it properly or building a new one. The church had very little money in its coffers, and there seemed no chance of donations coming their way. The churchwardens began to tighten up on finance. Several vestrymen, who had for years been entrusted with the disbursement of certain charitable funds, were known to have a surplus, which they had not returned to the church. They had not rendered regular accounts, either, and they were now asked to submit an audit, and to repay any moneys left in their hands. The vestrymen had no alternative but to agree to this procedure—with the exception of one of their number, John Keele. This rugged individualist refused to submit to any audit, and challenged the Vestry to take legal proceedings against him if they wished. The Vestry accepted the challenge, and sued him in Kingston Court. The surprised John Keele thereupon climbed down, and asked them, in a much more subdued manner, to cease from suing. They got their money.

Valentine Leaver was engaged to re-build the church steeple. "First he is to make the Tower a Plaine Plinth" with such stone as he should find in the churchyard, "and to make the rest of the Battlements a plaine Coping answerable to the thickness of the Wall." He was to do a great deal more work, and to find all the labourers and finish it in good time, for the sum of £30 down and 20 nobles to come. But when Valentine Leaver went to the Vestry to justify a debt of drawing lime, sand, laths, and bricks he had used in the work, he was told that the parish was unable to pay old debts. Valentine not only forgave them his bill but gave them a donation.

It was an offence to allow property to become ruinous. The landlord of the Red Lyon was fined "for that his house was dilapidated", and James Medlecoate, Gent., a tenant of property in Brewers Lane, not only had neglected to pay his rent to the lord of the manor for some years, but allowed his premises "to fall down and go to ruin for want of Reparation", and so the bailiff and officers of the court were sent to seize the premises and evict the tenant.

During the Commonwealth, the Vestry elected the incumbent of the Parish Church, and having heard several prospective ministers preach, selected Mr Samuel Hinde, being satisfied "with his Certificates and Testimonials of his good abilities and conversation, and of his conformableness to the present government." Mr Hinde lasted two years, and was succeeded by Mr Abiel Borfett, who was promised £100 a year, including the small tithes. Mr Borfett continued as minister for thirty-six years, in spite of the fact that he always had difficulty in getting his stipend paid.

There are few entries which stress "conformableness" to the central government, of whatever complexion; the emphasis in the records is naturally on local affairs. It was laid down that "no Butcher shall keep any more Sheep or Cattle upon Richmond Green or the Common than the land they hold will allow them to keep by the Custom of the Manor—10^d for each offence." The inhabitants were ordered to erect a pillory. The ducking-stool of Richmond was to be repaired and mended before the following Michaelmas, "or else the inhabitants of the Town to Forfeit to the Lord of the Leet, 10s."

Being ducked—the sentence usually pronounced on "low, scolding and abusive women"—was a very unpleasant punishment. The ducking, or cucking, stool was a strong chair fixed by means of a swivel to a pole at the side of a deep pond, or river. The wretched woman was fastened in the chair, and ducked again and again in the water, being held below the surface so long that she came up gasping painfully. The curious thing is that the same women appear in the records more than once—apparently experience did not teach them a lesson.

There is an entry in 1653, noting that Thomas Cockdell "converted the Ducking Stool to his own use." He was told to mend the stool and set it again in the place where it usually stood or he would pay 10s. In the following year Thomas was again convicted of taking the stool "for his own use." He was ordered to return it to its proper place, by the side of the Great Pond, under penalty of forfeiting £3. Intriguing entries. Did he prefer to do a little domestic ducking on his own account?

Drainage, sewage, and the removal of ordure brought serious problems in the seventeenth century, and there are many references in the Court Rolls and the Vestry records to offenders

against the local regulations. Water was brought into the town
by means of ditches, and penalties were imposed on people who
fouled these channels. Sir James Butler was fined 6*s*. 8*d*. for not
cleaning part of the sewer running past his house on the Hill.

The Court did not scruple to put the town to the expense of
dealing with surplus water. "It is ordered that at the charge of
the Town the Rain which descends from the Hill to the Green to
the nuisance of the King's House there be conveyed into the
Vault in the Green either by a paved channel or Vault." This
seems to dispose of the belief, held by many, that there are secret
passages under the Green running along the site of the palace.
Most of these 'passages' are old sewers or channels for fresh water.

In 1654 the inhabitants of Pensioners Alley (later Golden
Court) were arraigned for "throwing dirty water and soap suds
out of their houses so that the filth ran out to the Green." They
defended themselves, declaring that they had to do this for want
of a suitable sink. It was accordingly ordered that their landlord,
Richard Burnham, should provide a sufficiently large sink to be
placed in the alley, or else forfeit 50*s*. to the lady of the manor.
And if the tenants of the alley didn't use the sink each offender
was to forfeit 2*s*. 6*d*. a time. Brewers Lane was in the courts
in 1656, the inhabitants being accused of throwing dirt from their
cottages on to the Green. It had already been ordered some time
before

> that all Householders within the Town of Richmond that have
> any dunghill or lay shales [peelings] before their several doors in
> the Streets, Lanes or Allyes do remove and take away the same
> respectively before the First Day of February next Upon Pain
> everyone to forfeit 2*s*. 6*d*. to the Lord of the Leet.

There was no suggestion as to where the dung and lay shales
were to be taken.

Continual efforts were made to control the nuisance of domestic animals being allowed to roam at will. Jeffrey Smith was
warned against allowing the inhabitants of the house near the
Green to be "annoyed by the Stench of Hogs in Brewers Lane."
Roger Veasy was warned not to allow the inhabitants to be annoyed
"with the Stench of the Dung of Hogs or other Cattle" which he
allowed to wander in Church Lane, and was fined 1*s*. This kind
of offence crops up throughout the seventeenth and eighteenth

centuries. Perhaps the local authorities had begun to associate the
filth allowed to lie openly about the town with the plague, recurring at this period even more often than it had done in previous
centuries. The melancholy subject of the plague comes up many
times in the State Papers of the time. Thomas Povey wrote in
1665 that he had been daily providing for infected persons, more
than 300 having died in Brentford and Isleworth: "Death has
become so familiar and the people so insensible of danger that
they look on those who provide for the public safety as tyrants."
The pest-house at Richmond was crowded, but the Vestry tried,
by strict measures, to keep infected persons isolated, and so
avoid a major outbreak in the town.

The steward of the manor and the Vestry were both very careful
of local rights. William Best built a wall 6 feet beyond the ancient
fence in Marshgate, "and in so doing hath quite Debarr'd all Foot
passengers from Going their Usual way to their great Annoyance."
He was bidden show his authority for his high-handed action,
and, producing none, was ordered to erect a convenient foot-stile
for passengers, failing which he was fined two shillings and six-
pence a month until it was done. Personages with considerable
influence were treated no differently from their humbler neighbours. "The Highway leading from Petersham towards Ham and
Kingston, which is the Highway of Carriage and Horse and has
been so used Time beyond the memory of man is obstructed with
a Hedge and Ditch by W^m. Murray Esq." Murray owned a large
estate at Petersham and had been an official at Charles I's Court.
He was fined 20s. and ordered "that he reform same before the
Feast of St. John the Baptist next under pain of 30s."

An ancient highway for horse and cart from Richmond Green
to the Thames, formerly fenced as a right of way going between
"the little Park and the late Court Wall" was stopped up by Sir
Gregory Norton, who took down the fence and put up posts,
rails, and a gate, "to the prejudice of the Tenants and Inhabitants
of Richmond for want of free Passage for them and their Cattle
to go to the Thames." He was ordered to take down the posts,
rails, and gate and to replace the fence, forfeiting 20s. for every
month the work remained undone. Clement Maunder, a tanner,
had without leave or licence of the lord of the manor erected a
cottage on the Common,

which if it be suffered to continue is likely to prove prejudicial to our Custom and much offensive to the Tenants in General, whose Cattle kept upon the Common are likely to be infected by the water issuing from his Tan Pitts into the Common Pond. We therefore Pain the said Clement Maunder to pull down and take away his said Building between this and Bartholomew Day next or forfeit for every month, besides the Penalties of the Statute, £1.

Thomas Cockdell—he of the ducking-stool misdemeanours—was again in trouble, this time for "erecting certain Posts before his House upon the Hill to the endangering of Passengers, and if he remove them not between this and Michaelmas next they Pain him 10s." Passengers—foot passengers—were endangered in more terrible ways.

We find upon the confession of Matthias Cox and his servant Edward Jones by chance drove a Coach and horses over some part of the body of Katherine Strawberry which was the occasion of her death, and Find . . . her Death was worth £3.

William Sherman, James Wells, and others were 'pain'd' for keeping bull dogs, contrary to the Law, and "to ye endangering of the King and Queen's Liege people."

The parishioners were always being burdened by strangers who came into the town, lodged with landlords until their money ran out, and then claimed assistance from the parish. There was also the danger of strangers being carriers of infection. The Vestry forbade anyone to build a house or cottage with the intention of taking in lodgers, and the town constable was instructed to keep his eyes open for any contravention of the order. Thomas Raymond had to remove his mother-in-law out of the parish, though he was obviously a more responsible individual than Francis the Miller, fined 6s. 8d. for harbouring vagrant and idle persons in his barn "who could give no good account of themselves."

Women had to watch their tongues. Mary Crome was ordered to remove the Widow Latherwaight out of her house under penalty of 40s. "because the said Widow Latherwaight is a common Scould." Widow Latherwaight was next ordered out of the house of Michael Flewellyn, carpenter, under a penalty of 40s. The scolding widow was fortunate to escape the ducking-stool.

A PROSPECT OF RICHMOND

The same petty offences, common in medieval times, continued throughout the seventeenth century. Bakers were fined amounts up to 6*s.* 8*d.* for selling underweight loaves. William Hucker, of Ham, "a common Baker of bread, at different times hath baked unwholesome Bread" and was pain'd in the sum of 3*s.* 4*d.* Robert Webb "sold cheese and butter at different times, by illicit and false measures", and was fined 10*s.*

There were penalties for those who offended against the accepted conventional codes of conduct. Nicholas Austrell was fined 5*s.* for being "a Common Eave Dropper." George Cutler was fined 2*s.* 6*d.* for "keeping and suffering Company to be in his House Drinking in the Time of Divine Service on the Sabbath Day." John King, another ale-house keeper, was fined 10*s.* because "he allowed bad Conversation by Night as by Day." John Yeomans had to pay 12*s.* penalty as "he continually kept bad Rule and Government in his home in Richmond to the great nuisance and disturbance of his neighbours and contrary to diverse Statutes."

It was an offence to refuse to assist the arm of the law. William Saule was fined 3*s.* 6*d.* "for that he hath not obeyed Assistance to the Constable with a prisoner", and, at the same court, Thomas Howses was fined 12*s.* "for that he hath refused to carry a Hue and Crie." To assault the constable in the execution of his office was much more serious; Edward Olden incautiously tried fisticuffs on this dignitary and was fined £5. The usual fine for "drawing blood" was 6s. 8*d.* The arm of the law might find himself facing the Bench. James Matthews, the constable of Ham, was fined 3*s.* 4*d.* "for not providing a pair of stocks there"—which throws new light on what the town constable had to provide out of his pay.

Contempt of court was a heinous misdemeanour. Thomas Fenner, carpenter, appearing before the court on some charge, "then and there spoke indecent words." He was enjoined to keep silence, but "obstinately refused to Obey the Order of the Court in Great Contempt and Disturbance of the Court and to a bad Example of all sitting and others our King's Liege Subjects then present." He was fined 100*s.*—a very large sum.

CHAPTER EIGHT

Eighteenth-century Richmond

A PROCESSION of kings and queens from the eleventh century onward had made the royal village on the Thames known
to succeeding generations of nobles and rich merchants. By
the eighteenth century, Richmond was established as an agreeable
resort in its own right. Fashionable Londoners might travel to
Tunbridge Wells or Bath to take the waters, living in lodgings;
but they built houses at Richmond, and many of them stayed in
the lively little place for the entire summer.

What had been a country lane winding up the Hill, began to
be a road, as more and more houses were erected. With the discovery of a mineral spring near what is now Cardigan House,
Richmond took on the added glamour of a "spaw", and soon there
was an aristocratic colony up the Hill, and along the riverside.
Defoe rowed from Kingston to London, and thought the Richmond
reaches of the Thames among the prettiest he ever saw, "with
gentlemen's houses on the banks, very fine."

There had been several houses round the Green in Elizabethan
times, but these had been altered, added to, or demolished to make
way for the new houses of Queen Anne's day, the beginning of
that age of fine design in domestic architecture which was to
become the delight of later generations. Stand on the Green and
look at the south-east side. Here is a great sweep of beautiful
houses, Queen Anne and Georgian. There is much variety and
complete unity: each house stands happily by its neighbour, whatever the difference in style.

Queen Anne, whose name for posterity indicates some of the
most gracious of the old houses in the town and neighbourhood,
did not, in fact, have much to do with Richmond, except as
hereditary lady of the manor. She had succeeded William and Mary,

[73]

whose chief connection with Richmond had been a sporting one; they liked hunting in the New Park. There was no longer a suitable residence for a reigning sovereign; the remains of the palace, except for the gate house and the wardrobe, had long been cleared, and the land leased to various people. Then, in the eighteenth century, the age-old royal connection with Richmond was unexpectedly renewed—as the result of a violent quarrel.

The cause of this sudden thrusting into prominence of a small riverside resort was well known and fully exploited. From the early 1700s onward, Richmond's fortune was made. Three out of the four Georges who sat on the English throne became closely connected with the town, and it is worth studying their background and some aspects of their characters, for they had an undoubted influence on eighteenth-century life. When the reigning monarch is dissolute, self-indulgent, and indifferent to the well-being of his subjects a powerful aristocratic class follows his example, with consequent repercussions on the middle class, and what was then called "the lower orders."

The nation was not consulted when, on the death of Queen Anne, the Elector of Hanover was invited to become King of England as George I. There was a party in the country which would have liked the return of the Stuarts, but memories of that family's misrule were long. As Thackeray cuttingly remarks: "The German Protestant was a cheaper, and better, and kinder King than the Catholic Stuart in whose chair he sat, and so far loyal to England that he let England govern herself." The Elector was married, but—himself a "cold, selfish libertine of a husband"—he had incarcerated his wife in a Hanoverian fortress because she had ventured to have a love affair of her own. Prince Frederick George, their son, now unexpectedly Prince of Wales, came to England with his father. He was married to Caroline of Anspach, and it was not long before the Prince and Princess of Wales found that they could not live under the same roof as the autocratic and evil-tempered King. They looked round for another home, and chose Richmond Lodge, a house which stood in what is now the Old Deer Park.

The mansion had been originally built in the sixteenth century by Dean Colet, the founder of St Paul's School. At the beginning of the eighteenth century, it was occupied by the Earl of Ormonde, one of the Jacobite aristocrats who had schemed to get the Stuarts back. The Earl's estates were confiscated to the Crown, and Richmond Lodge was eventually sold to the Prince of Wales for £6000. The Prince and Princess held their own Court at their new home; the Princess's Maids of Honour lived in the row of elegant houses built for them on the Green. It was a gay, pleasure-loving Court at Richmond, attracting the wittiest men, the loveliest women, in London. The enchanting Molly Lepell was often there: even now, the mention of her name gives a lustre to that long-vanished Court at Richmond. The daughter of Major-General Nicholas Lepell who owned the island of Sark, Mary Lepell had been, as a girl, according to Lady Louisa Stuart,

> singularly captivating . . . gay and handsome; never was there so perfect a model of the finely polished, highly bred, genuine woman of fashion. Her manners had a foreign tinge, which some called affected—but they were gentle, easy, dignified, and altogether exquisitely pleasing.

She married Lord Hervey, who was a close friend of the Princess of Wales and held a position at Court for a number of years when the Princess became Queen, so lovely Molly Lepell, who had "from the currish Pope extracted praise", came to know Richmond well.

Another Court beauty often seen at Richmond Lodge was Mary Bellendon, "incontestably the most agreeable, the most insinuating, and the most likeable woman of her time—made up of every ingredient likely to engage or attach a lover." Miss Bellendon, if aware of her considerable attractions, was careful where she bestowed her favours, for when the Prince of Wales made advances to her, counting guineas into his hat before her eyes, she kicked the hat out of his hand and laughed in his face before running out of the room.

Caroline of Anspach was attracted by clever and distinguished people; Pope, Horace Walpole, Hervey and others who could present "a handsome person with an engaging address in his air and manners, and the dignity and good breeding which a man of quality should and can have", were welcomed in that lively circle. That the Prince of Wales had a roving eye was something which Caroline accepted as a fact of nature; his father had a bevy of mistresses, and in the eighteenth-century world of fashion, marital faithfulness was considered estimable but rare.

The village of Richmond, now spreading into a small town, was not slow to provide amusements and entertainment for all the fine folk who came down from London by road or by water, bent on tasting the delights of pleasure in surroundings which had the added glamour of a royal Court—and one, moreover, which was the reverse of strait-laced. The pleasure-grounds of Richmond Wells,[1] at the top of the Hill, were laid out in a most attractive manner, and if, "under the pretence of taking an aperient water, a vast amount of unhealthy dissipation was carried on", the local tradesmen did not worry. The post-houses were always in a state of bustle, with the constant coming and going of chaises and carriages, the confectioners and other shops which sold comestibles did a thriving trade, there was plenty of employment for young persons in the houses of the Quality, and a pleasing air of gaiety and good living pervaded the place.

Glamour and gaiety at Richmond Lodge, spicy gossip about the Quality—these made up the tuppence-coloured strands of life for the ordinary citizen of Richmond. The everyday business of living was another thing, and with the Vestry so active, and the local manor courts apt to come down heavily on the wrong-doer, the aforesaid ordinary citizen had to walk warily. A golden guinea was a great deal of money, and if he found himself up before the justices, he was 'pain'd' where it hurt most—in his pocket.

The Court Rolls of the eighteenth century echo many of the offences which figure so largely in the records during the previous century. In 1707, Daniel Ellicoe was admonished for not keeping the King's Head Inn in repair, "it being ready too fall down", and was told to pay 6s. 8d. for every month he continued to leave it in that state. At the same court, several inhabitants complained that the land adjoining the footpath leading to the Ferry was in such bad repair that they could no longer "goe the antient way as formerly." The court held that this was deliberate on the part of the tenants concerned, and fined them each and severally. In 1714, the Honourable General Cholmondeley was heavily fined "for

[1] Page 154

[76]

ordering the Digging of Gravell to the Injury . . . of the high Road
on the top of Richmond Hill . . . for nearly 40 yards to the Danger
of his Majesties subjects."

The Vestry was continually on the alert for encroachments on
common land, and did not hesitate to bring actions against anyone, of high or low estate, who tried to take what did not belong
to him. In 1717 there were complaints of taking gravel from
gravel-pits without permission against Dame Elizabeth Saint
Aubyn, Cutts Barton, the Duke of Montague, and others. There
was also a charge

> that a Barr Gate had been placed across, and locked up, near the
> messuage of Thomas Pownall Esq., that the Hill common was full
> of great holes, and that the big houses discharged their filth on it.
> Also that the foregoing people were planting trees without
> permission, which might at some future time obstruct the view.

The prospect from the top of the Hill was already famous, and the
Vestry were determined to preserve it. They recommended that
the tenants of houses on the Hill should be absolutely forbidden to
plant trees which would grow above a certain height.

Provision was being made for the education of poor children. A
new building had been erected in 1713 on the site of a mansion
at the corner of Brewers Lane and the Green, and a large room
was made available as a charity school for children. A few years
later, another charity school was established in the middle of High
Street (George Street), supported by annual subscriptions from
inhabitants, and by a yearly church collection. It was conducted
on the monitorial system, senior pupils being set to teach the
younger ones, and it took in the children of the poor residing in
the parish who were not able to get into other schools.

George I died in June 1727, while he was in Hanover on a visit.
When the news reached England, Sir Robert Walpole called for
his horse and galloped from his Chelsea home along the country
roads to Richmond to carry the news to the Prince of Wales at
Richmond Lodge. He met with a cool reception. George Augustus
did not like his late father's Prime Minister. Ignoring Walpole's
questions about the Council being summoned, or the date for the
proclamation, the King said brusquely: "Go to Chiswick, and take

[**77**]

your directions from Sir Spencer Compton." The new reign ha
begun.

Sir Robert Walpole left Richmond and rode to call on the man
who was now chief Minister of State, as he himself had been to
George I. Thackeray describes Walpole as broad-faced, jolly-looking
corpulent, a sporting squire who rode boldly after the fox in the
hunting-fields of Norfolk. He was no saint. He passed his Sunday:
tippling at Richmond—which had many inns and taverns—and se
bishops and other important clerics by the ears with his ribaldries
He was, however, a clever statesman and a great patriot, and Sir
Spencer Compton, "a plodding, heavy fellow, with great applica
tion but no talents, his only pleasures, money and eating", re
ceived Walpole with much friendliness, and was soon asking hi
advice on matters of State.

George II turned out to be choleric and temperamental. He
kicked his coat and wig about when he got into a rage, and was
in the habit of calling his Ministers rogues, dirty buffoons and
impertinent fools to their faces; but he soon realised that high
political talent was rare, and before long he decided to bring Sir
Robert Walpole back to power. The course he took was simple. He
ordered Compton and Walpole each to write a speech on the
dissolution of Parliament. Compton's effort was lamentable.
Sir Robert Walpole was back in the saddle, and was again to be
seen, from time to time, drinking and roystering in Richmond pot-
houses with boon companions, when he felt he needed a little free
and easy company.

Every town has its black sheep, and Richmond had a clerical
black sheep in the eighteenth century, who caused his flock a great
deal of head-shaking. Mr Comer, minister of the Parish Church
in 1749, must have had a powerful personality, for he took advantage of the fact that Vestry meetings were infrequently held to
stop them altogether, and he was actually able to prevent further
meetings being held until 1766, when the first Act of Parliament
was passed

for the relief and employment of the poor and for repairing the
highways, paving, cleansing, lighting, and watching the streets,
and other places in the Town and Parish of Richmond . . . [which]
is large and populous, and the poor belonging thereto very

numerous, and maintained at a great expense; and whereas the highways within the Parish of Richmond were in bad repair, and the streets of the said town ill-paved, and not properly cleansed, lighted or watched, and are subject to many annoyances and incroachments.

There was plenty more, but the newly appointed Vestry had enough to be going on with. The chairman, Sir Charles Asgill, and the thirty persons who were appointed trustees to put the Act into execution, met in the Great Room of the Greyhound Inn at Richmond and speedily got down to business. They appointed overseers to collect rates, engaged "two able men to protect and clear the streets from all idle and disorderly persons, and to watch at night: to proclaim the hour of the night, and also the weather." Beadles were to be paid £20 a year and were each provided with "a brown surtout coat, the cape and cuffs to be faced with scarlet, trimmed with gold lace, and a gold-laced hat." These resplendent beadles had jurisdiction in the town, but they had no authority to protect the inhabitants from the pests of the roads between towns, the highwaymen—even if they had been courageous enough to try conclusions with those well-armed robbers. There are many entries in the records like this one, in 1737: "William Monson, Esq., his Lady and two daughters, travelling from Richmond to Chertsey, were robbed on Hounslow Heath by two highwaymen of a gold watch, four guineas and a diamond ring." Then, the Awful Warning. "Samuel Caton, an apothecary, was sentenced to death at the Surrey Assizes for robbing Tobias Wall of Richmond on the highway between Lambeth and Clapham."

The Vestry had, as always, to deal with problems relating to sanitary conditions. The Earl of Cardigan applied to the Vestry to lease a piece of waste land abutting on his house at the top of Richmond Hill "because it is mostly a dunghill and a great nuisance to the said Earl of Cardigan . . . and to all the Inhabitants of the Houses lying near the same." He obtained his land on payment of one guinea, and a rent of a shilling a year.

Then there was the Town Pond, which was "out of Repair for want of sufficient Purging and Scowering so that the same is not only a Nuisance to the Public but very Dangerous to the Inhabitants living thereto being full of loose mud and very Deep." The town Fathers kept a close eye on this amenity, Jurors of the Court

Leet having examined it earlier and found it to be "a Dangerous Place" on another count, for "unless Railed at the Head . . . it will be dangerous to both Man and Horse."

The mid-eighteenth century was a busy time for the widening of streets in Richmond. Among the many improvements carried out was the widening of part of the Green, in response to a petition made by Earl Brook and George Wood, tenants of a house with a view of "the Lane or Way leading from the Green to the River Thames situate between the Site of the old Palace of Richmond and certain land there called the Fryers." They considered that "this part of the said Green is not only very narrow but hath two sharp turnings and thereby hath often been dangerous to Foot Passengers passing up and down the same from coaches and other carriages."

It turned out that Mr George Wood owned a little parcel of copyhold land at the end of the lane by the Fryers, and was willing to give it up if the lord of the manor would grant an equal piece of land to make the widening effective. The lord of the manor's steward said, in effect, "Fair enough", and the work was put in hand.

George II, when Prince of Wales, had been Regent during his father's absences in Hanover. In those days he had frequently declared his dislike of everything German and love for everything English. Now that he occupied the throne himself, George II changed his mind. "No English cook could dress a dinner; no English player could act; no English coachman could drive or English jockey ride." He did not, however, denigrate the charms of the English ladies of the Court. Mistress succeeded mistress. "He used to pass those evenings he did not go to the opera or play at quadrille . . . talking a little bawdry to Lady Deloraine, who was always of the party", remarks Hervey, and then his tone sharpens as he describes this unamiable monarch's behaviour to Queen Caroline.

The King, who never used to be civil to the Queen even when he was kind, was now abominably and perpetually so harsh and rough, that she could not speak one word uncontradicted, nor do any one act unreproved.

Lord John Hervey was in a position to see Court life from the nside. Born in 1696, he was Vice-Chamberlain to the royal household, and was a great favourite with Queen Caroline. He disliked George II, but was always careful to conceal his feelings in that quarter, while taking in everything that went on. His quick eye for detail, his ear for nuance, his biased but often shrewd judgments, are of the utmost value to anyone trying to understand the eighteenth-century scales of values and habits of thought. Horace Walpole, amusing gossip that he is, can light up a scene for you in a dozen phrases and sum up a character in a dozen devastating words; but it is Hervey who is one of the classic sources for the Court of George II, for he actually lived in it.

On his accession George II and his consort had, of course, moved to London, and in due time there was a family of princes and princesses at St James's Palace. It was not a household which could be held up to the nation as an example of domestic felicity. George II was brutally unmannerly to his wife in public as in private; he flaunted his mistresses in her Drawing-Room, and talked about his bastards in the same breath as his legitimate children. The Queen bore it all with patience. She had an acuter intelligence than her spouse, and she was as devious as he was boorish. She had made a friend of Sir Robert Walpole, and George II would have been greatly surprised if he had known that a good deal of policy which he thought he had laid down himself came originally from the poker-faced Caroline, filtered through the Prime Minister and served up to His Majesty in casual asides. What is more astonishing still is that Caroline of Anspach really seemed to be devoted to this man who humiliated her at every opportunity. Thackeray says: "One inscrutable attachment that inscrutable woman has . . . save her husband, she really cares for no created being . . . she would chop them [her children] up into little pieces to please him."

The two were united only on one head: their unnatural aversion to their eldest son, Frederick, Prince of Wales. He had been a difficult child who had grown into a rebellious youth, and he was continually quarrelling with his parents: it was an appalling case of history repeating itself. There were not wanting mischievous gossips ready to catch up angry words and run from one to the other; and as the Prince had inherited many of his sire's loutish traits, there was plenty of fuel to add to the fires.

A PROSPECT OF RICHMOND

The Prince of Wales had married the seventeen-year-old Princess Augusta of Saxe-Gotha, and had his own suite of apartments in St James's Palace. George II, the Queen, and their other children went to Richmond Lodge every week, and then on to Hampton Court. When the Princess of Wales was expecting a baby the King insisted that the child should be born at Hampton Court. The Prince of Wales declared that the birth should take place at St James's, and the baby was, in fact, born there in 1737. George II reacted with more than his customary choler. He wrote a long letter to his son, setting out the Prince's faults and failings, and ending: "It is my pleasure that you leave St. James's with your family."

Frederick had his own income as Prince of Wales. He took a house in Leicester Fields, and a country house at Kew, and set up his own Court. White House, at Kew, which was also called Kew House, has disappeared: it stood near the present palace in the Gardens. It belonged to Richard Bennet in the seventeenth century, and came into the possession of the Capel family through marriage. The Capels were well-known horticultural enthusiasts. Evelyn notes in his Diary that he visited Sir Henry Capel's at Kew, where the "orangery and myrrhetum are most beautiful, and perfectly well kept. He was contriving high pallisadoes of reeds to shade his oranges during the summer."

The Prince of Wales engaged the celebrated William Kent to enlarge the White House and landscape the grounds, and a very handsome place Kent made of it. The break-away party of George II's Court found Kew more amusing: "The most promising of the young gentlemen . . . and the prettiest and liveliest of the young ladies, formed the new Court", and the Prince and Princess of Wales, with their growing family, delighted in their new house and fine gardens. They were popular with the leading personalities of the day, and with the Services. A London newspaper mentions "Admiral Boscawen has presented a Green Turtle, brought from the West Indies, and weighing 476 lb., to the Prince of Wales, residing at Kew, probably the first introduction of this delicate luxury to the table of this country."

The memoirs of the time are full of accounts of the delights of these rival royal establishments. "Fiddles sing . . . wax-lights fine dresses, fine jokes, fine plate, fine equipages, glitter and

Interior of Theatre on the Green, Early Nineteenth Century

By courtesy of Richmond upon Thames Libraries Committee

Trumpeters' House

Kersting.

St Mary Magdalen
Parish Church,
Richmond,
Eighteenth Century

*By courtesy of
Richmond upon Thames
Libraries Committee*

Anne's Church, Kew
Eighteenth Century

*By courtesy of the Director,
Royal Botanic Gardens*

Old Red Lion Inn, Early Nineteenth Century

By courtesy of Mr S. O. Ellis

A Day's Pleasure (View from the Star and Garter Inn) about 1845

es Scott, after Edward Prentis.   *By courtesy of Richmond upon Thames Libraries Committee*

White Cross Tavern, Early Nineteenth Century

Castle Hotel, 1844

T. Allon.

sparkle there; never was such a brilliant, jiggling, smirking Vanity Fair. . . ." The jiggling and smirking extended beyond the shores of England. George II, who was the Elector of Hanover like his father before him, also took to travelling to his German dominions. Hanoverian mistresses were, after all, more to his taste than the English high-born strumpets. Queen Caroline was well aware of the main reasons for his absences, but there was nothing she could do. She acted as Regent when he was away, stayed often at Richmond Lodge, and occupied herself in improving the gardens there. She laid out a pleasant walk along the river bank, and amused herself by erecting curious structures: a Grotto and Cave, filled with life-size wax images of historical personages— a kind of miniature Madame Tussaud's. She also set tongues clicking by "taking up" one of the garden labourers, Stephen Duck, who wrote poetry and aspired to higher things than digging. He was actually an individual of extraordinary powers, considering his origins, as he educated himself to the point of taking Holy Orders—with the Queen's help—and was appointed to the church at Kew, where he drew great crowds by his oratory.

These various activities of the Queen's cost a great deal of money—far more than she could personally afford. George II was frequently sarcastic about her "rubbish and nonsense", and he would have given way to other emotions if he had known that his Prime Minister was quietly settling the bills to the tune of thousands upon thousands of pounds. Caroline's long friendship with Sir Robert Walpole was paying dividends.

Queen Caroline died in 1737. George II was deeply distressed— but his main concern was that the Prince of Wales should not inherit Richmond Lodge. He was assured that it would remain his for his lifetime, and it would then inevitably pass to the Prince. With this assurance George II turned to his current German mistress, much consoled.

The Prince of Wales did not live to enjoy the possession of Richmond Lodge. He died unexpectedly, after an illness, leaving a large family. The Princess of Wales, now the Princess Dowager, decided to remain at Kew, and to devote herself to the upbringing of her children and especially to the training of her eldest son, George Frederick, who was now the heir to the throne. She also began that work of enlarging and improving the already splendid grounds round her house, with such intelligent expenditure and on such a scale as to make them the most famous botanical gardens in the world.

Besides the men and women of fashion who were always to be seen at Richmond, many of the prominent literary personages of the day often came down to pay courtesies to their patrons, or simply to see and be seen in the popular little resort, departing again with a flourish in coach or chaise, on horseback or by water. Richmond had a resident poet, however, who made his home there and of whom the town is understandably proud. This was James Thomson, the author of *The Seasons*, whose features, habits, and friends have been delineated for us, incongruously enough, by his barber, William Taylor of Richmond. The Earl of Buchan had the opportunity of talking to Taylor on Richmond Green, and the barber came out with a spate of reminiscences about the poet:

> He had a face as long as a horse . . . his hair was soft as a camel's—it grew so remarkably that if it was but an inch long it stood upright on end from his head like a brush. . . . He was pretty corpulent, and stooped, rather, when he walked, as though he was full of thought. He was very careless and negligent about his dress.

The details flowed on: Thomson walking from London to Richmond at all hours of the night, Thomson drinking with the actor, Quin, and not in moderation, either. Thomson, amazingly indolent, though capable of tremendous bursts of energy when the spirit so seized him. Did the poet keep much company?

> Yes, a good deal of the writing sort. I remember Pope . . . he used to wear a light-coloured great-coat . . . he was a strange ill-formed little figure of a man: but I have heard him and Quin . . . talk together so, that I could have listened to them for ever.

James Thomson was born at Ednam, near Kelso in Roxboroughshire, in 1700, the son of a Presbyterian minister. He was himself intended for the ministry, and probably would have taken orders but for the reprimand which he received from the Professor of Divinity for preaching his probationary sermon on the 119th Psalm in language so lofty and poetical as to be unintelligible to an ordinary congregation.

Thomson was encouraged to try his fortune in London, and had the ill-luck to be robbed soon after his arrival, which meant that he had to earn some money as soon as he could. He had already begun the poem *Winter*, the first of his famous *Seasons*, and he obtained twenty guineas from the gentleman to whom it was dedicated—a welcome sum, which supplied his immediate necessities, including a badly needed pair of shoes. The remaining poems, *Summer*, *Spring*, and *Autumn* were successively published and well received, but Thomson could not make an income out of his poetry. Neither was he a successful playwright when he turned to the drama; the noted line, the ultimate in bathos, "O Sophonisba! Sophonisba, O!" was parodied by one of the wits: "O Jemmy Thomson—Jemmy Thomson, O!" and was echoed through the town.

Thomson had true poetic sensibility, nevertheless, and his friends loved him for his kindness and unassuming character. One of them, the influential Lord George Lyttelton, was able to get for him the office of Surveyor General of the Leeward Islands, and after paying a deputy actually to go and live there—a common practice—Thomson had about £300 a year left to live on, to which was later added £100 a year by a new patron, Frederick, Prince of Wales. He is buried in Richmond Parish Church, but one is most conscious of James Thomson on the Terrace, where one remembers the lines which will always endear him to those who love Richmond:

> Which way, Amanda, shall we bend our course?
> The choice perplexes. Wherefore should we choose?
> All is the same with thee. Say, shall we wind
> Along the streams? or walk the smiling mead?
> Or court the forest glades? Or wander wild
> Among the waving harvests? Or ascend
> While radiant Summer opens all its pride,
> Thy hill, delightful Shene? Here let us sweep
> The boundless landskip: now the raptur'd eye,
> Exulting swift, to huge Augusta send,
> Now to the Sister Hills that skirt the plain,
> To lofty Harrow now, and now to where
> Majestic Windsor lifts his princely brow,
> In lovely contrast to this glorious view

A PROSPECT OF RICHMOND

Calmly magnificent, then will we turn
To where the silver Thames first rural grows.
There let the feasted eye unwearied stray:
Luxurious, there, rove thro' the pendant woods
That nodding hang o'er Harrington's retreat;
And, stooping thence to Ham's embowering walks,
Beneath whose shades, in spotless peace retir'd,
With Her the pleasing partner of his heart,
The worthy Queensb'ry yet laments his Gay,
And polished Cornbury wooes the willing Muse.
Slow let us trace the matchless Vale of Thames;
Fair-winding up to where the Muses haunt
In Twit'nam's bowers, and for their Pope implore
The healing God; to royal Hampton's pile,
To Clermont's terrass'd height, and Esher's groves,
Where in the sweetest solitude, embrac'd
By the soft windings of the silent Mole,
From courts and senates Pelham finds repose.
Inchanting vale! beyond whate'er the Muse
Has of Achaia or Hesperia sung!
O vale of bliss! O softly-swelling hills!
On which the Power of Cultivation lies,
And joys to see the wonders of his toil.
Heavens! What a goodly prospect spreads around,
Of hills, and dales, and woods, and lawns, and spires,
And glittering towns, and gilded streams, till all
The stretching landskip into smoke decays.

From the Works of James Thomson, with His Last Corrections
and Improvements (London, MDCCLXVIII, Printed for A
Millar, and Sold by T. Cadell, in the Strand).

One of the most charming impressions of eighteenth-century
Richmond, seen through the eyes of a traveller, is given by
Charles Moritz, who came to England in 1782 with little in his
purse and *Paradise Lost* in his pocket, which he intended to read
in the land of Milton. He was a young Prussian clergyman
liberal in sympathy in days of iron-fisted Continental dictator-
ships, and it is clear that he had long saved up for a visit to the
country which seemed to him to be, above all others, the land of
the free. He apparently had only enough money for a stay of
seven weeks, three of which he spent in London, where "In the

morning it is usual for a gentleman to walk out in a sort of negligée or morning dress, your hair not dressed, but merely rolled up in rollers."[!] When he came to the end of his stay in London, "four guineas, some linen, my English book of the roads and a map and pocket-book, together with Milton's Paradise Lost, which I must put in my pocket, compose the whole of my equipage."

He travelled by stage-coach to Richmond, the first town on his list, then on foot to Windsor, Oxford, Birmingham, and Matlock. On these journeys he saw for himself what freedom meant:

It strikes a foreigner as something particular and unusual when, on passing through these fine English towns, he observes one of those circumstances by which the towns in Germany are distinguished from the villages—no walls, no gates, no sentries, nor garrisons. No stern examiner comes here to search and inspect us or our baggage; no imperious guard here demands a sight of our passports; perfectly free and unmolested, we here walk through villages and towns as unconcerned as we should through a house of our own.

The fare on the stage-coach to Richmond was two shillings, a shilling for each of the two stages. They drove by way of Kensington and Hammersmith, the road on both sides being lined with houses. The young pastor admired the beautiful villas and the country seats which succeeded the rows of dwellings, but was glad to get out of the coach after a five-hour journey. He found an inn, drank some tea, and set out to explore Richmond:

Even this town, though hardly out of sight of London, is more countrified, and more cheerful than London . . . the people appeared more sociable and more hospitable. I saw several sitting on benches before their doors, to enjoy the cool breeze of the evening. On a large green area in the middle of the town, a number of boys . . . were enjoying themselves, and playing at trap-ball. In the streets there reigned here, compared to London, a pleasing rural tranquillity, and I breathed a purer and fresher air.

I went now out of the town over a bridge, which lies across the Thames, and where you pay a penny as often as you pass over it. The bridge is lofty and built in the form of an arch, and from it you enter immediately into a most charming valley, that winds all along the banks of the Thames. It was evening. The sun was

[87]

just shedding her last parting rays on the valley; but such an evening, and such a valley! The terrace at Richmond does assuredly afford one of the finest prospects in the world. Whatever is charming in nature, or pleasing in art, is to be seen here

The prospect before and all around him was one, he was sure that he would remember always. Treading on "that fresh, ever and soft verdure which is to be seen only in England," he admired the little swelling hills, the green meadows, the shelvy banks, and smooth lawns rising like an amphitheatre on the other side of the Thames, with white houses glimpsed here and there through the dark foliage of luxuriant trees. Sundry family parties walking arm in arm along the river bank made him regret the days he had wasted in London; he should have left "that huge dungeon" earlier and come to Richmond. He resolved to return to the inn, go to bed early, rise betimes, and look on this delectable view in the early morning, when it would be even more beautiful, glistening in the dew.

When he returned to the town he found, however, that he had forgotten the name and sign of the inn. "It cost me no little trouble to find it again", and when he did, he could not get to sleep for a long time as the landlady talked so much and so loudly to her servants. He rose at 3 A.M.,

and was now particularly sensible of the great inconvenience they sustain in England by their bad custom of rising so late, for as I was the only one in this family who was up, I could not get out of the house.

He spent three irksome hours until 6 o'clock, when a servant at length opened the door and Moritz rushed out to begin climbing Richmond Hill. Disappointment awaited him at the top, for within a short time the sky was overcast, cloud came down, and most of the view was hidden. There was still much to enjoy, in spite of everything—the alley of chestnut-trees at the top of the hill, the row of well-built gentlemen's country houses behind. "I never saw a palace which, if I were the owner of it, I would not give for any of the houses I now saw on Richmond Terrace", Moritz wrote, and many a later traveller has echoed that sentiment.

George III became King in 1760, and anyone more unlike his

grandfather and great-grandfather would be difficult to imagine. He had been brought up very strictly, with his brothers and sisters, at Kew, and he was the only one of the Princess Dowager's sons who did not later turn to wild ways as a result. When she was accused of keeping them in seclusion the Princess said

she would gladly see her sons and daughters mix in the world if she could do so without risk to their morals. But the profligacy of the people of quality alarmed her. The young men were all rakes; the young women made love instead of waiting till it was made to them.

The new King was, as a result, unsophisticated and pliant. He was kind, friendly, with simple tastes and a liking for a regular life. He married a princess with similar tastes. Charlotte-Sophia of Mecklenburg-Strelitz was seventeen when she came to England, and she is reported to have said, after fifty years of marriage, that she never knew real sorrow until the King's illness caused their temporary separation. Sorrow she had in plenty, for the King's malady consisted of attacks of insanity—something the Princess Dowager had not mentioned during the marriage negotiations. Nevertheless the couple settled down to a happy, well-ordered existence, coming to their country house, Richmond Lodge, for the summer, and whenever they could leave London at other times.

The Queen gave birth to a son and heir, and there was much rejoicing. The Court continued to come to Richmond every summer, and the local people appreciated the vastly increased trade which resulted. The main street of the town was re-named George Street. The royal pair were popular, and, as they were approachable, the inhabitants did not hesitate to ask them to redress wrongs. Thomas Fuller of Richmond, Butterman to the Earl of Cholmondeley, petitioned the Queen in a well-reasoned document that she should carry out an obligation of her predecessor's. Caroline of Anspach had pulled down his parents' cottage, as it had stood in the way of her gardens between Kew and Richmond, and had built them a "tenement" in another place. This habitation was now in a ruinous state. The father was dead, the elderly widow was living in a house which was now all but tumbling about her ears, and she would be destitute of a habitation. Queen Caroline had meant the house to be kept in repair, argued the Butterman, and was it not her present Majesty's duty to do something about it? The widow was too poor to have anything done herself, but he was willing to contribute to the cost.

Thomas won his petition, though whether the Queen accepted his offer or not is not recorded.

In 1769, George III decided that Richmond Lodge had become too small for his increasing family; the Queen had had three more children. He asked Sir William Chambers to draw up plans for a new palace. A part of his gardens round Richmond Lodge was marked out as a private garden for the proposed palace, but an additional piece of ground, not in the royal manor, was thought to be necessary "for the purposes of elegance and convenience." This would have to be purchased from the town authority—the Vestry.

The Vestry refused to sell; it was considered that His Majesty had enough ground for his garden. George III was very angry; he had, in fact, instructed Chambers to begin building, and it was galling to be refused. He determined to leave Richmond Lodge and remove to Kew.

It was the first but not the last time that George III was to come up against the Richmond Vestry, those loyal and incorruptible guardians of the rights of the town and its inhabitants. George III was respected as a pattern of domestic rectitude, and a great improvement in every way on his predecessors—but he possessed the Hanoverian obstinacy, and a tendency to behave as if the divine right of kings was an established law instead of a concept that had vanished with Charles I.

The Vestry had now a very large parish to administer, and they were faced with the usual difficulties inherent in their office. They tried continually to improve the amenities of the town, but it was uphill work; it needed influence in London before they could use any powers to make real progress. Improvements did, however, come. The Act of Parliament of 1776 had stated in plain language that all the highways were in bad repair, the streets ill-paved, ill-lighted, and not properly cleansed. Rates were to be levied, the highways repaired and paved, the lighting improved, cleansing to be done regularly, and sign irons (advertisements) removed. The road from Kew Road to the Bear Inn, at the beginning of the town, was to be amended and made commodious for passengers and carriages, and "His Majesty, or any other person occupying Richmond Lodge, should keep the said road in good and sufficient repair for ever."

It was all very well to authorise rates to be levied, but the Vestry found these very difficult to collect—and there were always strong protests at any increases to meet rising costs. The Vestry took no chances where public money was concerned; when the office of Clerk/Treasurer became vacant the successful candidate was to give £500 security himself, and also to find two sureties for £250 each. The salary was £50 a year.

There was the perpetual problem of refuse disposal, but in 1785 a partial solution was found—a dustman. John Andrews was engaged "to take away the dirt from the paved streets and squares and lanes and shovel them up in heaps, and also the dirt and dust and ashes from the inhabitants for one year for one pound one shilling."

Proper lighting of the streets was decided upon. The Vestry resolved that a number of lamps "not exceeding 200 be lighted the ensuing winter, and that lighting them should begin in September and continue until March." They were to be lit at sunset each evening and continue burning until 5 o'clock in the morning. Also, the "two able men" who had at first constituted the watch were no longer sufficient; twenty-two men were now employed as watchmen during the winter months, eleven of them to cry the hours alternately, to begin at nine o'clock in the evening "and not to leave off until they have gone their rounds after 5 in the morning, till 25 March." The pay was "1*s.* 6*d.* a night for each man every night they shall be on duty."

The spiritual and moral as well as the physical welfare of Richmond were well to the fore in the minds of the Trustees of the Vestry. Attempts were continually made to discourage trading on the Sabbath day.

> Ordered that the Beadles do give notice to the several shopkeepers to shut their shops every Sunday morning at 10 and to continue the remainder of the day, or in default the Beadles are directed to lay informations before a magistrate against the persons so offending.

The Vestry also kept a stern eye on any stranger likely to tempt the inhabitants into wicked ways. In March 1787

> A Mountebank having erected a stage in this Town and having obtained large sums of money by Lottery and other illegal practices Ordered that the Beadle do immediately remove the posts of the before mentioned stage and also inform the said Mountebank if he exhibits any more in this Parish the Vestry will prosecute him as the Law directs.

It was the gambling which upset the Vestry more than the Mountebank's pomping. Lotteries were common, and some offered valuable prizes. A Mr Hinton of Hammersmith set up a lottery which had twelve large Richmond houses among the prizes.

It was not easy to hold down man's natural sinfulness. The London newspapers of the day kept Richmond well in the news: "A convivial Party returning from Richmond to town, owing to the coachman being in liquor, they were overturned. The coachman broke a leg, two ladies were badly hurt, and the Gentlemen cut and bruised." Then there was A Gentleman of Richmond, "who for some time had paid his Addresses to a Young Lady of Fortune in the Neighbourhood, fixed on Tuesday last for the Celebration of their Nuptials, but as they were going to Church his Conscience touched him and he owned he had a wife living in Gloucestershire." Any Total Abstainers on the Vestry would have been hard put to it to deal faithfully with the servant girl in a house on Richmond Hill "who put arsenic in some bottles of brandy, which was found out by a footman before the family had drunk much. She said she had no intention of hurting anyone; she had only meant to spoil the brandy."

While the King took umbrage and moved his family and Court to Kew, and the Vestry worked conscientiously to look after the public sevices and public morals, and the Quality built fine houses and enjoyed their wealth and leisure in any way that pleased them, the solid core of Richmond's inhabitants earned a living, brought up their families, visited their relations, cultivated their gardens, and went to church on Sundays. There were Dissenting Chapels in the town, but the Parish Church was still the centre of community life, and the minister was an important and greatly respected individual.

The egregious, autocratic Mr Comer had been the only man of
his cloth to have incurred the dislike and disapprobation of the
parishioners. The Wakefields more than made up for Mr Comer.
The Reverend George Wakefield was minister of the parish, as
well as being vicar of Kingston, in the 1760s, and his two sons,
Thomas and Gilbert, also took Holy Orders. The Reverend Mr
Bailey, of Langley in Derbyshire, who was the patron of the
livings, presented them to George Wakefield for an unusual
reason.

"I am satisfied with my present situation," said Mr Bailey, and
went on:

> Now were I to go to Richmond, the King would be my
> parishioner: I must consequently go to Court. Then I shall be
> looking forward, of course, to a prebend or a canonry. As soon as
> I am settled in a stall, I shall grow uneasy for a bishopric, and
> then eager for a translation to a better. In due time Lambeth will
> be the fond object of my wishes, and when I am stationed there,
> I must be miserable because I can rise no higher. Had I not then
> better be quiet in my present condition, than be always wishing,
> always obtaining, but never satisfied!

The Reverend George Wakefield seems not to have been
worried by such scruples; he is described as a man of plain good
sense, benevolence, and piety. He was followed at Richmond by
his son Thomas, who was minister for thirty years, and much
liked. Gilbert Wakefield, the younger son, was a remarkable
character. An eminent scholar, he received deacon's orders after
graduating, but within a short time found himself opposed to the
Liturgy and doctrine of the Church of England. When he visited
Thomas at Richmond he was on perfectly amiable terms with
the brother, though he argued with the minister. He did not stop
at arguing. He began writing Dissenting pamphlets, and from
there went on to the more dangerous ground of politics. "He
thought fit to censure the policy of the administration in the war
against France during the Revolution," and when the Bishop of
Llandaff published a pamphlet addressed to the People of Great
Britain, supporting the war, Gilbert Wakefield replied with a
sharply critical pamphlet which brought down on him the wrath
of the Establishment.

Ruin followed. He was indicted, along with his publisher, for seditious libel, and was sentenced to two years' imprisonment in Dorchester County Gaol. The sentence created an immense sensation, but Wakefield, "who would have accepted poverty with peace of mind rather than a bishopric with an uneasy conscience", was prepared to suffer for his beliefs. He served the sentence, dying of a fever shortly afterwards. He is buried in Richmond Church, "a high, undaunted soul."

CHAPTER NINE

---◆•••◆---

Kew

KAYHOUGH, Kayhowe, Kyahoe, Keyhowe, Keye, Kaiho, Kayo, Kewe—Kew. The village was certainly a very old one, as the variations of spelling indicate. Fine houses stood there in the early part of the sixteenth century, and Queen Elizabeth honoured Sir John Puckering with her presence at his house on Kew Green in 1595, when he was Lord Keeper. It was an expensive business entertaining the great Tudor Queen, with her shrewdness and acquisitive instincts. The Lord Keeper found it

> great and exceedingly costly. At her first alighting she had a fine fan, with a handle garnished with diamonds. When she was in the middle way, between the garden gate and the house, there came one running towards her with a nosegay in his hands and delivered it with a short, well-penned speech; it had in it a very rich jewel, with many pendants of diamonds, valued at £400 at least.

After dinner, in her privy chamber, the Queen received a fine gown and juppin (petticoat), which pleased her, "and to grace his lordship the more, she of herself took from him a salt, a spoon, and a fork of fine agate."

There had been a chapel at Kew in the early sixteenth century, but by the beginning of the 1700s it was not big enough for the needs of the inhabitants, and leave was asked of Queen Anne to build a larger chapel. The Vicar of Kingston, whose parish included the hamlet of Kew, supported the petition, and Queen Anne gave her assent. She presented the village with a site on Kew Green and a hundred pounds towards the cost of the chapel. The nave and chancel were built 1710–14, and the church was named St Anne's. It was enlarged from time to time, and "the character of the edifice was considerably changed," but it retains a certain classic grace, and the many monuments on its walls bear witness to the famous people who lived in the neighbourhood.

The triangular Green was once used as a regular place for fairs, until these were stopped because of the rowdiness which grew increasingly annoying to the inhabitants. Cricket was played on the Green in the early eighteenth century; there is a record of a match played there in 1737, captained on one side by the Prince of Wales and on the other by the Duke of Marlborough. A few years later, a London newspaper grows indignant about the popularity of the game:

"The cursed spirit of Gaming, Idleness and Extravagance, which has been raised by the great, has run like wild-fire throughout the kingdom, and been productive of the most shameful and dreadful consequences." A striking example of this was seen at Kew Green two or three times every week, where two or three hundred men, most of them labourers, "assemble at this critical and important season, to divert themselves with playing at the game of cricket." Notwithstanding that these labourers had been earnestly solicited to assist in the harvest field, and tempted with an offer of five shillings for each day, they had absolutely refused to work, preferring to watch cricket on Kew Green.

Meanwhile the Princess Dowager, widow of Frederick, Prince of Wales, went on enlarging the botanical gardens. "In her connection with Kew," says Garnett of the Princess, "she laid the nation under the greatest obligation, for from her proceeded the scientific impress which has given it its unique place among national possessions, and its supreme rank among the botanical institutions of the world."

In 1759 the Princess engaged William Aiton to establish a "physic garden", and two years later William Chambers built for her a greenhouse that was over 100 feet long, as well as an orangery. The gardens already contained a great collection of shrubs, trees, flowers, and herbs, and others were continually being added. The Princess had as her adviser the Earl of Bute, who was an able botanist.

Chambers was the architect of Somerset House, and one of the founders of the Royal Academy. He had visited China several times, which accounts for the Great Pagoda, still the best-known landmark in Kew Gardens today. Chambers also built, for the Princess, several garden shelters in the form of classical temples; the Temples of Arethusa, Bellona, and Aeolus still survive.

The Princess Dowager died in 1772, and the King and Queen moved to the White House. They now had eight children, and the house was too small for their growing family. The older children were placed, with their tutors and servants, in the Dutch House near by, and the other children lodged in various neighbouring houses. The Dutch House (now called Kew Palace) was built on the site of an Elizabethan house called the Dairy House. In the seventeenth century it came into the possession of a prosperous London merchant of Dutch extraction, who rebuilt it; the gables of the façade are reminiscent of Dutch architecture of the time. The date of the rebuilding can still be seen above the main entrance—1631. The Dutch House had already been leased by the Crown for members of the royal family on several occasions, and now George III and Queen Charlotte took it for a nursery, eventually buying the freehold.

Here indeed was a Court firmly founded on the domestic virtues. We get detailed pictures of its everyday life in the memoirs of the delightful Mrs Papendiek, whose father, Herr Albert, had come over from Strelitz with the Queen and was a Court official. Mrs Papendiek was born and brought up in England, mostly at Kew, and she was an observant girl. Completely unselfconscious and unaffected, she later set down a record of her life at the Court of George III which is a pleasant change from Walpole's malicious pinpricks and Hervey's obstinately partisan loyalties in the preceding Court. Fanny Burney is another classic source for the third George's Court, but she naturally concentrates on her experiences as Maid of Honour to Queen Charlotte later in the reign; if there had been central heating at Windsor Castle, Miss Burney might have written more enthusiastically of being Second Keeper of the Robes, for she felt the cold woefully. Mrs Papendiek's memoirs of the earlier home at Kew give a more intimate picture of the private life of the royal couple and their family.

"Their Majesties rise at six o'clock and call two hours their own." After breakfast, the elder children worked at their lessons, and the little ones were taken by their nurses into the royal gardens. In the afternoon, the Queen sat at her needlework while the King read to her. Once a week, the King and Queen, with their whole family in pairs, made a tour of the Gardens. Queen Charlotte had a small cottage, roofed with thatch, built for herself on the southern verge of the Gardens, and sometimes took tea there. (The cottage still exists.)

The Ha Ha, the ditch or sunken fence alongside the towing-path between Kew and Richmond, was constructed in 1767, to prevent cattle from straying from the royal grounds on to the towing-path. George III, "Farmer George", took a great interest in dairy cattle, and in agriculture in general; his children were encouraged to study the growing of food as well as the art of horticulture.

Kew had become a fashionable rendezvous with the establishment of the Court there. The Richmond Gardens and those at Kew were parallel, divided by a road called Love Lane (later closed by arrangement with the Vestry; the present Holly Walk marks the site of the vanished lane). In summer, the public were admitted to the Richmond Gardens on Sundays, and to Kew Gardens on Thursdays, "for the amusement of all persons genteely dressed, by his Majesty's express order." On these days, Kew Green was covered with carriages, "more than £300 being taken at the bridge on Sundays." This was the toll bridge that had been built over the river at Kew in 1759, and which at that date had excited the tenants of near-by houses, who complained that the greatly increased traffic from the Ealing and Brentford side of the Green, on which they had been allowed to pasture "all manner of Cattle", would now be open to passing horses, and "the Herbage of the same would be greatly and unnecessarily destroyed and the copyhold Tenants . . . much injured in their right of Commonage."

The herbage seems to have been sufficient for all comers, at any rate up to Mrs Papendiek's time. The carriages continued to roll up to the royal residence, and their Majesties were to be seen at the windows, speaking to their friends, the royal children amusing themselves in their own gardens. Parties came to Kew by water, too, with awnings covering the decks, and bands of music playing spirited airs. "The whole was a scene of enchantment and delight; Royalty living among their subjects to give pleasure and to do good."

Royalty could not, however, control the weather. In 1770, a London paper reported that

The Distress of a numerous and brilliant Company in Richmond Gardens on Sunday was occasioned by sudden and long
continued heavy rain. Beaux and Belles, of all Ranks and Degrees,
were *everything but drowned*. Many were confined all night in
the Gardens, wet to the skin, while their carriages waited for
them in vain without. The Prince of Mecklenburgh . . . with
many persons of Rank and Distinction shared in the General
Misfortune. The Inns at Richmond were so crowded that Ten
Guineas was refused for a bed, and several persons of distinction
were obliged to lie all night in straw.

There are many eighteenth-century houses round Kew Green,
some of them, like the Gables, remodelled from earlier houses.
Sir Peter Lely lived on the Green in the seventeenth century; his
house is incorporated into the buildings belonging to the Royal
Botanical Gardens. Gainsborough was another resident, and is
commemorated in the church. Zoffany, the painter, lived at
Strand-on-the-Green, not far away, and often visited his friends
on Kew Green; Mrs Papendiek relates that she often met him at
the houses of their mutual acquaintance. Her father lived on Kew
Green himself for a time: "In 1776, several houses on the Green
were sold, and my father bought the one at the corner for £400."
   The friend Mrs Papendiek admired the most was the musician,
Johann Christian Bach, "the English Bach", son of a famous
family. He was the eighteenth child of Johann Sebastian Bach,
and after a period spent in Italy, settled in England, where he
lived for the last twenty-five years of his life. He was a concert
director in London, and music master to the royal family. Bach
had "an agreeable establishment at Richmond," and here he
would compose. "After dinner he sat down and wrote an enchanting first movement of a quintett in three flats." Mrs Papendiek
also relates that "a quartett party" practised at her home at Kew,
to which Bach sent a small pianoforte "for that purpose."
   The royal children were growing up. The Prince of Wales, later
to become George IV, was, at the age of twenty, "an elegant
person with engaging and distinguished manners." He was fond of
music, sang well, and played the violoncello with taste and preci-
sion. He had a house at Kew, with two equerries who had been
his former attendants. Mrs Papendiek did not care for these gentlemen, who, "while he had still lived with his parents, managed

the Prince's intrigue with the renowned beauty, Mrs Robinson, 'Perdita', by conducting her through the garden gate at the back of the house to the Prince of Wales's apartments."

Mrs Papendiek went to London and Windsor when the Court removed there, but she was always happy to return to Kew. There were visits to the theatre at Richmond, and calls paid on interesting friends. She liked pretty clothes, and gives descriptions of gowns "in alternate stripes of white and buff" and of bonnets "of a Quaker turn." The fashion of powdering the hair was a nuisance. "As I found it very inconvenient to dress my hair, powder being then worn, I cut it off, beautiful as it was, close to my head; but took care to have a cap most becomingly made. . . ."

Mrs Papendiek was in a coach which was stopped by highway-men on Barnes Common, and noted the fact as if it were not at all an unusual occurrence. The French traveller, de Saussure, had, earlier in the century, commented on

> a queer law [in England] to encourage counties to get rid of thieves. If a man is robbed of a considerable sum in the day time and on the high road, and if he declares his loss to the Sherriff of the county before sun sets, and can prove that the sum has been taken from him in such and such a place, the county is obliged to refund him the sum.

If this was indeed the case, the county of Surrey must have had an expensive time of it, for there were numerous highway robberies between Kew and Richmond alone. The Lord Mayor of London and his suite, including the swordbearer, were robbed by a highwayman as they were returning from a State visit to the King at Kew in 1776.

George III engaged Sir William Chambers to build an observa-tory in Richmond Gardens, not far from the site of Richmond Lodge, which had become derelict. The Hanoverian Herschel was appointed astronomer, with a grant of £4000 to assist in the construction of the great telescope. This graceful observatory is still to be seen in the Old Deer Park. Less successful was the crenelated palace which the King commissioned the architect Wyatt to design under his own directions. It was an extraordinary structure, all Gothic towers and turrets; Wraxall called it "an

[100]

image of distempered unreason", referring to the King's unfortunate recurring malady. It was built on the banks of the river,
not far from the Dutch House, but was never completed, and
was later pulled down.

The Richmond Vestry had been firm with George III over its
rights, but the King was not one to bear malice, and he was often
to be seen in the town, usually on his way to inspect the two
farms which he owned there. He was also ready to strike a bargain.
In return for the closing up of Love Lane, which divided the
Richmond Gardens from those at Kew and so provided a public
right of way, the King agreed, in 1788, to let the Vestry have
Pest House Common and to build a new workhouse there. A workhouse in the town for the destitute poor already existed, held on
lease at an annual rent of £26, "in tolerable good repair and in
every respect clean and decent." It had seventy-two inmates and
thirty-five "pension poor." The yearly bill for their upkeep was
£752, which included 124 barrels of beer. No Geneva brandy or
spirituous liquors were allowed in the workhouse, and no person
there was to "smoak tobacco."

The new workhouse on Pest House Common was to be available
for the indigent poor of Kew as well as for those at Richmond and
Petersham. The old building was let to Richard Howard for his
"manufactury of calico printing", at a rent of £12 per annum.
The old building was to be pulled down "by this day fortnight, and
the widow Hooper who resides therein upon sufferance only, have
notice to quit the same within that time." Eviction! Soon after
the new workhouse was built, the King had one of his attacks of
madness, which, however, did not last long. On his recovery,
there were rejoicings in the town, and the inmates of the workhouse "had some legs and shoulders of mutton and a pint of strong
beer each for dinner." The watchmen of the town were to get "one
shilling extraordinary to encourage them to be in attendance at
the festivities in case any accident may be occasioned by the
intended illuminations."

As his malady increased, George III found it advisable to live at
Windsor, and he did not often return to Kew after the turn of the
century. His sons had houses there; Ernest, Duke of Cumberland,
lived in a house on the north side of the Green, and the Duke of

Cambridge in the house with the portico, near the church. Queen Charlotte spent the last summer of her life at Kew, and died in the Dutch House in 1818.

The name Kew means, for most people who are not residents, Kew Gardens. The Royal Botanical Gardens are unique; they contain the most complete arboretum in existence, the largest and most complete herbarium in the world, splendid research facilities. Gardeners and botanists come from all parts of the globe to study the plants and flowers there. The eighteenth-century Princess Dowager, by spending munificent sums on gardens for her own delight, left a heritage without parallel for future generations.

CHAPTER TEN

Ham and Petersham

HAM is a very ancient village; in medieval documents the place is styled Ham-with-Hatch. The word Ham means a house, and Hatch comes from the Saxon word for a gate. In the sixteenth century it was known as Hamme-juxta-Kyngeston, and the palace was probably a cluster of cottages at the boundary of the Common, standing near a gate placed there to keep the cattle from straying.

The village is known, of course, because of the Jacobean mansion made famous, or notorious, by Charles II's Cabal—Ham House. This is commented on later in the chapter. A number of fine houses were built round the Common in the eighteenth century, one of the best being Ormeley Lodge, on the west side. It is early eighteenth-century, with wings, well-matched to the central portion, added a century later. Wrought-iron gates set off a handsome doorway, with Corinthian pilasters and a plasterwork frieze of palm-leaves and cherubs' heads. A row of small cottages between Ormeley Lodge and the main road dates from the early part of the nineteenth century; the end one, Sudbrook Cottage, is a charming example of a well-designed small dwelling, and has a notable garden created by the writer, Beverley Nichols.

St Andrew's Church, on the Common, was built in 1832, a period when several well-known people occupied near-by houses, including Maria Edgeworth, who lived at Langham House.

William Cowper, the poet, often visited a kinsman, General Cowper, who lived at Ham in a house near the Common. William's cousin, Theodora Jane, was often there, too, and he fell in love with her. (She is the Delia of his early poems.) Her father, Ashley Cooper, objected to the match: the poet, he said, could hardly support himself, let alone a wife. William objected to Ashley Cooper's green hat with its yellow lining, which, William declared, made the gentleman look like a mushroom. Relations became even more strained. William finally accepted the fact that he was *non persona grata* with the Ashley Coopers, and did not appear to be particularly heartbroken at the rejection of his suit. Theodora Jane did not take the disappointment so calmly. She grieved for William all her life, and it was a long life, for she was ninety when she was at last buried in Petersham Churchyard.

And now we are in Petersham, reputed to be the most elegant village in England. The twentieth century is sweeping through it, straightening out corners, driving roads over ancient fields, covering old roofs with television aerials. Blocks of flats block out once-familiar vistas, and 'development' is always a threat. Yet, astonishingly, the spoliation is only skin-deep. The great Stuart and Georgian houses remain, splendidly aristocratic behind their tall gates. There are still parklands, and cottages in trim gardens, unexpected little streets leading down to the river, cows in the water meadows. There is inevitable change, but no decay.

The earliest mention of Petersham is found in the records of the Benedictine Abbey of St Peter, Chertsey, in 666, when certain lands in Piterichesham were given to the abbey. In the Domesday Survey of 1086 it becomes Patricesham, and in 1303 it comes up in a slight argument between the Vicar of Kingston and the Prior of the Convent of Merton as Petrosham (and in the same paragraph, referring to "gardens, curtilages, and all that is dug with the foot," as Pettresham). Spelling was never an exact science in medieval times.

There was originally a Saxon church at Petersham; part of it was rebuilt in Norman times. Aubrey says that the village was a place of sanctuary, where nobody could be arrested, or if arrested at any other place, could not be brought through the village, adding that "by long and scandalous neglect this valuable privilege is lost." He was writing in the seventeenth century, when many would have found it useful to take refuge in this sanctuary.

The manor was held in turn by the villagers, then by various sovereigns as far as Charles I, who granted a lease of the manor to William Murray, who appears to have been, according to Burnet, "a great favourite but not an estimable person"—an understatement, judging by references to him in the records. His

daughter, Elizabeth, married Sir Lionel Tollemache, and obtained
the titles of Baroness Huntingtower and Countess of Dysart from
Charles I. After her husband's death, she married John, Earl of
Lauderdale. An unforgettable impression of the two is given in
an old parish magazine by Mr Mills, who was vicar of Petersham
for many years, retiring in 1962:

> On 17th February 1672, a wedding took place in Petersham
> Church. The bride was Elizabeth, Countess of Dysart: a widow
> who had borne eleven children to her previous husband, six of
> whom had died. She had once been a beauty, but "covetousness,
> ambition and pride had ravaged her comeliness and left their
> marks on her face." The bridegroom was John Maitland, Duke
> of Lauderdale, "a great gorilla of a man, with uncouth body and
> a shambling gait, a massive head crowned with a disorderly
> tangle of red hair, and when he spoke he slobbered." And so this
> well-assorted pair were joined in holy matrimony by the Bishop
> of Worcester, whom they had brought with them in their
> carriage.

The new Duchess, a woman of considerable personality, is said
to have mixed more than superficially in politics:

> She sold places, and she was wanting in no method that could
> bring her money, which she lavished out in a most profuse vanity.
> It is more than likely that she had a finger in that unsavoury pie,
> the Cabal, which will ever be associated with her home, Ham
> House.

Now a Stately Home under the direction of the Ministry of
Works, which you can visit on payment of a modest fee, Ham
House is a Jacobean mansion built in 1610 for Sir Thomas Vavasour.
It came into the possession of the Dysart family about the middle
of the seventeenth century, and was furnished, according to the
diarist Evelyn, "like a greate Prince's." Much of the fine furniture
is still there, on show, together with tapestries, paintings, and
furnishings which remain as they were after nearly three hundred
years. There are several richly decorated rooms, including the
chamber where the infamous Cabal is (erroneously) said to have
met.

This "committee of state", comprising Charles II's trusted
Ministers—perhaps confederates is a more exact word—were
known as the CABAL because of their several initials: Clifford,

Ashley, Buckingham, Arlington, Lauderdale. Charles II, who spent money as quickly as he got it, had no scruples as to where it came from. On his Restoration, he had taken over the entire control of foreign policy, and with the connivance of the Cabal, which held their secret meetings at Ham House, he concluded a secret treaty with Louis XIV of France, by which he undertook to subordinate English foreign policy to that of France for an annual pension of £100,000.

The Duchess of Lauderdale had a string of daughters by her first marriage, one of whom married the 1st Duke of Argyll. Their son, John, who became 2nd Duke of Argyll, was born at Ham House, and in about 1726 built Sudbrook House in the hamlet of Sudbrook, which adjoined Petersham. James Gibbs designed the mansion, which became famous because of the magnificent panelled room, a cube of 30 feet. The house now belongs to the Richmond Golf Club, which has made one of the finest courses in Surrey in the grounds.

The 2nd Duke of Argyll had distinguished himself as a soldier and now, at the beginning of the eighteenth century, he had laid aside his sword and had turned statesman. Queen Anne was on the throne, and it was a period of fierce political faction. Two noble families lived in unusual proximity at Petersham: the Duke of Argyll, the premier Whig peer, and the Earl of Rochester, a high Tory. It was noted that the Duke and the Earl were able to meet at dinner in the local big houses with commendable calm and politeness.

John Campbell, 2nd Duke of Argyll, was a remarkable man in many ways, not least when it came to choosing a wife. Handsome, witty, urbane, and charming, he became the idol of Queen Anne's Court. He had a wife, a chronic invalid; the marriage had turned out wretchedly, and the couple had parted long ago. The ladies at Queen Anne's Court who turned inviting eyes in the Duke's direction did not mind *her*. An estranged wife, and a crabbed one at that, was out of mind as well as out of sight. Now it so happened that the Lord Chamberlain gave a dinner to the Maids of Honour on the Queen's birthday, and when the cloth was removed, each lady was invited—as was the custom—to give a toast. Each made an innocuous choice, generally of an elderly gentleman; no young ady was going to give herself away publicly by naming the man he really admired. There was an exception, however. Jane Warburton, a country girl from Cheshire, not long appointed Maid of Honour to Queen Anne, saw no reason to dissimulate. Rather plain, unsophisticated, straightforward, and without pretensions, Jenny Warburton rose, lifted her glass, and toasted the Duke of Argyll. The company burst into laughter, a sad breach of manners for what was supposed to be a set of well-bred young women. But the idea of Plain Jane toasting the splendid Duke of Argyll was too much for their gravity. They continued laughing, and Jenny sat down, humiliated, and was soon in tears.

There was a ball that evening, and the Lord Chamberlain, finding the Duke near him, told what had happened, expecting laughter to greet the story. The Duke certainly smiled—and asked to be presented to Miss Warburton. He devoted himself to her for the rest of the evening, and other meetings followed. Lady Louisa Stuart noted in a letter that the Duke's attachment to Miss Warburton became "notorious and was as passionate as it was extraordinary." But the Duke already had a Duchess. It is probable that, passionate or not, any proposals that the gay gallant made would have been rejected by Jenny Warburton with northern bluntness. The Duke was allowed the privileges of a friend, no more. He sat and talked with Jenny in her lodgings as she sewed, and occasionally she allowed him to give her presents.

Then Queen Anne died, and the Whigs brought in the Hanoverian George. John Campbell, Duke of Argyll, the first of the Whig peers, became an important political personage. Jenny Warburton, the Duke's friend, was appointed lady-in-waiting to Caroline, Princess of Wales, who was un-Hanoverian in that she was very intelligent and sensitive. Jenny was happy with her royal mistress, and, apparently, quite content to go on allowing the Duke of Argyll to watch her sewing and listen to her pleasant but undistinguished conversation. But these Platonic meetings came to an end. The Duke's wife died in 1716. A ripple of malicious curiosity went round the Court. Would the Duke of Argyll make Jane Warburton, a dowerless country girl, his new duchess? They had not long to wait for an answer. The Duke offered Jenny his heart, his coronet, and his fortune. Jenny was of the opinion that he had acted with indecent haste so soon after the death of

[107]

his wife, and firmly told him he must wait. They were married some months later, and 'lived happy ever after'. Jenny had four daughters, and became even plainer as she grew older, but the Duke loved her faithfully to the last. When he died in 1744, it is reported that she looked down on his kind face and said: "Well, have been the wife of a great man."

Duchess Jenny remained in the village, making her home at Sudbrook and attending Petersham Church, her elder daughter Caroline, occupying the pew in the North Gallery after the Duchess's death. Caroline also rented three pews for her domestic staff: one for the upper servants, one for the livery servants, and a third labelled "Common Pew for Servants" for the rest. The hierarchy in the servants' hall was just as rigid as that in the drawing-room.

Douglas House, which is to the right on the east drive to Ham House, was built about 1700, and is closely associated with Catherine Hyde, Duchess of Queensberry—Prior's "Kitty beautiful and young and wild as colt untamed." She was a daughter of the Earl of Clarendon and Rochester. Kitty was no longer young when she came to Douglas House, but she still possessed considerable beauty, and her wildness was still untamed.

The lord of the manor, Lionel, 4th Earl of Dysart, lived at Ham House, next door. He was an eccentric, with cultivated tastes but an uncertain temper, and he quarrelled with the Duchess of Queensberry over a strip of land. Eccentrics are all very well, but when one is an earl quickly aroused to irritability, and the other a highly individual, undisciplined duchess, one expects the unexpected. Perhaps it did not come altogether as a surprise to their amused mutual acquaintance that Duchess Kitty should seize a stout staff while she and the Earl were on the disputed strip of territory and drive him from the field.

Many are the stories told of the Duchess of Queensberry, and even the apocryphal ones sound as if they ought to be true. She was one of those women who feel secure enough of their position in Society to let their personalities rip. A grand-daughter of Laurence Hyde, Earl of Rochester—"Lamentable Lorry" to his friends—she inherited many of his qualities and failings. She was often arrogant, obstinate, and self-willed to the point of mania

"Ham walls bound my prospect," said Horace Walpole, her neighbour at Strawberry Hill, "but thank God the Thames is between me and the Duchess of Queensberry." Swift relates that she insisted on keeping to her own fashions in dress and hair-style, refusing "to cut and curl my hair like a sheep's head or to wear one of their trolloping sacks."

She was, however, an outstanding figure in that world of eighteenth-century culture, with its sensibility, its fastidious taste in the arts, its appreciation of literary genius. She helped John Gay when he desperately needed a patron, inviting him to live in her house and taking care that he had the leisure and solitude essential to his writing. Kitty had a practical strain, too, where geniuses were concerned. Gay had no idea of money, and she "impounded his cash and doled it out to him as she thought he required it—sometimes too strictly, Gay thought at times." She also fought battles on Gay's behalf, quarrelling with no less a personage than King George II, because she thought Gay was being badly treated. Gay was accused of introducing political innuendoes into his plays so as to get laughs. (He did, of course.) The ridiculed politicians asked the Lord Chamberlain to stop his opera, *Polly*, being performed, on the ground of its immoral tendencies. In other words, certain Ministers of State had been caricatured. The Lord Chamberlain took action. So did the Duchess of Queensberry. She appealed to the King on Gay's behalf, and was rebuffed. Then she canvassed the entire Court for subscriptions to have *Polly* privately published. Affronted, the King barred her from the Court. Kitty replied with an extremely spirited letter which began in fine style:

> The Duchess of Queensberry is surprised and well pleased that the King hath given her so agreeable a command as to stay from Court, where she never came for diversion, but to bestow civility on the King and Queen; she hopes by such an unprecedented order as this that the King will see as few as he wishes at his Court, particularly such as dare to think or speak truth.

Four or five reigns earlier, she would have had that pretty, impertinent head struck from her shoulders for such a communication; but the eighteenth-century aristocrats thought themselves as good as, if not better than, any little Hanoverian whose father

had been brought over from Europe to sit on the Throne o
England, and the Duchess wrote to George II as she would have
written to anyone of her own rank who had acted in what she
considered an ill-bred manner. She stayed away from Cour
throughout the rest of the reign, and was quite consolable. The
pleasantest outcome of the affair was the success of the book. A
banned book, is, almost by definition, a best-seller, and Gay sold
over 10,000 copies of the well-publicised *Polly*, an enormous sale
in those days.

Montrose House, a handsome Stuart house still in an excellen
state of preservation, was built for Sir Thomas Jenner, on the site
of an "antient messuage formerly of Joanna Symonds", in the
reign of Charles II. He was a lawyer who rose to be Recorder o
the City of London and, under James II, a Baron of the Exchequer
When Catholic James had to flee, Jenner was committed to the
Tower on a charge of "subverting the protestant religion and the
laws and liberties of the kingdom." He was also charged later with
appropriating £3000 raised from fines on Dissenters. He was not the
only one to succumb to the temptation of easy money in a period
of "anything goes"; what is more remarkable is that he managed
to raise eleven out of his thirteen children at a time when it was
taken for granted that a high proportion of children in a family
inevitably died.

The house was given its present name when it was leased to
the Dowager Duchess of Montrose in 1838. There had been many
complaints that the right-angled corner on which Montrose House
stands was highly dangerous; there had been many accidents to
carriages. In the 1850s, there was a more than usually seriou
accident, when a coach hit the wall and driver, passengers, and
horses were badly injured. The residents of neighbouring house
were now very much alarmed, and joined together in a kind of
committee, calling themselves Trustees of the Roads. Led by the
Hon. Algernon Tollemache of Ham House, they managed to
extract a small piece of land from the owner of Montrose House
and softened the angle. It must have been a formidable bend, for
it is still a very sharp corner today.

Rutland Lodge, near Montrose House, is a notable example o
an aristocratic mansion. It was built in the 1660s for a Lord

Mayor of London, and another storey was added in 1720. The doorway, gate, and railings are very fine. The staircase, with a coved ceiling and good plasterwork, dates from 1740. Sir Thomas Jenner built or leased Rutland Lodge and left it to his daughter, Margaret. The Duchess of Rutland lived there between 1750 and 1760, and gave it her name.

Petersham House arrests one's attention immediately because of its elegant semi-circular domed portico with Ionic columns. It was built about 1674, but was altered towards the end of the eighteenth century (or possibly the early part of the nineteenth century—the records differ) when the top storey was added. The house contains a beautiful staircase, and fine panelling and chimneypieces.

Park Gate House, dating from the late eighteenth century, was the home of Daisy Ashford, author of *The Young Visiters*, who lived there as a child.

Other houses on Petersham Road include Gort House, built in 1674 and much enlarged in 1800. The Gort family, which had long associations with Petersham and Richmond, lived here for several generations. Elm Lodge was built at the end of the eighteenth or very early in the nineteenth century. Dickens rented the house in 1839, and wrote a large part of *Nicholas Nickleby* there. It is said that the duel scene in that book between Sir Mulberry Hawk and Lord Frederick Verisopht is set in a field beyond Ham House; Dickens often walked there. He wrote to his friends, asking them to visit him at Petersham. In a letter to Daniel Maclise, dated June 28th, 1839, he urged:

> Come down—come down—revive yourself with country air. I'll warrant you good health for 12 months at least. . . . The roads about are jewelled after dusk with glow-worms, the leaves are all out and the flowers, too, swimming feats from Petersham to Richmond Bridge have been achieved before breakfast, I myself have risen at 6 and plunged head foremost into the water to the astonishment and admiration of all beholders.

Ham Street, which runs from the Common to the river, has two fine Georgian houses: Greycourt, where Cardinal Newman spent his early childhood, and Manor House, once the home of Sir George Gilbert Scott, the architect, who lived there in the 1860s.

[111]

A PROSPECT OF RICHMOND

Many of the streets in Petersham have names which are links with the past. Lovell Road is named after the Lovel family, lords of the manor of Ham in the fourteenth and fifteenth centuries. Francis, the last male heir of the Lovels, was a favourite of the not very popular Richard III, and is immortalised in the couplet:

> The Cat, the Rat, and Lovel the Dog
> Rule all England under a Hog.

Mowbray Road is possibly called after Roger de Mowbray, lord of the manor of Ham from 1205 to 1220. Cleves Road recalls Anne of Cleves, and Sheridan Road was probably named after the playwright, Richard Brinsley Sheridan, who lived for a time at Downe House on Richmond Hill, and had many friends at Ham and Petersham. Murray Road has associations with William Murray, 1st Earl of Dysart; he owned a great deal of property in the neighbourhood.

Sandy Lane was marked as Blind Lane in an early nineteenth-century map of Richmond, and in 1837 it is noted as being "a winding lane with two or three houses and good hedges." It became known as Sandy Lane during the nineteenth century, probably because there was up to six inches of sand in dry weather, after a prolonged drought. It ran by the side of an orchard and a market garden, and was well below the level of these lands.

Some of the cottages have old names, usually connected with people who were well known in the parish in their time. Boxal Cottage probably belonged to Mr Boxall of Ham Vestry; he was an active member in 1817. Wiggins Cottage recalls William Higgins, Herdsman of the Parish 1851–52.

Modern development is taking place on the Bute Estate, which once belonged to the Earl of Bute, whose house stood opposite the Dysart Arms, and was pulled down in 1895. A modern church already stands there: All Saints', with an Italianate campanile built in the early part of the present century by Mrs Lionel Warde, a local resident.

You are soon back, however, in eighteenth-century Petersham you are never far away from the Age of Elegance in this charming village. Sudbrook Lodge, fronting the main road at the Common dates from the eighteenth century. There is a tradition that John Campbell, 2nd Duke of Argyll, built an annexe on to his house

Sudbrook Park, to insulate him from his five daughters, "the bawling Campbells", whose disregard of his need for peace drove him to this solution. This conflicts with another handed-down story that Nell Gwyn lived here for a time: Argyll belonged to the Court of Queen Anne, and Nell Gwyn belonged, so to speak, to Charles II.

A better authenticated tenant is Mary Anne Clarke, mistress of Frederick, Duke of York, Commander-in-Chief of the Army at the beginning of the nineteenth century—he who had ten thousand men. In 1809, there was a major scandal, as gossip grew into rumour and rumour burst into public indignation. Mrs Clarke had been selling Army commissions at a cut rate. There was a to-do. The Duke retired from his position as Commander-in-Chief, and Mrs Clarke tried to sell his letters for £10,000. How much she actually got for them is not clear, but she retired to her home at Petersham, and the Duke, after two years had elapsed, resumed his position as head of the Army.

It is said that on a dry day, if you were to look down from the air at the entrance to Richmond Park opposite the Dysart Arms in Petersham Road, you would be able to trace the outline of the foundations of what was one of the most famous of Petersham's houses—Petersham Lodge.

There were three houses of this name. The first was built by Gregory Cole, who sold it—no doubt under strong persuasion—to Charles I, when that monarch was enclosing the Park: it was pulled down. James II granted a lease of the place to Edward Hyde, and it descended to Lawrence Hyde, the leader of the old Tory party. Hyde lived mostly at his town house, but always came to stay at Petersham Lodge when he quarrelled with his relations, which was a fairly frequent occurrence. This house was burnt down in 1721. The site is opposite the Dysart Arms on Petersham Road. The Hyde connection is the most interesting.

Laurence Hyde died in 1711, and his son Henry succeeded to the title and the estate. Henry Hyde is described by Swift as being a simple, civil fellow. He captured as wife the most beautiful woman of her day, Miss Leveson-Gower ... "She did nothing, said nothing memorable, she just was." This lady was as kind as she was lovely, and became the Lady Bountiful of the village.

One of her two daughters married the Earl of Essex in Petersham
Church, and a contemporary account describes the wedding
ceremony as being solemnised with the greatest magnificence
"near 200 of the Quality" being invited to the nuptials. It is
interesting to picture this vast congregation crammed into little
Petersham Church—not much more than half the size of the
present building—and to imagine the ladies in their spreading
brocades, their hair dressed high and piled with flowers and
feathers; the grand gentlemen in curled wigs, their ceremonial
satins adorned with silver buttons and lace ruffles.

Fine houses and aristocrats. These lead back to Petersham
Church, and a sermon preached there by the Reverend Mr
Bellamy on Trinity Sunday, 1778. Mr Bellamy was a forceful
character, and he preached a forceful sermon. The small church
was full, as usual, and the congregation, also as usual, consisted of
some of the richest people in the parish, if not in England. Mr
Bellamy did not begin with a text, as was his normal custom:[1] he
started with a résumé of the duties and responsibilities of a minister
of the Gospel to his parishioners, and the equally important duties
and responsibilities of the laity, particularly in regard to providing
for the maintenance of their minister and the care of his parish
church. He then made a direct attack on his startled congregation.

> The House of God is almost the only house in the parish
> neglected, ruinous and sordid. . . . The splendour of the private
> buildings around it must impart a peculiar propriety to the
> Prophet's remonstrance: *Is it time for ye, O ye, to dwell in your
> ceiled houses, and this house lie waste?* It has been said that long
> familiarity will insensibly reconcile us even to wretchedness. It
> has not yet obtained its effect on me. I cannot hesitate to declare
> that I never enter this building, but I feel myself filled with
> astonishment—I had almost said, with indignation and terror—
> that it should be suffered to remain another year a disgrace
> perhaps a calamity to the parish. . . .

Mr Bellamy had prepared his sermon carefully, and he did not
stop. He spoke of "the numerous temples of Vanity and Vice
erecting their heads in triumph over this dejected edifice of piety"
and went on with renewed fire:

[1] The sermon and some of Bellamy's Memorials to the Bishop were published by
him in a small volume in 1779. Printed by Fielding & Walker, Paternoster Row,
London, and Ansell, George Street, Richmond.

Railway Bridge over Thames at Richmond

Cooke.   *By courtesy of Richmond upon Thames Libraries Committee*

Proposed Terminus of City of London and Richmond Railway

lunt.   *By courtesy of Richmond upon Thames Libraries Committee*

Cholmondeley House, Cholmondeley Walk

A. F. Kersting.

Morshead Hotel, The Terrace, Richmond Hill

J. S. Sanderson-Wells.

Kew Gardens: Mid-nineteenth Century

By courtesy of the Director, Royal Botanic Gardens

Kew Gardens: Edwardian Days

By courtesy of the Director, Royal Botanic Gardens

Election of Vestrymen
RATEPAYERS OF RICHMOND

The chief Curate and Lady Visitors are leaving circulars, and soliciting Votes for the following Candidates:—

F. BURDETT, Lt-Col.	T. J. KNIGHT,
W. ROBINSON,	H. T. CAUSTON,
T. M. CLARKE,	C. GREEN,
DR. HASSALL,	DR. WARWICK.

Are these the duties of Clergymen?

You are hereby cautioned that the majority of the above represent the extreme Ritualistic party so repugnant to the parishioners: as they are associated for one common object

REJECT THEM,

and shew your disapproval of their practices and interference.

You have plenty of good men to select from, *who will conscientiously attend to the general interest of the parish* without partizanship, and so teach the Clergy to mind their own business. **NO PUSEYITE.**

Election of Vestrymen, Poster,
Nineteenth Century

*By courtesy of Richmond upon Thames
Libraries Committee*

To the Gentlemen
OF THE
RICHMOND VESTR

SIRS,

The **LADY CANVASSERS** having busily employed in soliciting Votes for the **OFFIC** **PARISH BEADLE**, and from the strenuous exertions made in the **LATE ELECTION** for **VESTRYME** putting Mr. **JAMES MACKAY** at the Head of the I do hope they are **NOT** endeavouring to procure **OFFICE** of **BEADLE** for their **LATE FAVOURITE**

Should he be proposed, I do **CAUTION** you again **ILLEGALLITY** of such **PROCEEDINGS**, and **UNFAIRNESS** to the other **CANDIDATES**, in El one of your own **BODY** to such a **RESPONSIBLE** **IMPORTANT OFFICE**.

By the rejection of the Lady Canvassers **CANDI** or **NOMINEE** you will put an end to the system so in vogue of having **FEMALE** interference in **PA BUSINESS**, instead of attending to their **DOME** duties.

I remain, Gentlemen,

Your Obedient Servant,

A RATEPAYE

Richmond, October 31st, 1865.

To the Gentlemen of the
Richmond Vestry, Poster,
Nineteenth Century

*By courtesy of Richmond upon Thames
Libraries Committee*

Behold these walls, solemnly consecrated to the glory of the most high God! Mark their foundations! They have been pronounced ruinous, rotten, tottering to their fall. Now, brethren, let me ask a plain question. Would any of the noble and opulent possessors of the palaces that surround us, estimate this building competent for the reception of the lowest order of their associates? Would they venture to lodge the meanest of their domestics in so despicable, so mean a room as this? Contributions for luxurious purposes are ever ready. The temples of Baal are daily enlarging their borders, and every summons for their support and embellishment is obeyed with alacrity, and executed with a prodigal profusion: but here! though an incredible number of families, in and surrounding this village, will have no place for the public worship of the sovereign Dispenser of all things, you will not deign to issue your fiat, though nothing more has hitherto been required from your hands.

The sad fact was soon clear that these wealthy parishioners did indeed prefer to support the temples of Baal rather than their dejected edifice of piety. Mr Bellamy made this impassioned appeal from the pulpit as a last resort, and he failed to shake them from their indifference to the state of the church.

The fabric had been getting more dilapidated and ruinous every year. The original very small church had been enlarged in the seventeenth century, but by 1769, when an Act was passed forming Kew and Petersham into one ecclesiastical parish, the seating accommodation was quite inadequate. Mr Bellamy was appointed minister in 1740, and remained there for the best part of fifty years, during which time he made unceasing efforts to get the church repaired, enlarged, or rebuilt. There were no endowments; the minister's stipend came to under £100 a year, collected from pew rents. Bellamy had written memorials to the bishop, setting out in full the condition of the church, but very little was done. The famous sermon had equally barren results.

Mr Charles Warren, the historian of Petersham Church, finds it inconceivable that during Bellamy's long ministry, when the parish contained so many wealthy residents, the church could have been allowed to fall into such a dilapidated state, although, he adds, referring to Bellamy's ideas for enlargement,

in some respects it is fortunate that his schemes were not adopted, as the enlargement proposed by him might have involved the destruction of the Norman chancel, while the erection of a new church elsewhere in the parish might have resulted in the entire demolition of the old structure and the irreparable loss of it historical associations.

This would indeed have been a serious loss, as Petersham Church has some of the most ancient and interesting memorial in the county. After the minister's death in 1788 "the parishioner appear to have realised that the condition of the church called for some attention." Shades of Mr Bellamy! Alterations were carried out, and during the next hundred years the south transept wa widened, galleries were added, new pews provided, and othe improvements made.

The church is still very small, but it has great character, an the memorials which crowd the walls, and the tombs in the church yard, bear many famous names. The Hydes, the Douglases, the Murrays, the Montagues and many others of noble family are there; and then, on a tombstone, we find

Captain George Vancouver.
Died in the Year 1798
Aged 40

Vancouver was born in Norfolk and joined the Navy at the age of fourteen. He sailed with Captain Cook on two expeditions made a voyage of discovery round the Cape of Good Hope, surveyed the south-west coast of Australia, the coast of New Zealand, and the Pacific Coast of North America, where he discovered the island which was named after him. He returned to England in 1795, and finally settled down in Petersham at The Glen, a cottage in River Lane, where he wrote his *Voyage of Discovery*. A service is held at his grave every year, to which many visiting Canadians come.

Hannah, Mary, and Richard, the great-granddaughters and great grandson of William Penn, the Founder of Pennsylvania, are buried in the churchyard—another link with the New World.

If Petersham was not actually the home of the 'bluestockings' those literary ladies who adorned the *salons* in the late eighteenth and early nineteenth centuries, it was certainly the centre of a vigorous and lively cultural life which attracted most of the

celebrities of the period, the noted bluestockings among them. At
Douglas House, Lady Scott entertained writers and artists who
drove or rode out from London to enjoy the fresh air of the
Richmond meadows and the civilised conversation which was
always such a feature of Lady Scott's gatherings. Lady Louisa
Stuart, a frequent visitor, had considerable literary gifts; she was a
close friend of Sir Walter Scott, who profoundly respected her
judgment, describing her as the best critic he had ever had. She
was the first person to read *Marmion* and *The Lady of the Lake*,
and it was from her notes on the Richmond scene that he constructed the passage in *The Heart of Midlothian* that describes
Jeanie Deans' journey.

Another who achieved a kind of oblique immortality is Lady
Horton, who lived for a time at Sudbrook. She was a kinswoman
of Lord Byron, and it is said that she once met Byron when she
was at a ball, dressed in half-mourning, a star-spangled black
dress of some soft stuff—and this inspired the poet to write his
famous verses beginning: "She walks in beauty like the night."
Mrs Montague, one of the original 'bluestockings' and an authoress
of repute, often visited Petersham Lodge, and wrote "she could
turn Pastorella" in Petersham with great pleasure.

Lady Diana Beauclerk was a noted inhabitant of Petersham
towards the end of the century. She was a good painter, and
Bartolozzi's engravings of her pictures made her known to a
discerning public. The eldest daughter of the second Duke of
Marlborough, she married Viscount Bolingbroke, but divorced him
and married Johnson's friend, Topham Beauclerk, of whom the
great Samuel wrote to Boswell: "Such another will not often be
found amongst mankind." Lady Di, as she was called by her
friends, did not find happiness in her second marriage, either.
The Beauclerks lived at Little Marble Hill, which has since
disappeared; it is always described as "a very pretty house." After
her husband's death she moved to Devonshire Lodge, where one
of her friends was extremely pleased to "behold her in that sweet
home, released from all her cares, a thousand pounds at her
disposal, and her husband dead. Oh, it was pleasant, it was delightful, to see her enjoyment of the situation."

The most celebrated Petersham ladies of the time were the two sisters, Mary and Agnes Berry, immortalised as the friends of Horace Walpole. They became known throughout London Society, they appear in most of the memoirs of the period, and it comes as a surprise to realise that their fame did not rest on literary works or grand connections, but on the fact that they had a genius for friendship. It was the heyday of the *salon*, and Mary Berry, who had lived abroad a great deal, entertained her friends at *salons* modelled on those of the influential Parisian ladies. Her parties attracted the leading writers of the day, from the Continent as well as from the literary world of London. In their later days, the Berry sisters lived at Devonshire Cottage (later Devonshire Lodge), which they rented for the summer months from a friend, the widow of the Hon. George Lamb.

Mary and Agnes Berry were the daughters of Robert Berry, a Yorkshire barrister, who expected to be the heir of a rich uncle and therefore did not trouble overmuch about pursuing his profession with profit. He antagonised the old man by falling in love with a penniless girl and marrying her. Mrs Berry proceeded to make bad worse: she produced two daughters, and no son. The rich uncle, who wanted a male heir, turned to Robert's younger brother, William, an astute young man of business who had the good sense to marry a merchant's well-dowered daughter. She obligingly bore a son within a year of the marriage, and the rich uncle was well pleased. Robert Berry's misfortunes multiplied. He lost his wife after only four years of marriage, and when his uncle bade him seek another as soon as maybe, refused to comply. He did not wish to marry again, he said: he would look after Mary and Agnes, his two motherless children. The uncle decided to stand no more insubordination. He made William his heir, and Robert was left with his allowance of £300 a year and no expectations.

Mary was three years old, and Agnes two, when their mother died, and from their childhood Mary showed herself as possessing the stronger personality. They lived in Yorkshire with their maternal grandmother, who gave them lessons—there was not enough money for a governess. They were intelligent, lively girls, and went out in local society, where, in due time, they attracted plenty of young men, eligible and otherwise. The level-headed Mary records at one point: "Suffered as people do at sixteen from a passion which, wisely disapproved of, I resisted and dropped."

When the rich uncle died, William inherited a large fortune, and Robert was left a capital sum of £10,000. William made this up to an amount which brought in £1000 a year, and on this Robert Berry and his daughters lived. They travelled on the Continent, and lodged in London or in other places where they could be near friends, of whom they had many. In 1788 they rented a house in Twickenham, and there, at the house of Lady Herries, wife of the banker, they met Horace Walpole. Mary Berry was then twenty-five, Agnes twenty-four, and Horace Walpole was a bachelor of seventy-two. The beginning of the unusual friendship between Walpole and the two girls unfolds in a letter which he wrote to Lady Ossory on October 11th, 1788. He told her he had made the acquaintance of two young ladies of the name of Berry, who were the best informed and the most perfect creatures he ever saw at their age.

> They are exceedingly sensible, entirely natural and unaffected, frank, and being qualified to talk on any subject, nothing is so easy, and agreeable as their conversation. . . . Mary, the eldest, sweet, with fine dark eyes, that are very lively when she speaks, with a symmetry of face that is the more interesting from being pale; Agnes, the younger, has an agreeable sensible countenance, hardly to be called handsome, but almost. . . . They dress within the bounds of fashion, though fashionably; but without the excrescences and balconies with which modern hoydens overwhelm and barricade their persons.

Horace Walpole's admiration for the sisters, begun on such a high note, never changed. Soon the Berry family were visiting him regularly every Sunday evening at Twickenham. He found Mary an angel, "both inside and out", and Agnes, though less animated than her sister, delightful. Mr Berry was "a little merry man with a round face", and Walpole looked forward all through the week to his Sundays with the Berrys. Their mutual attachment grew stronger. Walpole wrote to them when they were away from the neighbourhood: he called them his "twin wives" or "beloved spouses." Mary was "Suavissima Maria" and Agnes "my sweet lamb." He declared he was in love with them both: "Were there but one of you, I should be ashamed of being so strongly attracted at my age; being in love with both, I glory in my passion, and think it a proof of my sense."

So he teased, but the relationship was neither misunderstood nor smiled at behind upheld fans. It was based on genuine affection and respect, and everyone knew it. All three parties to the friendship were gainers. Walpole, who liked talking, had two pretty and appreciative girls always ready to listen to him:

> Two charming beings, whom everybody likes and approves, and yet can be pleased with the company and conversation and old stories of a Methusalem. . . . At the end of my days [I] have fallen into more agreeable society than ever I knew at any period of my life.

Mary and Agnes, for their part, were introduced into the brilliant political, social, and cultural centre of what has been described as the most civilised society that has existed in English Society. For fifty years Horace Walpole had known everybody worth knowing, and he introduced his young friends to the powerful and prominent people who frequented his house. Mary and Agnes Berry were received everywhere in spite of their lack of rank and fortune. They were very happy.

The friendship continued without a shadow until Walpole's death, in 1796, at the age of eighty. He left the sisters Little Strawberry Hill, his second house at Twickenham, and legacies of £4000 to each of them, with the request that Mary should prepare a collected edition of his works: it was the edition of 1798, in five quarto volumes. She also edited a huge collection of letters—love letters!—which Madame du Deffand, celebrated for her *salons* in Paris, had sent to Horace Walpole. Mary Berry decided to publish selections of these letters because they gave such illuminating pictures of life in Paris before the Revolution. (It is said that Napoleon read this book in his coach on the road to Moscow in 1812. History does not mention what he read on the road back.)

The Berry sisters' lives had been interesting enough when Walpole was alive, but it was in their later years that they became really celebrated in their own right. Each had had an unhappy love affair, but they did not allow that to sour them. They travelled in France, and became friendly with Madame Récamier and Madame de Staël; they saw Napoleon: "He is not much like his busts . . . a little man, remarkably well on horseback, with a

sallow complexion and a highish nose." When they were in
England they lived at a small house in Curzon Street, but came
often to Twickenham and Petersham. They knew everybody,
and everybody knew the Miss Berrys, right to the end of their
long lives.

What was the secret of their fame? Their friendship with
Horace Walpole? Partly—but the truth must be admitted that
they turned into lion-hunters. They had seen the influence which
the French mistresses of *salons* acquired, and they brought the
salon to England. One met people who mattered at the Miss
Berrys' little dinner parties; novelists, poets, artists, up-and-
coming politicians, travellers. The Reverend Sydney Smith, one of
Mary's friends—of course—jeered at her but helped, all the same,
to persuade Charles Dickens to dine with the sisters when Dickens
was living at Elm Lodge on the Petersham Road, and Mary and
Agnes were at Devonshire Lodge. And some years later—"We
must have Thackeray," they would say, and did. Thackeray
sketched Mary at the beginning of his book, *The Four Georges*.

> A few years since, I knew familiarly a lady who had been asked
> in marriage by Horace Walpole, who had been patted on the
> head by George I. This lady had knocked at Doctor Johnson's
> door; had been intimate with Fox, the beautiful Georgiana of
> Devonshire, and that brilliant Whig society of the reign of
> George III; had known the Duchess of Queensberry, the patroness
> of Gay and Prior, the admired young beauty of the Court of
> Queen Anne. I often thought as I took my kind old friend's hand,
> how with it I held on to the old society of wit and men of the
> world. I could travel back for seven score years of time—have
> glimpses of Brummell, Selwyn, Chesterfield, and the men of
> pleasure; of Walpole and Conway; of Johnson, Reynolds, Gold-
> smith . . . of the fair maids of honour of George II's Court. . . .

Agnes Berry died at the beginning of 1852, and Mary at the
end of the same year. They lie buried in Petersham Churchyard,
resting, as is inscribed on their tombstone, "Amidst scenes which
in life they had frequented and loved."

The sisters were looked after for nearly sixty years by a devoted
housekeeper, Isabella Harrott, who died at the age of ninety and
was also buried at Petersham.

CHAPTER ELEVEN

The Park

MUCH of the area of what is now Richmond Park consisted, in the early seventeenth century, of waste ground, and Crown lands and commons. It had been a royal hunting-ground for hundreds of years; in the reign of Henry VIII it was still known as Shene Chase.

Charles I was exceedingly fond of hunting and field sports, and he had a great desire to make a large park for red deer, as well as for the more usual fallow deer, between Richmond and Hampton Court, where he owned large tracts of land and woods. There were numbers of gentlemen with estates and farmers with prosperous farms who had long settled in the area he coveted, and they were very reluctant to sell. The King pressed—he was determined to have their lands—and after much parley his surveyors were able to 'persuade' some of the farmers to sell. But "many very obstinately refused." A certain gentleman who had the best estate of all would by no means part with it, and "the King being as earnest to encompass it, it made a great noise, as if the King would take away men's estates at his own pleasure."

Archbishop Laud, who was Treasurer of the Realm, and Lord Cottington, the Chancellor of the Exchequer, tried to dissuade the King from going further with his infatuate scheme, not only on account of the public outcry, but because the brick wall by which Charles proposed to enclose his new park would not be less than ten miles round, and would cost far more money than they could provide out of the State funds. Lord Cottington, to whom the country people appealed to halt the almost compulsory purchase of their homes, tried by various delaying measures to stop the sale of the parcels of land; but Charles I would not be diverted from his purpose. Kingston sold him some of their common land,

nd in 1635 he obtained 265 acres belonging to the manor of
Petersham, and 483 acres belonging to the manor of Ham, 92 acres
of common and waste land in the manor of Richmond, and sizeable areas in Wimbledon, Mortlake, and Putney.

The long brick wall began to rise. Richmond was near enough
to London for strong criticism of the King's autocratic methods to
be made in many quarters. Charles I genuinely believed in the
divine right of Kings: any thwarting of his will seemed to him to
be worse than high treason. He ignored the ominous rumblings
of discontent, now widespread throughout the kingdom. The
dislike and intense anger gathering in Surrey over this royal rape
of the people's rights was now the general reaction to the King:
his obstinacy and megalomania had grown out of all proportion.

The wall round his new hunting-park lengthened, and was at
last finished. The park embraced land from six parishes. The
King paid fair value for all the land bought: he was an autocrat,
but no niggard. He gave orders that care should be taken that
communications between neighbouring towns should not be
hindered; gates were placed at Richmond Hill, East Shene,
Roehampton, Wimbledon (Robin Hood Gate), Coombe (Ladder-
stile Gate), and Ham Common. There were also step-ladders
against the wall of the Park for foot passengers. Two rights of way
across the Park were kept open, and poor people were allowed to
enter and gather firewood.

Charles I made full use of the New Park, as he called it; he
regularly came down to Richmond to hunt the red and the fallow
deer. As his trouble with Parliament increased, his hunting-
expeditions grew fewer, and presently ceased altogether. He was a
prisoner by 1647; in that year he was allowed to return for what
was probably his last hunt in Richmond Park. "The King was a'
hunting on Saturday, 28th August, in New Parke," wrote Colonel
Edmund Whalley. "Killed a Stag and a Buck: afterwards dined at
Syon." And a few days later: "The Duke of York, with the Lords,
were hunting in the New Parke at Richmond, where was good
sport—the King chearefull and much Company there."

The King was executed in 1649, and the House of Commons
passed an Act for the sale of all Crown lands, but they excepted
Richmond Park, presenting it to the City of London "for faithfull
services . . . to the Parliament and Commonwealth." Two keepers,

who had been appointed in Charles's reign, were retained unde
the Commonwealth. They were required to provide venison fo
City dinners, many a "brase of Fatt Staggs" being killed for thi
purpose.

In September 1658 Oliver Cromwell died, and the Common
wealth soon began to disintegrate. The monarchy was restored
and Charles I's son returned to England from his exile on th
Continent. The Lord Mayor and Aldermen of London attende
His Majesty Charles II, and they "gave him as a gift the New
Parke at Richmond", which his father had made. The wife o
Andrew Mollett, of Richmond, lost no time in laying informatio
that William Bentley, the late King's woodmonger, "had mad
havoc of timber and wood to the value of £20,000," and shoul
be exempted from the general pardon granted to all those who ha
retained office under the Commonwealth. There does not appea
to be a record of what happened to the late King's woodmonger
Petitions were soon submitted to Charles II for the title o
rangership of the Park. This was an office worth having; the range
was charged with overseeing and preserving the deer, and ther
were quite a number of perquisites, besides the nominal fee of 1s
a day. In 1660, Sir Lionel Tollemache, Baronet, of Ham House
and his wife, Elizabeth, Countess of Dysart, got the coveted offic
away from a rival, and two under-keepers were appointed—to d
the actual work. On March 7th, 1662, there was an order for "
warrant to pay Sir Lionel Tollemache, Bart, £300 for feeding th
deer lately brought to Richmond Great Park for the King'
disport", and on March 18th he received a similar amount. A fev
years later, however, a serious shortage in the numbers of th
deer was discovered by the King, and an inquiry was instituted
It was found that whereas there had been 2000 deer in the Parl
in 1660, there were not above 600 in 1669. Further results of thi
interesting inquiry do not appear to have been preserved. Si
Lionel Tollemache died in 1669, but his widow, presently marry
ing the Earl of Lauderdale, did not lose her share of the ranger
ship: her new husband was appointed ranger.
With the puritanical Commonwealth out of the way, people ir
power did not hesitate to make full use of their restored privileges
In 1673 and 1674, Charles II gave warrants for the Duke o

Lauderdale—the Earl had been elevated to a Dukedom—"to dig
and carry out of the [New] Park 1000 loads of gravel for his own
use", for Theophilus Tyrrell of London, Gent, "to dig any quantities
of gravel not exceeding 3000 loads . . . and to take away same and
dispose of it at pleasure", and for Henry Brounker, Esq. "to dig
up to 1000 loads"—no payment being mentioned in any instance.

The Duke had his troubles. Divers persons unknown put horses,
cows, and other cattle into the Park, to the prejudice of the feed of
the deer, and trespassers frightened the game. The wall round the
Park had continually to be repaired; over £3000 was spent in
mending it between 1660 and 1667.

In 1674, a receiver of Crown revenues for the county of Surrey
was appointed, with control of the Park and its houses, and a report
made a few years later on the improvements required—"The hay
that was mowed in the meads starved all the deer that winter and
will do so again, for the ground is one-third overgrown with rishes
this spring." In 1696, Sir William Parkyns and Sir John Friend
were executed for conspiring to kill William III on his return
from hunting in Richmond Park, "in a narrow and winding lane
leading from the landing-place on the north of the river [Strand-on-
the-Green] where he crossed by boat on his way through Turnham
Green to Kensington Palace."

Lauderdale had died in 1682, and Laurence Hyde, 1st Earl of
Rochester was appointed to the rangership "for two further lives",
in spite of the fact that the Duchess of Lauderdale had the right of
survivorship. But then "Lamentable Lorry" was the uncle of the
princess who later became Queen Anne.

Charles I had bought an estate and mansion at Petersham when
he had enclosed the Park, and this house, Petersham Lodge, was
now the home of the Hydes.

Anne succeeded to the throne in 1702. Henry Hyde, 2nd Earl
of Rochester, became ranger on the death of his father. The
Hydes were accused of neglecting the Park, leaving it "a bog, and
a harbour for deer-stealers and vagabonds." The second Earl
seems to have made some attempt to preserve the timber, at any
rate, for when the inhabitants of Kew petitioned the Crown for
eighty oaks from Richmond Park to complete the building of a
chapel-of-ease which they were having built on Kew Green, the

Earl protested that cutting down so many large trees might deface
the Park. In 1723, George I tried to raise £2000 by the sale of
wood in Richmond Park, but was told that the trees there were
rather for ornament than profit.

George II bought back the rangership from the Hydes for £5000
and bestowed it on Robert Walpole, the son of Sir Robert Walpole, his
Prime Minister. Now began a new era for the Park. Robert Walpole
was nominally the ranger, but it was his father who made most use of
the privilege. He took over one of the keeper's lodges which had once
been a farm—"there was not any mansion better than the common
lodge of the keepers", as Horace Walpole wrote to a friend—and enlarged it by the addition of wings. This became known as Old Lodge.
He also built a cottage for his huntsman on the north-eastern corner
of the Park, now known as Sheen Cottage. He enlarged an existing
small house, adding a thatched summer house in the grounds, the
walls and ceilings of which were covered with paintings attributed
to Angelica Kauffmann; this became known as Thatched House
Lodge.

George II built White Lodge, then called Stone Lodge, as a
"rural retreat when hunting." It contained a large banqueting
hall, as the King liked to entertain his friends well in this rural
retreat. White Lodge was a favourite resort of Queen Caroline,
and the broad ride bordered with oak trees on its western side was
named the Queen's Ride in her honour.

Pembroke Lodge, near Richmond Gate, appears in the Park
plans of 1754 and 1771 as "The Molecatchers." One of the game-
keepers occupied it in the eighteenth century, and the story goes
that he let apartments to the Countess of Pembroke, who was so
taken with it that she begged the King to give it to her. Horace
Walpole called her one of the most beautiful creatures in Europe,
and said she had a face like a Madonna. He especially noted the
grace and dignity with which she led the procession of Countesses
at the King's coronation. Shortly after this event, her husband, of
whom she was "doatingly fond", disguised himself as a sailor in a
black wig and ran away with another lady. This shattered the
Countess, but when her husband tired of his new love and returned
contritely to his home, she forgave him, hid her wounded feelings,
and continued life with the grace and dignity which had excited
Walpole's admiration.

It is evident that she could use her charm to some effect when
t came to asking favours of the King. He gave her "The
Molecatchers" and built another lodge for the gamekeeper nearer
:he Gate, "which however, on account of its ugliness, was eventually
demolished."

Sir Robert Walpole usually came down to Old Lodge at week-
ends "to do more business than he could in town." (The closing of
:he House of Commons on Saturdays dates from that period!)
George II had always liked hunting in Richmond Park, and had
gone there frequently when he had been Prince of Wales. Lady
Mary Wortley Montagu wrote to her sister in 1723:

> I pass many hours on horseback ... stag-hunting which I know
> you'll stare to hear of. I have arrived to vast courage and skill
> that way, and am so well pleased with it as with the acquisition of
> a new sense. His Royal Highness hunts in Richmond Park, and I
> make one of the *beau monde* in his train. I desire you after this
> account not to name the word old woman to me any more. [She
> was thirty-five.] I approach to fifteen nearer than I did ten years
> ago, and am in hopes to improve every year in health and
> vivacity.

His Royal Highness was now His Majesty, and in Sir Robert
Walpole he had a man after his own heart. Walpole joined him in
all his hunting-parties, and lively affairs they were, too. All the
royal family engaged in hunting in the Park.

The King and the Princess Royal hunted on horseback, the
Queen and Princess Amelia in a four-wheel chaise, Princess
Caroline in a two-wheel chaise, and the Princesses Mary and
Louisa in a coach. Sir Robert Walpole attended as Ranger,
clothed in green.

Some of the guests accepted invitations with trepidation. The
Countess of Suffolk wrote: "We hunt here with great noise and
violence, and have every day a very tolerable chance to have a neck
broke." Lord Delaware's lady and Lady Harriet d'Averquerque
were overturned in a chaise during a hunt; and on one occasion a
stag attacked Princess Amelia's horse, which threw her. The
Princess "happily quitted her Horse, tho' not without leaving
Part of her Habit upon the Crutch of the Saddle." This did not
deter her from re-mounting and continuing to hunt.

Sir Robert Walpole, having spent many thousands of pounds of his own money improving Old Lodge and Thatched House Lodge, felt he was entitled to privacy; many doubtful characters were able to get into the Park without much trouble. He removed the ladder-stile gates from the walls, and built small lodges at the gates in which he installed keepers, who were instructed to admit "all respectable persons" in the daytime, and such carriages as had pass-tickets, which could be obtained without difficulty. These tickets, or tokens, were made of brass, with numbers stamped on one side, and a baron's coronet with the letter "W" on the reverse side.

There was a quick reaction from the local people. "Some people of Richmond and the neighbouring villages went publicly to demand at East Sheen Gate, Richmond Hill Gate, and Ham Common Gate, leading into Richmond Park, liberty to pass thro' the Park with Carriages, on Horseback and afoot." They were refused admittance at all three gates, as they had no tokens. Sir Robert Walpole died in 1745, and his son, the ranger, carried on the same policy of making it difficult for people to get into the Park without special permission. The brass tokens were now stamped with the cypher "G.R." under a crown, with the baronet's coronet and the letter "W" on the reverse side.

On the death of Robert Walpole, George II gave the ranger-ship to his daughter, Princess Amelia, and she proved to be even more high-handed than the Walpoles had been. One of the first things she did was to carry out a plan of gradually curtailing admission to the Park, declaring that so many people crowded into the Park on hunting days, they interfered with the sport. Before long, the right of admission to "all respectable persons" was narrowed to a few special individuals. The Park, to which the people of Richmond and others had had free access since Charles I had put a wall round it, was now virtually closed to them. Indigna-tion began to mount high. There were memorials and petitions, reminding the ranger that there had always been free access to the Park, and asking her to restore the stiles or ladders, and to remove restrictions at the gates. Princess Amelia did not even reply to the petitions, whether from the Quality or the commonalty.

At last some gentlemen took action. Led by a Mr Symons, they went to one of the Park gates, and were refused admission by the gatekeeper, Deborah Burgess. Mr Symons thereupon laid an

ndictment against the deputy ranger, James Shaw, nearly £1100
being subscribed by the inhabitants of East Sheen for the expenses
of the case. There were twenty-seven witnesses for the prosecution,
who tried to prove a right of way for vehicles and foot passengers,
and thirty-seven witnesses for the defence, who asserted that anyone who would pay 2s. 6d. for a key could get into the Park. After
a two days' trial, judgment was given for the deputy ranger, and
things went on as before.

One Richmond inhabitant, however, was not content to accept
this reverse as final. John Lewis, a brewer, determined to go on
with the fight to get the townsfolks' ancient rights restored.
Gilbert Wakefield, brother of the Minister of Richmond Parish
Church and himself a person of tough and independent character,
tells the story—told directly to him by Lewis—in his *Memoirs:*

> Lewis takes a friend with him to the spot [East Sheen Gate];
> waits for the opportunity of a carriage passing through; and when
> the door-keeper was shutting the gates, interposed and offered to
> go in. "Where's your ticket?" "What occasion for a ticket: any-
> body may pass through here." "No: not without a ticket." "Yes,
> they may, and I will." "You shan't." "I will." The woman pusht,
> Lewis suffered the door to be shut on him, and brought his
> action.

The action was, in fact, put off again and again for three years,
but Lewis was patient and persistent. The trial took a day, and the
verdict was given in Lewis's favour. The judge asked him if he
preferred a door in the wall or a step-ladder to go over it. Lewis
realised that a door could not be left open because of the deer;
moreover, a door could have a bolt put on it. He opted for a step-
ladder, and in May 1758 ladder-stiles and gates were affixed to
the wall at East Sheen Gate and Ham Gate, and "a vast concourse
of people from all the neighbouring villages climbed over the ladder
stiles into the Park."

Some time later, when one of the judges, Sir Michael Foster,
again came on the same circuit, John Lewis complained to the
Court that such wide spaces had been left between the steps of the
ladders that children and old men were unable to mount them.
"I have observed it myself," said Mr Justice Foster. "And I
desire, Mr Lewis, that you would see it so constructed, that not

only children and old men, but old women, too, may be able to get up." The ladder-stiles were amended accordingly.

It is melancholy to have to record that John Lewis became poor in later life; he was given an annuity by the inhabitants of Richmond. He died in 1792 in his eightieth year, and was buried in Richmond Parish Church; his epitaph is written in the inscription on the engraving made from his portrait, painted by a pupil of Reynolds:

> Be it remembered, that by the steady Perseverance of John Lewis Brewer, at Richmond Surry, the Right of a Free Passage through Richmond Park was recovered and established by the Laws of his Country (notwithstanding very strongly opposed) after being upwards of twenty years withheld from the People.

Encouraged by Lewis's success, several owners of estates in the neighbourhood brought an action to try to establish a carriage and bridle way through the Park, but this case went against them. Princess Amelia, angry at all the publicity which was raising such a wave of unpopularity against her, left White Lodge, where she had been staying. After the death of her father, she sold the rangership to George III for an annuity of £1200 a year.

The Park was a haunt of footpads and criminal characters who now found it very easy to get over the wall. Sir Horace Mann's sister-in-law had her coach stopped by a highwayman in the Park one afternoon: "The prudent matron gave him a purse with very little money, but slipped her watch into the bag of the coach."

In 1793, several of the Richmond vestrymen met the perambulators of the Park as they went the bounds along the freeboard outside of the Park walls. (A rod or 16½ feet on the outside of the Park wall has always been left for workmen to repair or rebuild the wall; this strip is called the freeboard.) The perambulators stated that His Majesty wished to make a path, 16 feet wide, in addition to the freeboard. The vestrymen pointed out that this proposed path would go over land belonging to the parish. They then registered a formal objection, saying that such a requisition would no doubt be compiled "with alacrity", but they had their duty as trustees of the parish. His Majesty countered their objections very neatly: he was graciously pleased to direct the putting up of a pump and reservoir for water to be brought to the end of the proposed new road, for the use and accommodation of the inhabitants. At the next Vestry meeting, the vestrymen had no alternative but to vote that His Majesty should have his new road, at a peppercorn rent for the land.

George III put up the present gate and lodge at the Richmond Hill entrance to the Park; they were designed by Lancelot Brown—Capability Brown—and replaced former wooden gates and a ladder-stile.

Many domestic animals were kept in the Park at the beginning of the nineteenth century; in 1806 we read of 400 sheep and 300 lambs being pastured at the ranger's farm, as well as cows and oxen. During the Napoleonic Wars some of the Park near Sheen Gate was under cultivation. In 1814, Princess Elizabeth, daughter of George III, was given the rangership, and during the next twenty years several areas were enclosed and planted: Spankers Hill, Sidmouth, Isabella, and other plantations familiar today. Carriages were allowed into the Park if the bell at the gate was rung and an admission order produced; at Richmond Gate the lodgekeeper was "remarkable for his civility." These orders were abolished in the middle of the century, and free access to the Park allowed.

In 1834, Petersham Park was purchased and incorporated in Richmond Park; a high fence was removed, and the Terrace Walk continued from Richmond Gate to the Pembroke Lodge stables, near the place where the memorial to James Thomson now stands. The deputy-surveyor of the Royal Parks, a great lover of trees, tried to discourage persons cutting their names on the splendid beech-trees in the Terrace Walk, a practice, he surmised, "which is, perhaps, exclusively English."

The Pen Ponds, situated almost in the centre of the Park, are artificial; there are conflicting accounts of their origin. Princess Amelia is said to have constructed them from gravel-pits. There is evidence that a large pond existed there earlier, but the large amount of gravel dug and carted away from the Park a century earlier indicate that they were possibly excavated pits originally. They were called "The Canals" in Eyre's plan of 1754, but in Dr John Evans's guide-book of 1824, he refers to them as "the Upper and Lower Canal, commonly called the Pen Ponds." On the Ordnance Survey of 1867–69, they are called the Pen Ponds; in other maps and books they are variously referred to as the Penned or Pend Ponds. The Sanctuary at the head of the Upper Pond is a charming nature reserve, with waterfowl and many waterside plants. There are fish in the ponds—bream, roach, carp, and eels. Large pike are also there, but are not often caught. Pike are aggressive fish; in February, 1935, a terrier was attacked and its tail bitten by a pike while swimming in the Upper Pond. Another pike, when caught, was found to contain a duckling.

There are many species of birds in the Park; bird-watchers have noted greenfinches, goldfinches, warblers, linnets, crossbills, magpies, rooks, golden-crested wrens, tits, white-throats, and other of the more common birds. There are also kingfishers, grebes, owls, doves, shovelers, and numerous birds which are not so common.

Sidmouth Plantation possesses a heronry; the birds arrive in February and leave again in the autumn. Edward Jesse wrote in 1834:

> A large assemblage of herons takes place at certain times of the year in Richmond Park. . . . Sometimes they may be seen on the tops of trees, and at others on the ground at a distance from the ponds, appearing perfectly motionless until they are disturbed. This assemblage is very curious.

The Park is still a royal demesne, and several of the houses are in private occupation. At the present time Princess Alexandra of Kent and her husband, Mr Angus Ogilvy, live at Thatched House Lodge, and the ranger of the Park in another house. White Lodge has been made available for the school of the Royal Ballet.

Pembroke Lodge ceased to be a private house at the end of last century. Lord John Russell occupied it for many years, and entertained there most of the political figures and other notabilities of his day. Bertrand Russell (Earl Russell), a grandson of Sir John, lived with his brother at Pembroke Lodge after the death of their father. The house is now divided into living-quarters for Park staff, but a restaurant and coffee-room have been opened to the public on the ground floor, facing the splendid views over the Park and the valley; and the superbly kept gardens are also open.

There is a mound in the grounds, not far from the entrance

nearest Richmond Gate, which is popularly supposed to be the spot on which Henry VIII stood, watching for smoke from the signal gun fired from the Tower of London to announce the execution of Anne Boleyn. John Gloag, in his fascinating book, *2,000 Years of England*, makes out a strong case for a neolithic origin of this mound; it was in all probability an ancient barrow. In an early seventeenth-century map it is called "The King's Standinge", and in old documents it is variously referred to as "King Henry's Mount", "King Henry VII's Mount", and "Henry VIII's Mount." The Tower of London could be seen from the Mount before the present Sidmouth Plantation was made, so it is not impossible that Henry VIII could have seen the ascent of a rocket. It is, however, improbable. On the day Anne Boleyn was executed, Henry VIII spent the evening at Wolfe Hall in Wiltshire, 60 miles from Richmond. He was waiting to marry the next lady, and it is just possible that he was at Richmond at noon, watching for the signal, so as to make sure he was safely off with the old love before taking on the new. It would have meant some pretty hard riding to cover the 60 miles to Wiltshire, and arrive in time for the ceremony that evening.

There is no hard-core evidence one way or the other, but the legend has grown over the centuries, and is as much alive today as ever. The mound is there: "King's Standing" or "Henry VIII's Mount." With old, unhappy things of long ago well behind you, it is an exceedingly pleasant spot when the daffodils are out, and with the roses about to bloom.

CHAPTER TWELVE

Pleasures and Palaces

THERE have been public entertainments in Richmond since the days of Queen Elizabeth. Mr Cundall states that Shakespeare took his company of players to act before the Queen at Richmond Palace, and puts February 1603, two months before her death, as the last time he was there. As Shakespeare and his fellow-players were sensible business men as well as professionals, it is more than likely that performances were also given for the inhabitants of Richmond, either on the Green or in one of the Common fields. Joseph Taylor, whom Shakespeare taught to play Hamlet and other major parts in his plays, was manager of a troupe of comedians at Richmond in 1614, and was later appointed Yeoman of the Revels to Charles I.

The best-known place of amusement in the early part of the eighteenth century was Richmond Wells, which stood on a site adjoining the present Cardigan House. Chalybeate waters had been discovered at this place in the reign of James II, and diversions provided for those who came to take the waters. By the 1720s there was regular formal entertainment: an advertisement in the *Daily Post* in 1722 promises

> a good Set of Musick, that play every Morning and Evening; and on Thursdays and Saturdays it will be accompany'd with the Trumpet, French Horn, and German Flute. A commodious pair of Stairs will be provided for the convenience of Company that come by water.

Then an enterprising showman leased the place and changed the tone. An advertisement in the London *Craftsman* for June 11th, 1703, reads:

> This is to give notice to all gentlemen and ladies that have a mind either to raffle for gold chains, equipages, or any other

curious toys, and fine old china; and likewise play at quadrille, ombre, whist, &C. And on Saturdays and Mondays during the summer season there will be dancing, as usual.

A traveller to Richmond describes it at this time as a place

where you will find one's own stamp to converse with. . . . If you will make love, a stranger is everywhere welcome. At play, they will indeed be a great deal too cunning for you; even the ladies think it no crime to pawn handsomely; and for drinking, you may be matched from night to morning.

He visited the Wells, and enjoyed himself immensely.

What had been a gay little spa-house was now a palace of all the pleasures. It was obviously no longer a place for respectable citizens and their families, and the local inhabitants complained to the Vestry on more than one occasion that the Wells was giving Richmond a bad name. The Vestry could do nothing, unless there were statutory breaches of the peace. Noise, music, and raucous laughter did not constitute a statutory nuisance, and the shrewd owner of the establishment knew it. He advertised widely in the London papers, and attracted a raffish clientele which could be relied on to spend money—gamblers, dissolute young gentlemen on the road to ruin, rich merchants and their doxies out on a spree, women of the town certain of custom. There were also many aristocratic parties who came out of curiosity, spending money with equal liberality, and welcome because they gave a certain air to the equivocal proceedings.

By the 1770s, however, the Quality no longer found the place amusing, the raffish element made more noise and spent less, and Richmond Wells began to go down. In the end, it was not the Vestry which closed the Wells, but Rebecca and Susanna Houblon, who lived at Ellerker House on the Hill. They had for years suffered from the noise across the road, which disturbed their rest. They bought the freehold of Richmond Wells for £400, closed it down, and allowed the buildings to fall into a dilapidated state, until at last the ruins were pulled down altogether.

Further down, off Hill Street, the comedian, Will Penkethman, had opened a theatre in 1719, but it was not successful. The actor, Chapman, built a theatre on the lower part of the Hill in 1733, playing *Don Quixote* and farces, tickets to be had at the Three Compasses Tavern. This theatre likewise did not do so well, mainly because of an Act of Parliament which imposed penalties on un-licensed comedians. Theophilus Cibber, the son of Colley Cibber, took over the theatre, and found a way of getting round the Act. An announcement in the *General Advertiser* for July 8th, 1756, states blandly:

> Cibber & Co. *Snuff Merchants*, sell at their Warehouse at Richmond Hill most excellent *Cephalic Snuff*, which, taken in moderate quantities (in an evening particularly) will not fail to raise the spirits, clear the brain, throw off ill humours, dissipate the spleen, enliven the imagination, exhilarate the mind, give joy to the heart, and greatly improve the understanding! Mr. Cibber has also opened at the aforesaid Warehouse (late called the Theatre) on the Hill, an *histrionic* academy for the instruction of young persons of genius in the *art* of ACTING; and purposes, for the better improvement of such pupils, and frequently with assistance, to give public rehearsals—without hire, gain, or reward!

In spite of his ingenuity, Theophilus Cibber had as little luck with his venture as had his predecessor, and in 1774 the playhouse was converted into a meeting house for Protestant Dissenters.

There were many attempts to provide entertainment on a smaller scale. In 1722, E. Marriott's Great Room on the Green offered "an extraordinary Concert of Music from the Opera", with "music performed on the Hautboy and German Flute and Little Flute." In 1738, the Widow Boddicott at Richmond announced that she would open her house for an Assembly every Tuesday, but no person would be admitted who was not a subscriber. They could, however, have Coffee, Tea, and Chocolate on any day of the week.

The best-known theatre in Richmond in the eighteenth century was the Theatre Royal, often called the Theatre on the Green, situated at the north-west corner of the Green. There are conflicting accounts of its inception. One source says it was built in 1765–66 by a Mr Sanderson for a lady named Horn for a relative, James Dance. He was an actor whose theatrical name was Love, and was known for his rendering of the character of Falstaff. Another source states that a playhouse and Assembly Room were built in the north-

west corner "and abutting on a lane or cartway leading from the
said Green to the river Thames commonly called Palace Lane"
(now Old Palace Lane), and that it was built by Adam Jellicoe and
leased to James Hubbald "for the just sum of £1000 of good and
lawful money of Great Britain." In 1767 it appears "in the occupation of James Love." Both accounts agree that the building was
modelled on the Theatre Royal, Drury Lane, and that many
distinguished players appeared there. David Garrick wrote a prologue for the opening, in June 1765, which was printed in that
month's issue of the *Gentleman's Magazine*. It began:

> The ship now launched, with necessaries stored,
> Rigged, manned, well built, and a rich freight on board,
> All ready, tight and trim from head to poop,
> And by commission made a royal sloop
> May Heaven from tempests, rocks and privateers
> Preserve the Richmond! Give her, boys, three cheers!
> > (Three huzzas behind)

The theatre had been carefully planned so that a good view of
the stage could be had from every seat, though there were pillars
supporting the gallery, and the scenes were well painted. Boswell
wrote on September 18th, 1769:

> I had promised to pay a visit to my old friend, Mr. Love, to see
> him in his greatness as manager of the Theatre Royal on Rich-
> mond Green. So I this morning set out in the Richmond Stage.
> . . . It was a most delightful day. Richmond seemed delicious.
> Mr. Love's theatre is a very handsome one, having everything in
> miniature. . . .

Boswell reached Richmond in good time for the performance,
and later dined with Love and Miss Radley, apprentice to the
manager, "a fine little actress and a very good singer and a very
modest girl." Boswell was quite taken with Miss Radley, who made
tea for him and showed him one of the high boxes in the theatre.
He later sat in her dressing-room, "with band-boxes and laced caps
and I know not how many pleasing objects all about me."

The theatre is mentioned in many memoirs and diaries of the
time. Dr John Evans, in his guide-book, describes it as "the
prettiest little theatre in the kingdom." Well-known London actors
were pleased to come to Richmond and tread the boards; Charles

A PROSPECT OF RICHMOND

Mathews the Elder made his début in public there in 1793, as the Earl of Richmond in Richard III, paying the manager seven-and-a-half guineas for the privilege. Litchfield played the lead. Mathews wanted to show off his skill as a swordsman, and later described his part in the performance:

> I cared for nothing except the last scene of Richmond, but in that I was determined to have my full swing of carte and tierce. I had no idea of paying seven guineas and a half without indulging my passion. In vain did the tyrant try to die after a decent time, in vain did he give indications of exhaustion. I would not allow him to give in. I drove him by main force from any position convenient for the last dying speech. The audience laughed, I heeded them not; they chaffed, I was deaf. Had they hooted I should have lunged on unconscious of their interruption. I was determined to show them all my accomplishment. Litchfield frequently whispered "enough", but I thought with Macbeth, "Damned be he who first cries hold, enough!" I kept him at it, and I believe we almost fought literally "an hour by Shrewsbury clock."

Kean, Macready, and Charles Young attracted the crowds, as did Mrs Jordan, who lived on Richmond Hill with her lover, the Duke of Clarence, and sometimes played at the Theatre on the Green. Mrs Siddons, "in compliance with the repeated solicitations of several families of distinction in Richmond and its neighbourhood", came down from London one night to play Lady Randolph in the tragedy of *Douglas*—a feather in the cap of the manager, Beverley. A later manager, Klanert, brought off a greater triumph: he persuaded Edmund Kean to act at his theatre. Kean drew the Town as well as audiences from Richmond, and on the nights of his performances, highwaymen and cut-purses gathered a rich harvest. The management advertised that they employed a number of armed men to patrol the roads leading to Richmond, but it was still hazardous for the nobility and gentry to come in their carriages and coaches from London, though many took the risk.

Klanert was always ready to pay London salaries for star actors, and he paid Kean very highly indeed, giving the actor more than half the receipts. Kean insisted on being paid before the end of a performance, but he could not keep his money in his pocket. We find him writing to Klanert from his lodgings at the Castle Inn,

sking for a loan of ten pounds "till Wednesday." Open-handedness
s one thing, but a less pleasant trait in his character was his jealousy
f other actors. On one occasion when he acted Richard III at
Richmond, his supporting players were so good that the public
pplauded them as enthusiastically as they did Kean in the star
art. Kean was furiously angry, and left the theatre immediately
fter the performance. Next day, a letter was delivered to Klanert:

> My dear Sir,
>   I have the greatest respect for you, and the best
> wishes for your professional success; but if I play in the Richmond
> Theatre again—*I'll be damned*.
>
>   Yours Sincerely,
>   EDMUND KEAN.

He did play in the theatre again, for the benefit of a member of
he company, so it is unlikely that he was damned, at least very
much: he was fundamentally a kind man.

In 1831, Kean wrote to Mr Bunn, the then-lessee, that he would
ike to end his days in the quiet seclusion of Richmond Theatre. He
ffered to hire the theatre.

> I am weary of scampering over His Majesty's domains. . . . A
> good company well appointed and governed by a man of forty
> years' experience would fix upon my retreat both pleasure and
> profit, until I make my final bow to the British public.

He took a lease of the theatre, and wrote to his wife, whom he
ad treated badly, and from whom he had been separated. The
etter was headed "Theatre Royal, Richmond", and ran:

> My dear Mary, let us be no longer fools. Come home, forget
> and forgive. If I have erred it was my head not my heart, and
> most sorely have I suffered for it. My future life shall be employed
> in contributing to your happiness and you, I trust, will return
> that feeling by a total obliteration of the past.

There is no record of his wife returning to him. He lived
n rooms near the Green, apparently alone. Time dimmed his
opularity, and he took to the bottle, drowning his disappointments
nd trying to deaden physical pain, for he had become a sick man.
There is a touching story of an incident in his last days. Kean had
lways had a passion for music, and he possessed a true singing

voice. Dr James Smith, his doctor and old friend, entered Kean'
house one night—it adjoined the theatre—and heard the acto
accompanying himself on the piano. The doctor listened. Kean wa
singing one of Moore's melodies; after which he sang *Those Evenin,
Bells.*

His voice at first was clear and sweet . . . then thick, as if wit
emotion. Then it died away, and there was silence. The listene
entered the room. The singer's head was bowed down upon th
piano, and when he raised it a moonbeam fell upon the keys
They were wet with tears.

Kean went on acting, at Drury Lane and at Richmond, but th
fires had burnt out. He died at Richmond in May 1833 and i
buried in Richmond churchyard. An enormous crowd attended hi
funeral, and it is said that Grimaldi, the clown, who had come witl
a large party of theatre people, raised his hat and called out
"Bravo, Teddy, you've drawn a full house to the last!"

Helen Faucit, a well-known Shakespearean actress in the earl,
part of the century, began her career at the Theatre on the Greer
She was born in 1817, the youngest of a theatrical family; both he
parents were on the stage, and three of her four brothers had gon
into the profession. Her only sister, Harriet, took to the stag
directly she had completed her education. It was decided that Heler
who was shy and dreamy and rather over-burdened with sensibility
should not become an actress, though her great passion was readin
the plays of Shakespeare, and she knew the leading female parts—
Juliet, Ophelia, Rosalind, and the rest—off by heart at an earl
age.

The sisters went to boarding-school at Greenwich, and spent al
their summer holidays together at Richmond. Their parents ha
parted for good and the family was split up; Harriet, who was eigh
years older than Helen, became like a second mother to her. The
stayed with friends "at a little house on Richmond Green opposit
the Theatre", and they were very happy there. Helen was alway
to retain a great affection for Richmond, "where every step of th
Green, the river banks, the fields round Sion House, the Hill, th
Park and Twickenham meadows, were all loved more and more a
each summer enlarged my sense of beauty."

One of her earliest recollections was of seeing Edmund Kea

rolling on the Green with his aunt, Miss or Mrs Tidswell. She sent
an account of her first meeting with the great actor to a friend,
Mrs S. C. Hall, the novelist, years later.

I saw . . . a small pale man with a fur cap, and wrapped in a
fur cloak. He looked to me as if come from the grave. . . . He was,
in fact, ill at the time. A stray lock of very dark hair crossed his
forehead, under which shone eyes which looked dark and yet
bright as lamps. So large were they, so piercing, so absorbing, I
could see no other feature.

Helen Faucit did go on the stage, and she began in unusual
circumstances. At that date, 1833, a Mr Willis Jones was the lessee
of the Theatre on the Green; he was a gentleman of independent
means who had ambitions to be more than an amateur actor, and
he had an eye for talent, engaging the best companies from London
to come and play at Richmond. Helen Faucit was walking with her
sister one hot day towards the river, during their yearly holiday
at Richmond, and passed the theatre on their way. The stage-door
was open, the interior dim, mysterious, invitingly cool. Harriet had
already had some experience as an actress playing in London.
The theatre was empty, the stage set with a balcony. This was
tempting; they both knew *Romeo and Juliet* almost off by heart,
and soon they were up on the stage, declaiming the lines, Helen
taking Juliet and her sister Romeo. It was all rather a lark, but a
few days later, to their consternation, they learned that there had
been an unseen listener, who had now traced them. This was Mr
Willis Jones himself; he had been in a box, and had been surprised
to hear voices on the stage. Once he began listening, he knew he
had at least one good potential actress there. He told Helen and her
family that she had a future in the theatre. It took some time to
persuade them, but he succeeded in the end, and Helen made her
debut at Richmond as Juliet. She was so nervous on the first night
that she crushed the supposed phial of poison in her hand, and a
thin red stream trickled down her pale satin dress. She staggered to
the bed on the stage, and fainted so realistically—it was a real faint
—that she might have taken the poison in good earnest. After that
they gave her a wooden phial.

Three years later Helen Faucit was again acting Juliet, this time
at Drury Lane under the management of Macready. The Romeo
was "of too mature an age for so young a Juliet," and so vehement,

that her sister would not trust her in the tomb alone with him,
he shook it so violently, the whole fabric would have dropped
pieces on her head if the sister, who played the part of a caryati
had not been there to hold it up.

There was a very strong puritan element in the town which hel
that all theatres were temples of sin. In 1839, the Reverend I
Hoare made a strong attack on the Theatre Royal, which brougl
even stronger reactions from theatregoers. One of these wrote
the papers, calling Mr Hoare

> a blind enthusiast, or something worse, and should be treate
> accordingly. As to any effect the expression of his foul-mouthe
> prejudice can have, we laugh at it as we should at admonitio
> from the lips of a fool . . . the saintly bigot.

Another correspondent asked:

> Who is the Revd. E. Hoare, the Richmond fanatic, that h
> should take upon himself to castigate players and playgoers? Is h
> himself a model of such excelling virtue that he is qualified
> read lectures to . . . more worthy men? Has he the vanity t
> believe that his preachments against the drama can have . . . th
> least weight in influencing the public to shun the theatre? Whe
> the reverend worthy thought proper to designate actors "knaves
> and actresses "harlots", he forgot the world's opinion of men o
> his cloth.

There were several managers of the Theatre on the Green durin
the next thirty or forty years. Sothern played Dundreary there
Madame Celeste appeared and drew full houses. Royal patronag
returned; the Duke and Duchess of Teck, then living at Whit
Lodge in the Park, attended several performances, and the Duches
of Cambridge brought a party from Kew. Distinguished patrons
however, could not save the theatre when the general public n
longer gave their support. Communications between Richmond an
London had vastly improved with the regular railway service, an
it was easy to attend the theatres in Town and return home, all i
an evening. The local theatre was an attraction on Bank Holidays
special efforts being made to present popular stars, but the run-of
the-mill performances were poorly attended. The Theatre Roya
was closed in the early 1880s and pulled down in 1884; and a
"imposing villa" was later built on the site.

There had been visiting companies of entertainers at Richmond
since the days of the strolling players in medieval times, and they
still found the town a good 'pitch' in the eighteenth and nineteenth centuries. In 1846, the Ethiopian Serenaders, "having met
with the most flattering reception from a fashionable and crowded
audience on Monday last", gave an additional black-and-white
minstrel show at the Richmond Institution, which included *You'll
see Them in Ohio* and the Phantom Chorus from the opera *La
Somnambula*. This troupe were the originators of the Nigger
Minstrels. In 1852, Mr W. Abbott announced to "the Nobility,
Gentry and Inhabitants of Richmond" that he was bringing singers
from London to the Castle Hotel to give a performance of Handel's
Messiah, and assured them that the band and chorus would be on an
efficient scale.

The Castle Hotel Assembly Rooms had long been used for
entertainments. In April 1890 it became the "New Theatre." The
prologue on the opening night, written by Frederick Bingham of
Richmond, was spoken by Lily Langtry; there were recitations and
songs, and a performance of *Bardell v. Pickwick*. Gilbert Hare, later
a very popular London actor, appeared "and was well received,"
and the young Mrs Patrick Campbell, then unknown, was glad to
take a small part in a play at Richmond. But the New Theatre
proved to be no more successful than the others had been, and it
eventually reverted to its original function as an Assembly Room
and ballroom.

F. C. Mouflet, the proprietor of the Assembly Rooms, was not
discouraged. He was sure that there was a public for plays in
Richmond, and he decided to build a proper theatre, finding a good
site on the Green. The theatre was designed by Frank Matcham—
who appears to have been singularly insensitive to the rest of the
architecture on the Green—and opened in 1899 as the Theatre
Royal and Opera House. The first play was *As You Like It*, with
the Ben Greet company.

There was a good deal of interest in the venture at first, but the
continuing success which Mouflet had hoped for did not come. The
name was changed to the Richmond Hippodrome, and then to the
Richmond Theatre. Every kind of theatrical show has been presented in the last sixty years, from Shakespeare to farces and
pantomime: some successful, some not. The theatre continued to

have its ups and downs—like many others in country towns—b
it survived. In 1959, a non-profit distributing Company was form
to run it, with a board of Honorary Directors. The theatre no
presents fortnightly plays, and has become very well known, n
only as a repertory company with a high standard, but as a try-o
theatre for London.

A supporting organisation, the Friends of Richmond Theatr
continually widens public interest in the theatre by arrangir
meetings at which personalities in the theatrical world speak c
matters connected with their profession.

Amateur societies had long flourished in the town. The Richmor
Musical Society was established in 1858, and the Literary ar
Scientific Institution lived up to its name with mixed programme
one of which was a lecture on comic songs (with specimens),
lecture on conchology, and a Mrs Balfour speaking on "The Obl
gations of English Literature to Female Writers."

There have been Thespians and an Athenium, and variou
musical and dramatic societies, but the outstanding society in th
last thirty years has been the Richmond Shakespeare Society. Th
was founded in 1934 by Gladys Eriksen, an ex-repertory actre
whose aim was to present the plays of Shakespeare "as living, vit
things." She persuaded the Town Council to allow her to stag
plays in the Terrace Gardens, and there have been yearly produ
tions there ever since, usually in July. The Gardens make a perfec
setting for the plays, and imaginative lighting at the evenin
performances brings a touch of magic to the scene.

The Society has also acquired its own Little Theatre in Cardiga
House, where the dramatic fare ranges from Wycherley an
Labiche to Shaw and Chekhov, performed on a microscopic stag
but full of character and panache.

So there is again a theatre at the top of the Hill, within touchin
distance of the eighteenth-century spa-house which set out t
provide entertainment for the pleasure-loving Georgians. It i
unlikely, however, that any present-day Miss Houblon woul
attempt to close the Little Theatre: she would be more likel
to join the Shakespeare Society and take her friends to th
performances.

CHAPTER THIRTEEN

The River

AN anonymous poet, returning to London from a journey on the river in 1606, wrote lyrically about

> The bubbling beauty of fayre Thames
> The silver christall Streame.

Paulus Hentzner found it fascinating, especially in London: "The wealth of the world is wafted to it [London] by the Thames." The produce from dozens of riverside villages in Surrey and Middlesex was also wafted to the metropolis, and especially from Richmond and Hampton, which had many market gardens. London women 'codders' journeyed to Richmond in the pea-gathering season, much as East-enders now go hop-picking in Kent, and anyone walking by the river on a summer's morning might see a fleet of sailing barges going downstream on the tide, laden with open wicker baskets piled to the brim with peascods, potatoes, salad stuff, green vegetables, and the fruit in season.

The swans were a feature of the Richmond river scene. Hentzner noted: "This river abounds in Swans, swimming in flocks; the sight of them, and their noise, is vastly agreeable." Swans were royal birds, and there were strict regulations governing them. All the swans on the river between London and Henley belonged to the Crown, the Vintners' Company, and the Dyers' Company, and every year there took place the 700-year-old custom known as "Swan-upping", a custom which is kept up to the present day. Three swan-masters, one representing the Sovereign and the other two the companies, row from Tower Pier in stages to Henley, identifying and marking the year-old cygnets. Those belonging to the Vintners and Dyers are marked, those belonging to the Crown remain unmarked.

Another early eighteenth-century river event which has turne
into a tradition was the annual race for Doggett's Coat and Badg
This was instituted in 1715 by Thomas Doggett, a popular actor a
Drury Lane, to mark the first anniversary of George I's accession t
the throne. It is a race for young watermen just out of thei
apprenticeship. There are trial heats from Putney to Hammer
smith, and those chosen row in the final, which is always agains
the tide, on a course from the Swan Inn at London Bridge to th
Swan Inn at Chelsea, "on August 1st when not on a Sunday.
Thomas Doggett gave a fine, orange-coloured coat ornamente
with a silver badge to the winner; the Fishmongers' Company
which now administers Doggett's bequest, gives money prizes to th
runners-up. It was the ambition of all young watermen up an
down the river to win Doggett's Coat and Badge, and the honou
went to Richmond on many occasions.

"Sailing on the river" was a favourite recreation all through th
eighteenth century, and the watermen made a good living in
reasonably fine summer. There were hazards, however. One Sun
day in 1725, six young men took a boat and waterman "on a part
of pleasure to Richmond", became intoxicated at an ale-hous
there, refused to pay the waterman, and on their return to Swa
Stairs, Thames Street, upset the boat. Assistance was immediatel
given, but "two out of the six passengers sank to rise no more."
In 1763, the Thames was frozen over, and a fair was mounte
on the ice at Richmond "for the sale of divers commodities in th
same manner as at Whitehall in the last great frost in 1739–40.
There are references in contemporary memoirs to the rive
entertainments given in the mansions in and around Richmon
and Petersham, references that give an impression of splendour bu
few details. Horace Walpole, writing to his friend, Sir Horace Man
in June 1763, gives an account of a grand party he attended a
Richmond House, in Whitehall, which fits in so well with some o
the local references to ducal and other festivities that it was almos
certainly like those which took place at Richmond on specia
occasions:

Last night we had a magnificent entertainment at Richmon
House, a masquerade and fireworks. A masquerade was a ne
sight to the young people, who had dressed themselves charm

View from Richmond Bridge looking towards Isleworth

D. Harding, 1832.   *By courtesy of Richmond upon Thames Libraries Committee*

Cholmondeley Walk, Nineteenth Century

By courtesy of Richmond upon Thames Libraries Committee

The Thames frozen over at Richmond, 1858

"*Illustrated London N*

Preparing the Ice-rink at Richmond, 1946

By courtesy of Mr Ronal

"Gosling's Dressmakers at Play", probably 1912

By courtesy of Richmond upon Thames Libraries Committee

Royalty at Richmond Royal Horse Show, 1913

By courtesy of Richmond upon Thames Libraries Committee

The First Aircraft made in Richmond in the 1914–18 War

Whitehead Aircraft Co., Ltd.

By courtesy of Mrs Hélène W

Richmond Bridge, 1913

*By courtesy of
Richmond upon Thames
Libraries Committee*

ingly. . . . The Duchesses of Richmond and Grafton, the first as a Persian Sultana, the latter as Cleopatra—and such a Cleopatra! The whole garden was illuminated, and the apartments. An encampment of barges decked with streamers in the middle of the Thames, kept the people from danger, and formed a stage for the fireworks, which were placed, too, along the rails of the garden. The ground rooms lighted, with suppers spread, the houses covered and filled with people, the bridge, the garden full of masks, Whitehall crowded with spectators to see the dresses pass, and the multitude of heads on the river who came to light by the splendour of the fire-wheels, composed the gayest and richest scene imaginable, not to mention the diamonds and sumptuousness of the habits.

There had been a ferry at Richmond, from Ferry Hill (now Bridge Street) to the Twickenham Meadows, for at least three hundred years. In the Privy Purse accounts of Henry VIII, Queen Mary, and Queen Elizabeth I, there are many references to payments for ferrying royal personages or their servants from Richmond to the opposite shore. In 1622, the ferry was leased by the Crown to Edmund Cooke and Edmund Sawyer, and as the document mentions their "Executors, Administrators and assigns," it looks as if the privilege had been converted into a family affair, with rights of inheritance. There were two boats, one for passengers, and a much larger vessel, the 'horse-boat', for the conveyance of horses, small light carts, and bulky goods. Carriages could not be taken; they had to be driven round by way of Kingston Bridge. The ferry rent was 13s. 4d. per annum.

In the late eighteenth century, the lessee of the ferry was a Mr Windham, and the rent had gone up to £3 13s. 4d. a year. In 1773, Mr Windham decided that it would be very advantageous to build a bridge over the river, and charge tolls. His ferry lease still had twenty-six years to run, and he offered to sell this remainder to the Crown Commissioners for £6000, and pay for the erection of a bridge. He presented a petition to the House of Commons for leave to bring in a Bill; he did not expect opposition from anyone. He was mistaken. The inhabitants took alarm. Mr Windham's bridge was to be of wood, and he proposed to erect it from Ferry Hill, which had an exceedingly steep approach. "Indeed the declivity was so great that a poor woman . . . gained a small livelihood by keeping a few chairs for invalids and aged persons to rest upon."

There were meetings, and the inhabitants drew up a repor
opposing Mr Windham's scheme on several counts: it was to be
privately owned, it was to be built of wood, it was to be built in a
highly inconvenient place on the Richmond side. They agreed tha
a bridge was desirable, and suggested a stone structure, and a bette
site, at the end of Water Lane. A correspondent who signed himsel
"A Friend to the parish of Richmond" wrote a letter which wa
published in *Lloyd's Evening Post*, February 18th, 1772, putting
the case in blunt terms:

> At a meeting of many respectable inhabitants of this place,
> found that the remainder of a lease of the . . . King's Ferry wa
> sold to the Proprietor, Mr. Windham, and that he intended to
> build a bridge on that spot, to be passable in 6 months. It is to be a
> wooden bridge—what a cat-stick building must this be, to be
> executed in so short a time! Methinks I hear Old Thames groan
> to be so vilely strode. . . . If our view up and down that delightfu
> River must be obstructed . . . let it be an elegant and free bridge
> and not for the emolument of any one individual.

The writer advised that the bridge should be built to enter the
centre of the town, by pulling down the Feathers Inn,

> and those houses in Water Lane which, at present, is the sink and
> disgrace of the place, and also, at the other end of the street
> removing a nest of houses which is very properly called Bug
> Island; by this means you will have the finest street in the
> kingdom, and a full view of near a mile, without interception

The Trustees of the Richmond Vestry energetically backed the
opinions of the inhabitants, and in the end Mr Windham withdrew
his Bill. Plans for a stone bridge were put in hand, but the commissioners, having already bought out Mr Windham, were in no way
inclined to spend more money. The cost of the bridge, £26,000
was raised on Tontine shares of £100 each. Under this system, a
shareholder got a proportion of the tolls until death; his shares were
then added to those of the other shareholders. The Tontine could
not lapse until the death of the last survivor.

The chief clash with the commissioners was over the siting of the
bridge. On the Middlesex side of the river opposite Water Lane was
land belonging to Twickenham Farm, the proprietor of which
angrily opposed the Water Lane suggestion. Everyone on the

Richmond side, except Mr Windham, the lessee of the Feathers Inn, and the inhabitants of Water Lane, thought the only logical thing to do was to widen that Lane and let the highway run straight on to the bridge at the end of George Street. It was pointed out that there was a palpable inconsistency in building the bridge from Ferry Hill (which was much steeper then than it is now). Why should wagons with heavy loads have to be drawn up a steep aclivity from the level of George Street, then turn sharply to the right and descend a sharp incline to the toll-houses? Surely this was beyond common sense?

His Majesty's commissioners were not concerned with common sense. They sided with Mr Windham, the lessee of the Feathers Inn, the inhabitants of the hovels in Water Lane, and the proprietor of Twickenham Farm. Richmond Vestry had no alternative but to put forward a Bill approved by the bureaucrats, Messrs Paine and Couse were engaged as architects, the bridge was begun in 1774 and completed in 1777. It was, and is, one of the handsomest bridges across the Thames—as it would have been one of the most conveniently sited, if the Richmond Trustees had been able to overcome the stiff-necked obstinacy of His Majesty's Crown Commissioners in London.

The City Livery Companies possessed splendidly equipped barges, which drew everyone to the river banks as they sailed by. One Tuesday in 1772,

> The Master, Wardens, and Assistants of the Company of Stationers, with their Ladies, accompanied by a band of music, went up the river in their Barge to Richmond, where an elegant entertainment was prepared at the Star and Garter. On their return, perceiving their Majesties, with all the Royal Children, walking down to the River, the Watermen were ordered to lay down their oars till their Majesties were got to the waterside, when several pieces of music were performed.

The accounts of these charming outings appear every summer, directly good weather can be expected. In 1778,

> The Skinners' Company, according to annual custom, went with their Ladies up the River in their barge, accompanied with a good band of music and every necessary preparation for an

elegant dinner on board thereof, on their arrival before the seat
of Sir Charles Asgill at Richmond.

Two years later:

> The city barges made a splendid appearance upon the Rich-
> mond Thames. The Merchant Taylors, the Grocers, the Iron-
> mongers and the Goldsmiths Companies paraded at Richmond,
> with their different bands of music, dressed up all in their pomp
> of colour and decoration. The day being remarkably fine, the
> shores were crowded with company, and the numerous parties
> attending them in pleasure boats, together with the salutes, and
> firing of guns all the way up the river, rendered it one of the
> gayest scenes of ancient customs at present remaining in this
> great metropolis.

There were many rowing-match wagers. A typical item of news
is of two eight-oared cutters, the Invincible and the Pitt, started
with the tide against them to row from Westminster Bridge for a
wager of sixty guineas. The long description of the race reads like
a running radio commentary, beginning: "At the starting pistol
the inattention of the people aboard the Pitt gave their rival a lead
of 3 strokes!" Pitt won, in spite of their initial inattention, and "the
large concourse of barges and boats" which followed them very
properly huzza'd.

The passenger barges went under sail, but there were large
numbers of smaller commercial barges which were drawn along
from the towpaths by gangs of men. In 1791, Dr William Battie of
Richmond was the promoter of a scheme for towing barges by
horses instead of men. Towing was reckoned by the ton carried, and
the work was very well paid. Dr Battie's scheme was not received
enthusiastically: "He narrowly escaped being tossed over Kingston
Bridge by the incensed bargemen." In Richmond, the bargemen
lived in Water Lane, which was convenient, as they were often
called upon late in the day, or at night, to give additional assistance
with heavily laden barges.

River excursions were as popular as ever in the nineteenth
century. In 1807: "A large party of Fashionables went up the river
in the Admiralty barge and landed at Richmond, taking tea at Lady
Herne's beautiful villa."

There were now three piers at the quay, and the Richmond watermen had the financial side of their business well organized. They owned the piers co-operatively and fixed the charges of the tolls, which were shared out every Saturday at the White Cross Inn.

In 1811, it was found that the stone steps down from Richmond Bridge to the waterside needed repairing. The estimated cost was: 294 feet of step at 3s. 6d., and 70 feet of paving at 1s. 6d.—a bill of over £56, which came out of the tolls. In 1814, the watermen and young people of the town marched in procession on Easter Monday to celebrate the downfall of Bonaparte; they dressed up as military commanders, with white cockades in their hats, and made rings round a Bonaparte "very ludicrously clad, with a ponderous cable round his neck and assailed with sarcasms on every side."

In 1816, an important court case came on in London. An information was laid by the Watermen's Company against the proprietor of river craft who had been engaging untrained young men on their boats at low wages. The company invoked an ancient statute which cited "that no person or persons shall be eligible to work a boat unless [they] shall have regularly served their apprenticeship." Counsel were engaged for both sides, as much depended on the decision—given for the Watermen's Company.

A year later, an unusual craft was seen on the river—one of Richmond's new steam-yachts, which accompanied the Lord Mayor of London's state barge from London to Richmond, where a fête and rowing-match were held to celebrate the coming-of-age of his Lordship's eldest son. There was a renewed outburst of gambling that year: scarcely a week passed without notices of wagers on rowing-matches: "Two gentlemen undertook to row a wherry from Woolwich to Richmond and back in 8 hours for 100 guineas." They won.

The steam-boats were growing more numerous, and by 1825 they were being extensively written up in the London papers:

The Aits, or Osier Islands, are picturesque interspersions on the Thames. Its banks are studded with neat cottages or elegant villas . . . the lawns come sweeping down like green velvet to the edge of its soft-flowing waters, and the scenery improves till we are borne into the full bosom of its beauty—the village of Richmond. On coming within sight of this, the most delightful scene in our sea-girt isle, the band on board the steam boat plays "The Lass of Richmond Hill" while the vessel glides on the translucent water, till she curves to the bridge foot, and the passengers disembark.

All this for a fare of 2s. 6d. each way and 3s. on Sundays. Passengers were recommended to enter the pleasant and comfortable Roebuck Inn, "which has nothing to recommend it but civil treatment and domestic conveniences," unless "an overflowing purse can command the preference of the Star and Garter."

Edmund Kean was always interested in the river, and gave a yearly prize—a truly noble one, a wherry—to be rowed for every year. On the occasion of the ninth race, in 1832, the newspaper account states that "the tragedian looked exceedingly well, but appeared to be troubled with his old acquaintance, the gout, in one of his legs." He and his theatrical friends were in the starting-gallery, and well-known Richmond watermen were represented in the sixteen rowers: two Rednaps and a Hammerton. Henry Hammerton and George Jackson, also of Richmond, won the prize wherry, which was conveyed to the Theatre Royal, on the Green, where a new ballet composed especially for the occasion was performed: "The Tenth of August, or the Jolly Lad That Won the Wherry."

A Richmond waterman, Mr Chitty, related, as an old man, how people travelled from Richmond to London when he was young, in the 1840s. There were few omnibuses on the roads; most travellers went by boat, heavy randans rowed by three men. They left Richmond on the outgoing tide, the journey taking 3½ hours to the landing-stage at Whitehall, and returned when the tide began to run upstream again. The fare for the single journey was 1s. 6d. and a passenger could take an oar if he wished.

The Duke of Buccleuch had a house in London as well as on the river bank at Richmond, and his watermen, assisted by Chitty, used regularly to row the ducal family washing from Buccleuch House to the town residence, Montague House, in Whitehall. There they collected the soiled washing and rowed it back to the duke's private laundry in Petersham Road.

Taking a water excursion to Richmond, which for centuries had been a pleasant way of spending a day, had become less so by the middle of the nineteenth century. Owing to the large and ever-growing quantity taken by water companies, the removal of Old London Bridge in 1833, the greater waterway of the new bridges at Blackfriars and Westminster, the dredging away of shoals, and the construction of the Thames Embankment—all allowing the tidal water to run away more rapidly—the level of low water fell to such an extent that huge mud banks were visible. A cricket match was once played on the bed of the river at Twickenham.

The Richmond Vestry and the Twickenham Local Board, in the 1880s, made several attempts to have a lock constructed "so as to impound some of the tidal water", but the Thames conservators opposed every scheme put forward. A committee of local residents lodged a Bill in Parliament to construct a lock at Isleworth, but the opposition was again too strong. The conservators compromised by dredging and embanking the river between Teddington and Kew Bridge, but this was inadequate. The locals persisted: the chairman of the Vestry made inquiries in various parts of the world to find a scheme which would be accepted by the conservators, and came up with Mr F. G. M. Stoney and his remarkable sluices. These could be so arranged between the piers of a footbridge as to hold up the water to the level of half-tide, and be drawn out of the water and stored under the bridge when that height was exceeded. A Bill to authorise the works was prepared—and some of the local inhabitants awoke to the fact that the footbridge and lock were going to cost the town money. Leaflets were distributed: "Do not Vote for Lock and Weir, Your Rates Will be Increased!" The Bill went through, however, "after meeting with the most strenuous opposition", and received the Royal Assent in August 1890.

The footbridge was built between Richmond and St Margaret's, and the lock was constructed. "A pretty and interesting view" was obtained from the footbridge, though the visitor was warned that to go to the bridge for the purpose of enjoying the view would cost him twice as much as to pass right over. The toll for crossing to the other side was 1*d*., "but persons who venture on to the structure and return whence they came are charged 2*d*."

The illuminated river fêtes at Richmond during the season brought hundreds of visitors down from London. Of one of these fêtes, the *Richmond and Twickenham Times* enthusiastically reported:

A PROSPECT OF RICHMOND

Nothing can exceed the beauty of the scene as the coloured lamps gleam out from the dark foliage of the trees, and the illuminated boats steal out from the shore, repeating their glow of purple and red and gold on every ripple of the river.

Music added its charms to the pleasures of the evening, "bands being stationed at suitable places along the banks."

On July 7th, 1893, a Grand Venetian Fête was held on the river to celebrate the marriage of the Duke of York to Princess Victoria Mary of Teck. This was an elaborate affair, with boats tricked out to look like gondolas.

Sometimes Richmond Bridge was illuminated, and Chinese lanterns and thousands of fairy lamps lit the scene. Decorated boats with cardboard classic temples erected on them glided past, and ascending rockets and bursts of fireworks "evoked the utmost admiration" until midnight. It was no easy matter to move about the town on the day of a fête; there were such crowds that one had to take the utmost care to avoid ending up under a horse's hooves, so many carriages, hansom cabs and wagons blocked George Street.

Swift's description of fishing as "a stick and a string, with a worm at one end and a fool at the other" has not deterred generations of anglers from following their sport. Richmond has always been a favourite place for fishermen, though the variety of the fish seems to be a great deal less than in Holinshed's time, for he wrote in the sixteenth century of "an infinite plentie of excellent sweet and pleasant fish . . . the fat and sweet Salmon dailie taken in this streame", and talks of "the store of Barbels, Trouts, Perches, Smelts, Breames, Roches, Daces, Gudgeons, Flounders, Shrimps" which were commonly to be caught in the Thames.

Salmon seems to have been a preserve of the lord of the manor since before Holinshed's time, for there is an entry in the Court Rolls for January 28th, 1525: "By Letters Patent the King granted pardon to John Perkens of Rychemound, convicted of salmon poaching on the grounds of Merton Priory at Keyoe" [Kew. The parish belonged to the Priory]. In 1750, it was reported that fishermen took several salmon between Mortlake and Richmond, though no prosecution appears to be recorded in this instance. Poaching was on the increase a year later, judging by the number of prosecutions, and the number of guards on the river increased,

[154]

but the local fishermen cared nothing for authority. They were a
continual nuisance, "erecting Stops in the River for the taking of
Lamperus [lampreys] so that there was scarce room for boats to
pass." The poachers were often defiant to the point of violence. A
water bailiff going to cut unlawful salmon nets at Richmond was
set upon in midstream, had his boat "beat to pieces", and nearly
had his head beat to pieces, too.

Fishermen with authorised permission to fish sometimes made a
graceful gesture. In 1769, a gentleman "catched a fine Sturgeon,
upwards of 6 feet in length", which he presented to the King. This
splendid fish was already very rare in the Thames, and few trout
were now to be found, though it is recorded in 1794 that Mr Daniel,
author of *Rural Sports*, caught a trout at Richmond Bridge that
weighed 2½ pounds.

The principal fish caught in the nineteenth century were barbel,
roach, dace, gudgeon, and eels; not such good eating as salmon or
trout, but as valid an excuse as any for sitting on the towpath anywhere between Petersham Meadows and Kew, quietly enjoying a
long, sunny day.

CHAPTER FOURTEEN

Inns and Taverns

THE World affords not such as England hath, either for good and cheap entertainment after the Guests own pleasure, or for humble attendance on passengers; yea, even in very poor villages. For as soon as a passenger comes to an Inn, the servants run to him, and one takes his horse and walks him till he be cold, then rub him and gives him meat, yet I must say that they are not much to be trusted in this last point, without the eye of the Master or his servants to oversee them. Another servant gives the passenger his private chamber, and kindles his fire, the third pulls off his boots and makes them clean. Then the Host or Hostess visits him and if he will eat with the Host, or at a common table with others his meal will cost him six pence, or in some places but four pence . . . yea, the kitchen is open to him, to command the meat be dressed as he best likes. . . . He is offered music, and it is the custom and no way disgraceful to have the remains of his supper for breakfast, he has his reckoning in writing, and if he give some few pence to the Chamberlin and Ostler, they wish him a happy journey.

Inn-keeping was so described by Fynes Moryson, a sixteenth century English traveller who knew the countries of the Continent as well as he knew his native land, and could therefore compare them. Richmond had more inns than most towns of its size, and by the latter part of the eighteenth century, the more temperate inhabitants had decided to approach Authority with a view to keeping the number of establishments down to a reasonable level. The jurors at a Court Leet in 1781 considered that there were too many ale-houses in the parish of Richmond. Not only did the victuallers have difficulty in gaining a livelihood, "but so large a number tends to promote and encourage idleness, tippling, quarrels and many other disorders to the great annoyance of the honest

Mr Bowles
Hare & Hounds Pub.Ho.
Mr Cheap
Mr Gandoli
Duke of Clarence
Mr Vanneck
Mr Coney
Mr Bowyer
Priest Bridge
Mr Gallard
BM
Barnes Workhouse
Lady Grantham
Mr Palmer
Lady Hoare
Hounds
2.5M
PUTNEY
1 Mr T. Hankey
2 Mr Jeradock
Fulham Palace
Bishop of London
Mr Sharpe
FULHAM
Miss Wright
Castle
Brickhaw
Mr Minns
Mr Meyricke
Rev. Mr Bower
Mr Drew
Old Wheat Sheaf Pub.Ho.
Mr Hoare
Mr Bennet
Walham Green
Dr Warren
Little Chelsea Br.
Holland Ho.
Earls Court
Mr Beaucroft
2 Miles from
Hyde Park Corner
Mr J. Hunter
Little Chelsea
Mr Grove
Old Queens Elm
Pub.Ho.
Queens Elm Gate pass
with Hyde Park Gate ticket
George
Adm.l Keppel Pub.Ho.
Mr Marsh
Mr Drake
S.r Geo. Warren
Mr Vere
Dr Devaynes
Hon. Miss Leigh
Rev. Mr Grimes
S.r R. Symons B.t
Mr Selby
L.d Glasgow
Brompton
Mr Holland
HYDE PARK
Knights Bridge
Pimlico
Side General Plan
Pimlico Gate
Hyde Park Gate
LONDON
LAMBETH
Marsh Gates
LONDON to RICHMOND

Published by J. Cary, July 1.t 1790.

INNS AND TAVERNS

London to Richmond

This late eighteenth-century map was designed to give the stage-coach traveller plenty of information to interest him on the five-hour drive from London to Richmond.

The staging inn, where horses were changed, are shown, together with "Gentlemen's Seats and villas belonging to the Nobility and Persons of Quality."

Reproduced by courtesy of Mr John Gloag

I N N S

Fulham	Richmond
Kings Arms	Star & Garter.
Putney	Castle & Talbot.
Red Lion	Greyhound

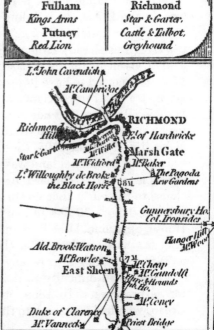

L.d John Cavendish
Mr Cambridge
RICHMOND
Richmond Hill
E.l of Hardwicke
Star & Garter
Marsh Gate
Mr Widford
Mr Baker
L.d Willoughby de Broke
the Black Horse
BM
The Pagoda
Kew Gardens
Gunnersbury Ho.
Col. Ironsides
Hanger Hill
Mr Wood
Ald. Brook Watson
Mr Bowles
East Sheen
Mr Cheap
Mr Gandolfi
Hare & Hounds
Pub.Ho.
Mr Coney
Duke of Clarence
Mr Vanneck
Priest Bridge

industrious and peaceable inhabitants." They therefore requeste(
that at the next Petty Sessions for licensing ale-houses, the numbe:
of these establishments should be reduced. No appreciable diminu
tion appears to have taken place, however.

There were several well-known posting inns at Richmond whicl
have now entirely disappeared. The most renowned was the Sta:
and Garter, on the crest of Richmond Hill, "more like the mansio»
of a nobleman than a receptacle for the public", as a contemporar»
noted. Other accounts of the building described it as "a fine, decen
house" and "a substantial house, pleasant enough", but all sub
scribe to the delight of being there, "to inhale the pure air, an(
exhilarate their spirits by contemplating a wide spreading circum
ference of rural scenery."

There is some evidence that an ale-house of the name stood ther(
at the beginning of the seventeenth century, or even earlier. Th(
local records state that the inn was built by John Christopher i»
1738, on a site which he leased from the Earl of Dysart at a rent o
40s. a year. It was given its name because the Earl was "a Membe
of the Noble Order of the Star and Garter." The inn was actually ¡
tavern and dining-house: it was too small to accommodate travel
lers. In the 1770s, the building was either enlarged or pulled dow»
and a bigger hostelry erected; accounts differ. The view overlookin₂
the river was already famous. George Vancouver, the explorer, no
a man given to flights of poesy, on entering the dining-room i»
1798, is reported to have stopped at the window and exclaimed: "I»
all my travels, I never clapt eyes on a more beautiful spot than this
Here would I live and here would I die!" He had his desire, for h(
took a small house in Petersham, and lived there for the remainde(
of his life, dying in 1798. (See page 116.)

In 1803, additional land was obtained at a rent of 60s. a year, th
lessee now being Richard Brewer. The new lease contained ¡
clause to the effect that no shrubs or trees were ever to be plante(
thereon "above 30 feet in height", so that the view from Ancaste
House, Sir Lionel Darell's mansion, should never be impeded. Th(
lawyer who formulated that clause did not allow for the fact tha
a 30-foot tree might grow any higher.

Brewer had difficulty in making the inn pay, and it was close(
for several years. In 1809, it was opened again by Christophe
Crean, who had been cook to the Duke of York; but it was not unti

1822, when Joseph Ellis took over the management, that the great days of the Star and Garter really began.

Ellis took pains to furnish the Assembly Room "in high style", and it soon became a favourite place for wedding celebrations. When Dr John Evans was there he saw "a respectable party of Quakers partaking of a wedding dinner, with all due sobriety and cheerfulness", and remarked that religion was no enemy to innocent enjoyment, and that the celebration of a marriage was deemed a period of festivity by every people under heaven.

This Assembly Room must have been a grand sight on gala occasions. It was 80 feet long and 30 feet wide, with a lofty ceiling and crystal chandeliers, as well as "every suitable embellishment, including an orchestra." Three balls took place during the winter, in November, December, and January, "300 of the nobility and gentry taking tickets." In the summer, the inn was a fashionable meeting-place, and it was also a popular rendezvous for runaway couples. The London *Evening Mail* reported in 1796:

Lieut. K-ll-y of the 12th Dragoons, stationed at Mitcham in Surrey, had made love to and married Miss M - e, one of the prettiest young ladies in the district. Previous to the ceremony, however, he had to contend with an unconsenting old uncle, who, on a movement of the lovers, followed them to the Star and Garter, at Richmond, and from thence to Croydon Barracks. At the last mentioned place, a negociation ensued, which ended in a peaceful contract, by which the hero acquired a beautiful little wife, a considerable sum of money, and the property of an Inn, called the Spotted Dog, at Mitcham.

Many London notabilities held banquets there. Charles Dickens gave a yearly dinner-party for his friends in a private room, to celebrate his wedding anniversary. Forster, Dickens's close friend and biographer, wrote to Marryat during the summer of 1843, inviting him to a dinner which was to be given for the actor Macready, before the latter went to America on a tour.

Joseph Ellis was noted for his amiable character, as well as for his pride in keeping to the highest standards of inn-keeping. The Victorian barrister, Serjeant Ballantyne, has left a highly individual account of the inn, where Mr Ellis, "the picture of a host", received his guests. The house itself was unpretentious, but the garden behind was a perfect picture of loveliness; the small garden rooms, with honeysuckles, jasmine and roses training themselves up the sides, with a lovely sweep of lawn, on which were scattered trees which had flourished there for many a long day, affording shade as well as beauty; one magnificent spreading beech, itself a sight, and an avenue of limes, forming the prettiest of walks at the bottom of the garden, with a view beyond; none fairer to be seen through the length and breadth of England.

On a Sunday, the garden was usually crowded; artists, singers, actors, and actresses came down from London and revelled in the landscape. There were well-known figures in the literary, political, and social worlds at the tables in the arbours: Balfe, the composer, with his beautiful daughter, and Delane, the editor of *The Times*, talking to Charles Lever, the witty Irish writer.

It was a tragedy, thought Serjeant Ballantyne, when the house was burnt down in 1870, and

a pretentious barrack of a place was built in its stead by a speculative company. Trees were felled, and in the place of flowers which seemed to flourish of their own free will, formal beds were stiffly planted. The lime walk was supplanted by a terrace without an atom of shade, and which was not improved by the perfume of the stables, over which it has been constructed.

No modern improver could ever make Richmond otherwise than beautiful, concluded Ballantyne, "but the loveliness of the Star and Garter is one of the things of the past."

Another fire in 1888 destroyed the last traces of the original building. A banqueting hall and additional buildings were raised on the site, but the character of the original inn had totally disappeared. The main part of the inn was eventually used as a temporary hospital, then demolished, the site being acquired for the erection of the Star and Garter Home for Disabled Soldiers.

The Red Lyon, which gave its name to the present Red Lion Street, was first established early in the sixteenth century, probably on the site of an earlier tavern. There is a record that Richard, a tapster there, fell a victim to the plague in 1625, and that in 1638, William Crowne was "created into the place and office of Rouge Dragon Pursuivant of Arms in Ordinary, at the Red Lyon Tavern or Inn," with all due forms and ceremonies. By the eighteenth century it had become a commodious posting-house, with a yard and stabling of considerable size. The coming of the railways diminished its importance, and it ended as an ale-house, which was pulled down in 1909, when the area was opened up and the road widened.

Another very popular inn was the Talbot Hotel, in Hill Street, at the corner of Ormond Row, which replaced the Dog Inn, a tavern that appears in the records as early as 1714. The Talbot was turned into a private residence in the nineteenth century, and the site is now occupied by the Odeon Cinema. The Talbot's proprietor, George Topham, tried to recoup his fortunes at the Royal Hotel, built where the tower now stands adjoining Richmond Bridge, but he lacked the equivalent of green fingers as an inn-keeper, and was as unsuccessful with the Royal as he had been with the Talbot.

Best known of all these vanished hostelries in the lower part of the town was the Feathers Inn, at the corner of King Street and Water Lane, which was demolished in 1908. It was originally a Tudor tavern known as the Golden Hinde, but the name was changed in honour of Henry, Prince of Wales, the popular son of the unpopular James I. The Feathers was a house of public entertainment in every sense; it had a fine Assembly Room at the back where subscription balls for the townspeople were held during the winter season. It was always a prosperous business. George Child, who kept the Feathers in the early eighteenth century, died in 1735, "having acquired a plentiful fortune." Proctor, a later landlord who had "a very gentlemanly way with him", did not disdain to tout for custom in front of his premises, "accosting strangers with a request, couched in the most polite manner, that they would step in and test the accommodation his house offered."

The Compasses, first mentioned in the Court Rolls in 1737, either stood near or replaced an older inn called the Rising Sun. It was pulled down in 1952 under a road-widening scheme, but the name is preserved in Compass Hill.

The ale-houses in Brewers Lane which appeared so often in the records have disappeared: the Lillie Pot, the Magpie, and the rest. So have the Angell and the Flying Horse, seventeenth-century inns which stood in what is now George Street, and the eighteenth-century Black Boy in the same highway. The Rose and Crown was a noted posting-inn with extensive stabling, at the corner of the main highway and what was then Duke Lane; and the original

Castle Inn, the best known of them all in the lower town, was on the opposite corner. It was here that the poet, James Thomson, and his bosom friend, James Quin, the actor, used to meet and imbibe. John Halford, the licensee, removed the licence to larger premises in Hill Street, and it soon became as well known as the Star and Garter. In 1830, John Cockerell took over the "respectable concern", and pointed out its eligibility for land and water parties. As for posting, every effort, he said, would be made "to obtain efficient Post Horses, respectable carriages, and careful drivers."

The new licensee could guarantee respectability in every department of his establishment. In 1833,

> A lovely lady . . . residing at Richmond, invited Sir E—— to tea at her Apartments in the Castle Inn. Suddenly the waiters below heard a loud report and stupendous smash of china. They immediately rushed to discover the reason, when lo! they met the gentleman descending the stairs full gallop, followed by the infuriated madame. The cause of the smash might easily be conjectured—the lady threw the tea-board at the gent's little head. The reason of this attack on his person may be *guessed* but cannot be *mentioned*.

The Castle is now a completely modern public-house, as are many of the old inns which survive.

The Cricketers, on the Green, was known as the Crickett Players in the 1770s, and is as popular with the cricketing fraternity today as when the gentlemen in flannels and top-hats played for substantial wagers. The Cobwebs, in Duke Street, was originally the Coffee House Tavern, and the registration under that name goes back to 1601. The licence remained in the same family until the nineteenth century. The last of the family was an eccentric who allowed cobwebs to accumulate on the ceilings and in the cellars; it is said that during his management no floor was swept and no bottle touched until it was needed. The tavern was well known for its indoor vine, which was trained to grow through a hole in the roof. During later rebuilding, a cement floor was laid over the roots, and the vine withered. The spiders have long since gone, but the nickname, The Cobwebs, became the licensing name of the hostelry.

The Greyhound, in George Street, was originally built in the 1730s. At the end of the nineteenth century it was owned by

Mouflet, who also owned the Castle Assembly Rooms. The Ship, on the King Street corner of George Street, retains its pleasant eighteenth-century façade to this day. It first appears in the Court Rolls in 1735, and is mentioned in 1766 as "the Sign of the Ship in Furbelow Street"—the old name for King Street. Down Water Lane you find the Waterman's Arms, first licensed in 1669. This was the favourite drinking-place of the eighteenth- and nineteenth-century bargemen. It has long been a tradition for the Swan-Uppers to stop and lunch at the Waterman's Arms on their annual journey up the Thames to mark the Royal and Vintners' cygnets.

The White Cross, facing the river at the end of Water Lane, is another eighteenth-century house, built on the site of a watermen's tavern and extensively rebuilt and altered. The original site was included in the precincts of the House of the Observant Friars, possibly on the site of their chapel. The Three Pigeons, on the Lower Road, by the river, was first licensed in 1735. The King's Head, which stands at the corner of Richmond Bridge, is a fine example of a seventeenth-century inn with a façade which still retains its original character. It was known as the Plough in the 1650s; the name was probably changed about a hundred years later.

The Roe Buck Inn, on the Terrace, now known as the Roebuck, first appears in the records in 1738. C. A. Johns, in his *Forest Trees of Britain*, states that the oldest weeping willow in Europe stood in the garden of the Roebuck Tavern in Richmond.

The Black Horse, in Sheen Road, was already an old inn, with stables, yards, gardens, and outhouses, in 1769. The licence passed in that year from Martin Bird to Thomas Prosser, victualler. Later that year, Mr Prosser humbly prayed the lord of the manor to remove a gate and bars, standing on the adjoining common, nearer to his ale-house, so as not to shut off part of the common.

CHAPTER FIFTEEN

Age of Progress

THE vigorous, thrusting "Victorian Age" did not, in fact, begin with the accession of the young Victoria. New inventions, new ideas, were all being tried out during the latter part of the preceding century, and they figured as curious items of news in the first four decades of the nineteenth century.

In 1820, Mr Duckett of Petersham invented a plough with two separate shares and coulters, a machine which was widely praised, and which was more immediately newsworthy to the inhabitants of Richmond than the inventions of the Stephensons, father and son, who were working devotedly on railways and locomotives in the north of England. The idea of such an extraordinary means of transport had not as yet struck anyone in Richmond as a practical proposition. The many visitors who came to enjoy the delights of the riverside resort travelled by stage-coach, in hackneys, or in their own carriages.

John Evans, compiling his handbook on Richmond, gave the independent traveller useful advice:

Leaving Hyde Park Corner, and proceeding through Knightsbridge, Kensington, Hammersmith and Turnham Green, we reach Kew Green, which crossing, we soon arrive at *Richmond*. But quitting Knightsbridge, and taking the left, we pass through Brompton, Walham Green, Fulham, over Putney Bridge, Barnes Common, East Sheen to *Richmond*. Should a retired way be preferred, we turn down at Hyde Park Corner by St. George's Hospital, into the *King's private Road*, along which, uninterrupted by carts, waggons or stage-coaches, and embellished on each side by extensive nursery grounds, we pursue, through Fulham and Putney, our peaceful route to Richmond.

It is expected that by *the Bridge* now building from Hammer-

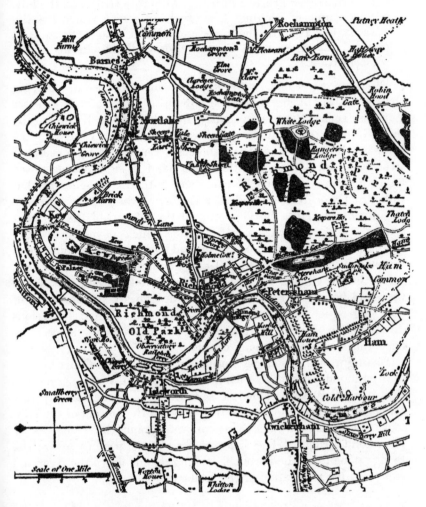

Environs of Richmond, Eighteenth Century

smith to Barnes, the distance from the Metropolis to Richmond will be shortened nearly a mile. .... At Spring Grove, on the left, within a mile of Richmond, we turn up a road which has the advantage of avoiding the town, and leads at once to the summit of the Hill, where burst upon the view all the charms of the adjacent country.

What an agreeable, pastoral scene this conjures up, driving through little villages which are now district numbers in Greater London. Today, the visitor coming from London to Richmond by bus, Green Line, Southern Railway, or District Line will see little on the journey, and the motorist, caught up in a ceaseless stream of traffic, takes his life in his hands if he attempts to see anything. But one thing he can share with the traveller in that unhurried world of a hundred years ago: when he reaches the summit of the Hill, the view of "all the charms of the adjacent country" will still be as beautiful as that which moved the usually cool John Evans to exclaim: "Richmond is only a village, but one of the pleasantest villages in his Majesty's dominions." It was, in fact, more than a village; it contained nearly 5000 inhabitants and a thousand houses in Evans's time. He describes it as consisting of one long street, with smaller ones branching from it in various directions; it had two stone town pumps, and a "respectable appearance superior to many country towns."

Distinguished personages were taken to Hampton Court by way of Richmond. When the King and Prince of Prussia, and the Emperor of Russia, came on a visit, both parties in separate carriages, the postilions, when they reached the bottom of the Hill, took the Russian by the Kingston route, and the Prussians by Richmond Bridge. "The King of Prussia on passing [over] the Bridge stood upon the Barouche looking up and down the river and expressed his admiration of the scenery."

Many people had praised the scenery at Richmond, and the early nineteenth century brought a spate of poems on the charms of this favoured town by the Thames. Alaric Watts let himself go in eleven verses in the *London Magazine*, beginning:

> Let poets rave of Arno's stream,
> And painters of the winding Rhine,
> I will not ask a lovelier dream,

A sweeter scene, Fair Thames, than thine;
As, 'neath a summer sun's decline,
Thou "wanderest at thine own sweet will,"
Reflecting from thy face divine
The flower-wreathed brow of Richmond Hill!

Richmond had a local authoress of whom the town was proud. This was Barbara Hofland, who lived at 2, Ormond Road for some years. She was born in Sheffield in 1778, and lost her mother at an early age. Her father married again, and Barbara was brought up by an aunt. She showed literary leanings, which the aunt encouraged, and appears to have had a happy and peaceful girlhood "without such domestic afflictions as those which beset her married life." When she was eighteen she married Bradshaw Hoole, "a young man of good social position, and respected alike for his manly disposition and uprightness." Barbara did not long enjoy domestic happiness: her husband died of consumption, leaving her with a four-months-old son. She began to write poems to support herself and the child, but it was a novel, *The Clergyman's Widow*, which brought a modest success. Then she married again—a young artist, Thomas Hofland. They moved to London to be at the centre of the artistic world; Hofland still had his way to make. Barbara was obliged to write hard, for her husband earned very little.

Hofland presently achieved some success, and began to neglect his wife. "His abilities and professional engagements drew him into that society whose allurements not infrequently prove themselves stronger than conjugal love," severely comments Barbara's chronicler. She was often hurt by Hofland's coldness, but there were compensations; she had a wide circle of friends, which included Miss Mitford and Maria Edgworth, who praised and encouraged her. Besides novels, Barbara Hofland wrote a topographical book, *Richmond, and Its Surrounding Scenery*, in which she set out "to display its familiar yet captivating lineaments." She was full of high flown sentiments about everything she saw, but one can clearly visualise from her descriptions the houses on the Richmond side of the Hill, "handsome structures with sloping gardens . . . well calculated for the entertainment of large parties." The entire bank of the river as far as Kew had "the convenience of a noble gravel walk, shaded by numerous trees." On the opposite shore, towards Twickenham, were Marble Hill and Ragland Castle, this last house

[167]

"the cheerful looking seat of Sir George Pococke," though, alas, "the beautiful clump of singularly elegant aspens" in the grounds is no more.

Thomas Hofland died in 1843, and Barbara had the further grief of losing her only son. She died at the age of sixty-six, and there is a memorial to her on the south wall of the Parish Church.

The scenery might inspire poets, and bring many admiring visitors to the town, but in the 1830s, the Vestry had to turn to the practical problems of lighting, water, and sewage. The lighting in the town was becoming modernised; the Brentford Gas Company agreed with the Vestry to lay the necessary pipes from their works at Brentford, and supplied Richmond with gas until the Richmond Gas Company was formed in 1853.

The water supply for the town had long been giving cause for anxiety. A private waterworks had existed in Richmond since 1767, but by the 1830s a growing population required more water. In 1835, the Richmond Waterworks Company was incorporated to supply the town. This was taken from the Thames and delivered unfiltered into the cisterns. By the middle of the century the inhabitants were complaining bitterly about the supply, and, forming a committee, applied to the West Middlesex Waterworks Company and to the Grand Junction Waterworks Company to arrange for a better supply. Unknown to the committee, the Southwark and Vauxhall Water Company made a take-over bid, subject to approval by Parliament, and bought up the Richmond company. The chairman of the Vestry happened to see a copy of this astute company's Bill for confirming the transfer (leaking information is not a new art) and discovered that the Southwark Company's charges were 1 per cent. higher than those of the Grand Junction Company. The chairman acted promptly. There were Indignation Water Meetings. Petitions signed by the inhabitants went before a committee of the House of Lords, which decided that the Bill should not proceed unless the Southwark Company agreed to reduce their rate, and not to charge extra for "high service, baths and water closets." The Southwark Company declined to accept these terms and withdrew their Bill.

The Vestry proceeded to sink artesian wells at Water Lane and in the Petersham Meadows, but these proved insufficient, and they were compelled to buy water from their foe, the Southwark and

Vauxhall Water Company. In 1866, the company demanded £240 a year instead of £120 for water used in watering the roads. When the Vestry held out the company accepted the usual sum. But it was not until 1873 that the real fight began: the company began charging 50 per cent. to 100 per cent. additional rate for water. A public meeting was held, and the Vestry were urged to make another attempt to get their own supply. They obtained a Royal Warrant to construct a reservoir in Richmond Park at a nominal rent of £10 a year, and permission was given for them to borrow £28,000 to erect their own waterworks

There were difficulties; again the supply was not sufficient for the demand. The company was jubilant, the Vestry patient and determined. Then—at the psychological moment—Mr Russ, one of the constructional engineers, knowing the geological strata round London, thought that there might be a large volume of water flowing from the springs in Richmond Park towards the Thames. He proved to be right. The Vestry made trials, analysed the water, and found it "most satisfactory." There was soon an abundant supply.

The Southwark and Vauxhall Company, appealing against its rate assessment later, was forced to admit that their income from Richmond which in 1876 exceeded £6400 per annum, was, in a year or two, reduced to less than £400 per annum, and of that £300 was accounted for by a long-term contract with the railway company. Mr Russ had saved the inhabitants of Richmond quite a sizeable amount of money every year, and, declared the *London Magazine*, "Whatever may happen in London, Richmond can claim to have completely broken down the power of the water monopolist."

Then there was the problem of sewers. In 1849, the assistant surveyor of the Metropolitan Commissioners of Sewers, instructed to report on the drainage of Richmond, disclosed that there was no proper system of sewage in the town, that the sewage was drained into cesspools, and that the general condition of the place was lamentable. Any responsible citizen of the town could have supplied the assistant surveyor with that information before: some, in fact, had been doing so for years. Having officially awakened to the fact that a lamentable sanitary condition in a town was undesirable, the assistant surveyor decided that proper main drains must be provided.

There followed a tug-of-war between the Vestry and the Metropolitan Commissioners of Sewers. Who was going to pay for the work? After a great deal of discussion and a certain amount of argument, the commissioners agreed to proceed with a joint scheme, but in 1851 they declared that they had no more funds. Neither had the Richmond Vestry, and in any case they did not possess the necessary legal power to proceed alone. They could not get the bureaucrats in London to go any further with the scheme; one sewer, constructed by the New Railway Company from Richmond Station to the Thames, was to be the main outfall for the entire sewage of the town.

In 1867, the Thames Conservancy Act prohibited the flow of sewage into the Thames, under heavy penalties. It took years of litigation and negotiation before Richmond, united for the purpose with the parishes of Barnes, Mortlake, Kew, and Petersham, was able to obtain a decent system of drainage, and a sewage disposal plant.

There were other signs of progress. Town constables and beadles had been employed in the town for centuries, and for the past hundred years a rudimentary local force of Vestry police had protected the inhabitants. In 1840, it was reported to the Vestry that the newly constituted Metropolitan Police Force was prepared to take charge of the town of Richmond; "the police commenced their duties and the police of the Vestry altogether ceased."

In 1849, the bargain which the then Vestry had made with George III, when they exchanged the right-of-way of Love Lane for Pest House Common, began to show dividends. A portion of the Common, which comprised the whole of the land on the east side of the present Queen's Road, as far as the top of Richmond Hill, was sold, and the money used to build a vicarage for the vicar of Richmond.

Progress was being made in the affairs of the church itself. One of the much-needed reforms which the Reverend Thomas Wakefield had made was in connection with the Parish Registers. Reforms were certainly needed. According to Challenor Smith, writing in the mid-nineteenth century:

> Richmond supplies a typical example of an ill-kept parochial record. Its parish clerks were for about two centuries members

of one family, who passed on, each generation to the next, a tradition of slovenliness and neglect in regard to their duty. There were hundreds of instances in which names were jotted down on pieces of paper, and lost.

The pieces-of-paper era was long over; the registers were now properly kept, and parish records of the period show a rising birth rate. The town was prosperous. George Street and King Street were the principal shopping streets, and the tradesmen formed "a respectable portion of the community." They had a social life of their own, governed by strict protocol. A writer in *Richmond Notes* of the period tells of the tradesmen's annual ball at the Castle Hotel, for which—

The niece of a worthy pastrycook applied for a ticket, but was politely refused, as, after some consultation, it was considered by the stewards that the lady in question scarcely occupied a position sufficiently elevated to qualify her for admission among the *elite* of the trade party.

But a dreadful revenge was taken. The uncle of this young lady was engaged to supply the greater part of the supper refreshments. Until the last moment he appeared to be making vigorous preparations, but when it was impossible to get anything elsewhere, he told the committee "that not one single article should they have from his establishment." A deputation waited upon him, but he was inexorable, and hunger and dissatisfaction reigned rampant among the visitors to the Richmond Tradespeople's Ball.

Here indeed was "Snobbery Punished". One of the London newspapers was even sharper in its comment on the tradespeople's patrons and customers, those ladies who employed their considerable leisure in one foolish pursuit after another:

The Richmond Minstrel. For some weeks past all the Dowagers, Widows and Maids have been running up to Richmond Hill of an evening to hear and see the performance of some fantastical itinerant, who, decked in a green tunic and inexpressibles, with a black Spanish hat and carroty moustachios, pretended to sing "Love's Young Dream" and other such airs, accompanying himself on a guitar. The fellow was a contemptible quack. We have heard a pig squeak more melodiously; and his ridiculous affectation of assumed gentility was all humbug. He gave himself out for a gentleman in disguise, and yet he greedily pocketed the shillings. We heard that certain persons, who ought to have known better, introduced this street musician to their wives and daughters. What may they expect?

It was becoming easy for audacious vagabonds to come to Richmond, fill their pockets, and be off again by the fast transport which was now linking the town with London. The four-horse coaches which had been the principal means of road transport were on the way out; the first horse omnibus had appeared in 1830, "and excited much interest as it passed along George Street." The omnibus could carry more passengers than the stage-coach, and fares were accordingly lower. People in a hurry would no longer be irritated by drivers like the proprietor of one stage-coach, who had so little idea of time while his horses were being changed "that he would sometimes keep his passengers waiting while he doffed his driving attire and went down a country dance at the Red Lion Tavern."

Railway communication with the town was discussed by the Vestry as early as 1837, but was turned down. By 1844, a more progressive outlook had prevailed, and the first railway-line, from Nine Elms to Richmond, was opened in that year—not without opposition. A circular headed "Ruin to Richmond" described in horrific terms what might happen to the town and the townsfolk if the railway scheme went through. The line was constructed, nevertheless, and the first train was welcomed by a brass band and artillery salutes. The public were invited to take free rides on any train that day, and the sanguinary expectations of the circularisers were happily unfulfilled.

For many years the headquarters of local official life was the old Vestry Hall in Paradise Road. The hall had been built in 1791, and by the middle of the next century had become "miserably inadequate for the purposes of the parish business." The rate collectors had no offices except their own dwelling-houses, and the room in which the Vestry meetings were held was so small that it was not possible to give all members seats at the table. When a deputation attended the Vestry the visitors had to stand in a corner with their backs to the wall; which was not without its advantages, remarks Charles Burt, a chairman of the Vestry at that period, "as it tends to discourage unnecessary deputating and prolonged addresses."

The Vestry tried to buy the old Castle Hotel premises, which were for sale, to convert into a Town Hall, but the price asked was considered prohibitive. Sir John Whittaker Ellis, a son of Joseph Ellis, of the Star and Garter Inn, was the town's Member of Parliament, and one of the great public-spirited men whose names will not be forgotten in Richmond. He purchased the whole of the property, on condition that a suitable municipal building was erected on the site, and a roadway made from Hill Street to the river, so that the public could have access to the waterside. The ballroom and Assembly Room of the establishment were sold to F. C. Mouflet, who transformed the Assembly Room into "a very pretty theatre." There were many discussions as to whether the proposed building should also contain a public hall for meetings and entertainments, but this suggestion was shelved. The design for the new Town Hall was thrown open to competition, and W. J. Ancell was chosen as architect. The building was opened in 1893 by the Duke of York.

The Terrace Gardens, one of the loveliest public gardens in Surrey, owe their existence to those members of the Vestry in the 1880s who had the ability and the will to make quick decisions which they knew would arouse strong hostility, but which they felt to be right.

On the site now occupied by the Gardens stood Lansdowne House, built in the early nineteenth century by a brewer called Collins and afterwards successively owned by the first Marquis of Stafford, the Marquis of Wellesley (brother of the Duke of Wellington), and the Marquis of Lansdowne. The mansion was demolished in the late 1860s and the land bought by the Duke of Buccleuch, who owned a house on adjoining land and wanted to secure the view. The Duke died in 1886.

At a Vestry meeting on May 18th, 1886, the chairman of the Richmond Vestry disclosed that he had been given private information the previous day that the entire property was to be put on the market; he was certain that speculators would seize the chance of buying it and covering the Hill with "desirable villas." He proposed that the Vestry should act immediately and buy the estate in the interests of the parish, keeping it in its natural state. The price he proposed to offer was £26,000; the asking price was

£30,000. The Vestrymen were naturally startled by the suddennes
of the proposal, but, with one dissentient, reacted favourably, and a
resolution in favour of purchase was passed. Next day, a repor
appeared in the *Thames Valley Times*, and protests immediately
began to pour into the Vestry from indignant ratepayers. Strong
letters were sent to the local newspapers, the most biting being from
a Mr Phillips, "who appeared like a bright meteor in the firmamen
of local politics when this question arose, but has since disappeared
from view."

The local newspapers, energetically favouring the proposal, were
supported by the London journals, and by artists like Holman Hun
and Sir Frederick Leighton, who contemplated rows of villas on the
Hill "with horror and dismay." An application had been sent to the
Local Government Board for permission to raise the money for
purchase, and when this was sanctioned the Vestry went quickly
ahead. Whittaker Ellis bought Buccleuch House for £6000, other
portions of the land were sold to supporters of the scheme, the
remainder of the money was found, and the famous view was saved.

The Richmond Corporation bought the house and demolished it
in 1937–38, adding the gardens to the rest, but retaining the name,
Buccleuch Gardens, to commemorate that part which belonged to
the house. The grounds were terraced and laid out; some of the
land from Cardigan House was added in recent times. The Terrace
Gardens are a fitting memorial to the town fathers of the late
Victorian Era, worthy successors to the Vestrymen of previous
centuries, who took great pride in their town, felt a sense of
responsibility towards their fellow-citizens, and were not afraid to
stand up for their opinions and principles.

In 1877, the Richmond Ratepayers' Association decided to press
for the incorporation of Richmond as a borough. They considered
that a corporation would possess much wider powers than a Vestry,
and it was time that a rising and important town like Richmond
should have the status of a borough. There were also a number of
would-be statesmen who disliked the way the Vestry was recruited
and wanted a more democratic method of election to the body which
ran the town's affairs.

There were objections to the idea of incorporation, and a long-
drawn-out and strenuous opposition, mainly from people who did

tot like any change at any time for any reason. A poll of the parishioners was taken, and the majority declared for incorporation. Meetings were held, committees were formed, visits were paid to the Privy Council Office. In the end, a draft scheme was published in the *Richmond Herald*. A good deal of argument ensued as to the division of labour between the proposed corporation and the Vestry, which would continue to function in some degree; but the lengthy business was at last resolved. Sir Edward Hertslet, Librarian of the Foreign Office and a local resident who had been prominent in public affairs, agreed to be Provisional Charter Mayor, and on July 16th, 1890, the charter was sealed with the Great Seal of England, and Richmond was henceforth a borough. On November 1st of that year, the gold chain of office was transferred to Sir John Whittaker Ellis, who became the first Mayor of Richmond.

Local politics were now matters of some importance to the townspeople, for the local council was elected by popular vote. The Richmond newspapers took their duties to the electorate seriously, giving as much information as they could about candidates for the council. In 1893, there were four contenders for the mayoralty, and the *Richmond and Twickenham Times* allowed equal space to the achievements of these well-known figures:

"Councillor Hilditch is a gentleman of retiring disposition and one who takes few positions of his own seeking, and yet who, when responsibility is cast upon him, works with dogged determination to ensure success." Alderman Szlumper was "one of the most genial and pleasant of men. Somewhat short in stature, and with an expressive countenance which suggests remarkable determination, Mr Szlumper possesses a personality which is at once the envy and the pride of the majority of those who come into contact with him." Councillor Albert Chancellor, continued the *Richmond and Twickenham Times*, needed no introduction: his name was a household word in nearly every home in the town. As for the last mayoral candidate, "To know Alderman Piggott is to love him."

In the event, Alderman James Weeks Szlumper was elected, and became the fourth Mayor of the Borough of Richmond. He had a very full year in office; the Footbridge and Lock were opened by the Duke of York, there were two visits to the town by Queen Victoria. During the second visit, the Queen knighted Mr Szlumper, and there was real rejoicing in the borough, culminating with a

demonstration of affection when a line of people of all ages joine
a procession through the town to the Mayor's house "to give him
hearty cheer."

The centuries-old royal connection with Richmond continued
In 1870, the Duke and Duchess of Teck came to live at Whit
Lodge, in Richmond Park. The Duchess had been Princess Mar
Adelaide of Cambridge, and had married a Würtemberg prince
They had three sons and a daughter, Princess Victoria Mary August
Louise Olga Pauline Claudine Agnes, who was destined to becom
the Consort of George V. James Pope-Hennessy, in his excellen
book, *Queen Mary*, relates how the stout, happy-go-lucky Duchess
the most extravagant of mortals, persuaded Queen Victoria to le
her have White Lodge as a country home, though the Duches
found it difficult enough to keep up her London residence, Kensing
ton Palace. The Duke developed a passion for gardening, and mad
the White Lodge gardens bloom the year round. He was also re
sponsible for the arrangement of the furnishings and furniture
The principal rooms were

> . . . loaded with ottomans and sofas draped with shawls, larg
> tables covered with Turkey rugs, small occasional tables a
> ubiquitous as mushrooms in an October field, elaborate inlai
> chairs, ornamental stools with twisted legs, and many palms i
> pots. Family portraits stood about on varnished easels, whil
> other pictures, small and large, peppered the brocaded walls a
> thickly as though they had been shot out at them from som
> gigantic gun. On the floors were strewn eastern carpets. The large
> pieces of furniture came brand-new from Maple's emporium.

Whatever gossip about the Duchess's irresponsible attitude t
financial stability seeped out through the servants' quarters o
White Lodge, there was no doubt about her popularity with th
people of Richmond. She sent dinners to destitute families, busie
herself energetically with numerous local charities, presided ove
committees, and saw to it that things really got done. She taugh
her children early in life that they must think of people les
fortunate than themselves, and try to help by personal service a
well as by giving money. She was a large-hearted woman, and th
people of Richmond could always count on her support for any goo
cause. They celebrated her Silver Wedding in June 1881, with zest

leaving the Duchess and her family in no doubt of their affection.

Princess Mary lived part of her early life at White Lodge, and it was at Sheen that an important moment in her life occurred: Prince George, Duke of York, second son of Edward VII, and now heir presumptive to the Throne, proposed to her in the garden of her cousin Princess Louise's house. They were married in 1893, and the following year their first child was born at White Lodge. The birth was expected to have taken place at Buckingham Palace, but the summer was so hot, Princess Mary decided it would be better to go to her parents' home in Richmond Park. She had been disconcerted by the publicity which accompanied this perfectly natural event, and disliked even more the uninhibited curiosity of the people who swarmed into the Park after the birth of the infant prince, crowds which grew so large that a temporary hurdle fence had to be erected at some distance from the railings, and extra constables put on duty to preserve order.

The Duke and Duchess of York, later George VI and Queen Elizabeth, lived at White Lodge for a short time after their marriage, and the next member of the royal family to live in the Park was Princess Alexandra of Kent, on her marriage to Mr Angus Oglivy. They came to Thatched House Lodge after their marriage in 1963, and a son was born to them there the following year.

The Richmond Athletic Ground is known far outside the confines of Richmond. The idea for a Ground was first mooted in the 1880s, when the Richmond Town Cricket Club, becoming dissatisfied with their quarters on the Green, wanted to rent part of the Old Deer Park from the Crown, but found the yearly hire prohibitive. Three members of the Club formed a limited company in 1885, and leased nine acres from the Crown. The new Ground was so popular that they soon had to add more land. Local groups, like the Shop Assistants' Early Closing Association, booked the Ground from year to year. The *Richmond and Twickenham Times*, reporting the Association's sports day in 1899, remarked:

"The little failures that were noticed last year, such as a faulty pistol for the starter, and insufficient dressing-room stewards, were remedied on this occasion, and a novelty was introduced in the shape of chairs on the central lawn . . . a good idea somewhat spoilt by the bad quality of the chairs."

A PROSPECT OF RICHMOND

The Royal Horse Show, held annually in June, dates from 1892 when it was founded by a local syndicate. There appear to have been horse races in Richmond, though no regular race-course in the district can be traced. In 1864, an item in the local press headed "A Few Remarks on the Starters in Richmond Races", includes pointed advice to would-be punters:

No. 7. PEPPER.   A Horse that has run many matches on the Green Sward, Many of his Friends have advised him to retire from the Course, being afraid of over-exertion.

No. 10. VARNISH.   A Horse that only goes in for Amusement, and to make himself more generally known in the Ring.

No. 12. SLIPPER.   A Horse of long standing, Honest in himself, rather Slow, but has been badly Jockey'd.

Cundall mentions pony and donkey races at Petersham, and this may have been the scene of the "Course."

The district had its modest share of inventors and inventions. One of the most interesting is the invention of rayon, which might be said to have been invented at Kew. Two chemists who had a laboratory there, Charles Frederick Cross and Edward Bevan, did some work which led, in 1892, to the discovery of viscose. Near their laboratory at South Avenue, Kew, Charles Henry Stearn, an expert on vacuums, ran an electric-lamp factory; he had been in partnership with Joseph Swan, the inventor of the electric lamp. Stearn was always experimenting, looking for new materials from which to make filaments. It is probable that Cross suggested viscose to him for this purpose, and Stearn and his assistants began fresh experiments with the newly discovered substance. For filaments, viscose had to be spun into fine threads by being forced through small jets and then hardened. Stearn did not find the results particularly successful for filaments, but he succeeded in making the viscose threads into artificial silk. This opened up great possibilities, and Stearn, Cross, and Frederick Topham, who had been working with them, formed a syndicate and set up production of artificial silk next to the lamp factory. They produced yarns with increasing success, and were eventually bought up by Samuel Courtauld in 1904.

Cricket on Richmond Green

. Ward.   *By courtesy of Mrs S. B. Ward*

Richmond Royal Horse Show: Coaching Marathon

By courtesy of the Directors, Richmond Royal Horse Show

Vigilance: 1896

By courtesy of Richmond upon T...
Libraries Com...

THREATENED VANDALISM

ON

RICHMOND HILL.

A renewed attempt is being made by certain members of the Richmond Corporation to destroy the old hedge upon the Terrace; also to erect an obtrusive iron railing.

A COMMITTEE OF RESIDENTS, of which Mr. T. W. STEPHENS, of Downe House, is Chairman, has been formed to resist this objectionable and unnecessary proceeding.

ALL PERSONS, resident or otherwise, anxious to preserve the existing natural features of the beautiful Terrace and the world-famed view from Richmond Hill are urgently invited to SIGN THE MEMORIAL lying HERE.

DECEMBER 31ST, 1896.

THE RICHMOND SOCIETY

A Petition to

The Minister of Housing and Local Government
c/o C. Hilton, Esq., B.A., A.R.I.B.A., N.T.P.I.

Planning Appeal, Star and Garter Hotel, Richmond, to be heard at RICHMOND TOWN HALL on JULY 7th, 1964

We, the undersigned, residents of, or visitors to RICHMOND, hereby record our deep objections to the Appeal for Planning Permission to build a 'skyscraper' hotel on the site of the existing Star and Garter Hotel. It would gravely damage the historic view of or from Richmond Hill, part of our national heritage and an important 'amenity', not only for residents of Richmond but for all London and countless visitors from all parts of Great Britain and Overseas.

NAME   ADDRESS

Vigilance:
1964

By courtesy of
the
Richmond Society

Chairman G E Cassidy BA FRIBA JP 67 Bushwood Road Kew Telephone RIChmond 3473
Secretary John Locke 4 Old Palace Terrace Richmond   Telephone Home RIChmond 1830 · Office WHItehall 5422
Treasurer Philip A Weston FRICS 16 Denbigh Gardens Richmond   Telephone RIChmond 3658
Membership Secretary Mrs D K Winslow 16 The Vineyard Richmond   Telephone RIChmond 1227

Traditional: Master Baker in
Sheen Road, Richmond.
One of the Few Left in Surrey

R. Wood.

Contemporary: Furniture Shop on Richmond Hill

K. B. Fleming.

Petersham House, Petersham

The end of the nineteenth century brought trouble in South Africa, but only the politically minded were unduly concerned. The Richmond "House of Commons" regretted the methods which the Government at Westminster had adopted in dealing with the South African Republic and the Orange Free State, prior to the breaking off of diplomatic relations, but were prepared to support the Government, nevertheless. The actual outbreak of war did not noticeably change the pattern of Richmond's daily life: South Africa was very far away. The 3rd Volunteer Battalion of the East Surrey Regiment, which included a corps of Richmond men, were invited to contribute one officer and forty men to the Lord Mayor's Imperial Volunteers for service in South Africa. "Truly this is a proud moment for the corps which some superior persons have been inclined to treat at times as little better than a plaything," said the *Richmond and Twickenham Times*.

As time went on, urgent letters began to appear in the local press from the colonels of Surrey and Middlesex regiments and the Lord-Lieutenants of the counties, appealing for volunteers for the army; but the main pages were full of the kind of news which does not make history, and is interesting only to the inhabitants. The Vicar of Ham walked in his sleep in the small hours of one Sunday morning, inadvertently broke a pane of glass, and was unable to take the services that day. A temporary wooden bridge had been erected at Kew while the new stone bridge was being built. A gentleman at the new Playhouse on the Little Green insisted on keeping on his chimney-pot hat because the lady in front of him refused to remove the enormous erection she was wearing. Councillor James Hilditch, who had scientific tastes, turned out to have been associated, in his youth, with A. F. Yarrow, the designer of shallow draught vessels, and had made telegraph instruments at the age of seventeen, the two young men connecting their respective houses by means of an over-house wire—the first telegraphic communication in London.

Local news predominated throughout the war: harvest festivals, weddings, local milk vendors fined, Lilley and Skinner selling off thousands of pairs of shoes damaged by smoke and water after a fire "from 6½d. upwards", Miss Braddon's latest novel, murders, thefts, discussions on the Ethics of Advertising. The small change of life in any country town as reflected in its local press.

CHAPTER SIXTEEN

Modern Times

THE Edwardian Era marked a highlight in the prosperity of Richmond. The land between the Hill and Sheen was now almost entirely residential; roads had been built, large houses erected, gardens fenced and walled. The town was decidedly a pleasant place to live in, and in 1901 the population was over 31,000.

It was becoming fashionable for Londoners to go down to Richmond for a day's outing on the river. The local watermen invested in small pleasure craft, and on a fine Saturday and Sunday, the river was a gay sight, punts poled by young men in regulation white flannels, while "a fair companion reclined gracefully against the cushions, delicately upholding a sunshade"; athletic characters pulled skiffs, families rowed comfortably in dinghies.

The tradesmen did well out of the visitors, and there was a constant demand for shops. Some of the Georgian houses in Hill Rise and Hill Street lost their front gardens; the owners were quite willing to sell for the substantial figures offered by speculators, who built shops on these valuable sites. If you look above the façades of the shops on the left-hand side going up the Hill, you will see several bow windows, and the graceful upper storeys of eighteenth- and early nineteenth-century houses.

The outbreak of the Great War in 1914 brought an echo of fifteen years before to the local press: patriotic sentiments and stirring exhortations appeared every week:

> The chief attraction at the Richmond Theatre this week is "Go Ahead!" It comes just at the right moment to give the eligible young men of this locality a gentle hint. Let them "Go Ahead" with their enlisting. They may not be wanted. But when

they have reached veteranhood it will be a proud thing for them to look back to this time, and remember that they would have been there if they had been wanted.

As the years passed, the tone altered. Lists of Richmond casualties were given every week. The advertisements for housemaids and cooks—"Reliable, abstainer, £20 a year and a good home"—grew ever more plaintive: there were few applicants, with munitions factories offering high rates of pay. The banqueting-room and ballroom of the now deserted Star and Garter Hotel had been turned into a hospital, and much of the local hard-core news was now of casualties, relief funds, homes for Belgian refugees, and Red Cross work.

On November 16th, 1918, Messrs Kempthorne and Phillips of George Street advertised "Flags! Flags! Flags! from 2d. each." The war was ended. Slowly peace returned, but Richmond had changed, together with the rest of the world. There was talk of reconstruction; some of the town councillors had begun thinking of the future, and the problems which increasing traffic was going to bring to the town. One of them even forecast that most householders would own motor-cars themselves before the century was half over, a remark that was greeted with some awe and a great deal of derision. How many ordinary people were ever likely to be able to afford £100 for a motor-car, in Richmond or anywhere else?

The years between the wars tell of the speeding up of life in general, and of anxieties which were continually being pushed aside by the determination to enjoy all the amusements available. The luxury cinemas which had been built in the town were always crowded; brassy organs rose from below the screen and brayed out luscious melodies between super-films and news-reels. Pathé Gazette began to show marching soldiers in Germany, and the watchful faces of statesmen in adjoining countries. After Munich in 1938, the Richmond Council started to make provisional preparations for evacuation, and air-raid precautions. On Easter Monday, 1939, 90,000 visitors came to Richmond by rail, and 70,000 to Kew Green. There were loud complaints from the residents about the litter left behind, but the chief news in the local papers was concerned with air-raid wardens, and auxiliary firemen, and reports of discussions in the Council Chamber whether Richmond should have deep air-raid shelters or not. By early May, trench shelters had been built in the Old Deer Park and the local recreation grounds.

Richmond's history during the next six years is one familiar in most towns in the London area: constant alerts, blackout, some bombing, and the grinding difficulties inevitable in a war in which civilians as well as soldiers are personally involved. The Town Hall was damaged during a raid, cottages in Old Palace Yard were reduced to rubble, houses in various parts of the borough were demolished or partly wrecked. On the whole, the town fared better than many towns in the Home Counties: the historic buildings escaped, and the casualties were mercifully few.

Richmond mourned a local hero in Wing Commander Brendan Finucane, D.S.O., D.F.C., who lost his life in the Battle of Britain. "Paddy" Finucane, a fighter pilot, was a legend in the Royal Air Force even at that early stage of the war. Possessed of unusually good eyesight and an extremely quick reflex action, he was a natural for command: gallant, confident, full of practical good sense. There was a sense of great loss among "the Few" in the R.A.F. when he was killed in 1942.

Twenty-three years later Richard Dimbleby, C.B.E., a world-renowned Richmond man, died at the age of fifty-two. He came of a family long connected with the town as newspaper-owners, and after some journalistic experience joined the BBC as their first 'news observer'. He became their first war correspondent, and quickly established himself as a skilled commentator; later he went over to BBC Television, where he was a much-loved figure. He was mourned by the nation in a memorial service in Westminster Abbey, which was televised.

Towards the end of the war, plans for reconstruction inevitably came up all over the country. The "Greater London Plan, 1944," was a bold attempt to plan for the future, and it contained a reference to Richmond in Chapter 8:

> The sprawling outward expansion of London has engulfed many towns and villages. Within the Suburban and Inner Urban rings they are now embedded in a vast sea of inchoate development. Here they remain the only real centres of community life despite the fact that the character of nearly all has been completely changed and most of their charm has been lost. Only a few have managed to resist the flow of disorderly building, and they

have retained individuality. It is by accident that their form remains, but it is noteworthy that within them is to be found a civic pride and healthy community life which is almost entirely lacking in the surrounding sea of incoherent housing. Unyielding barriers such as permanent open spaces and rivers have defended their integrity rather than local planning, which has been powerless to resist the stresses and strains imposed by the uncontrolled regional movement of population and industry. Richmond, which lies between the Thames and Richmond Great Park in one direction and between Kew Gardens and Petersham Common in the other, is an example of a well-defined community in the Suburban Ring which has stood firm.

The original plan for Richmond, an ambitious one, obviously could not be carried out within a few years. Compromises were inevitable, as practical difficulties arose from time to time. In the 1950s and early '60s, roads were widened, a system of one-way streets introduced, and various improvements made. In November 1962 the first outline proposals for the redevelopment for Richmond Town Centre were published.

Present-day Richmond is very different from the town which John Evans described in his guide-book over a hundred years ago; and my grandchildren, to whom this book is inscribed, will find the Richmond *they* knew different again.

The Borough of Richmond, as such, is no more. A Royal Commission set up when arrangements were being made for the old London County Council to be replaced by the Greater London Council reported, in 1960, that it was desirable to change the boundaries of some of the London boroughs so as to rationalise local administration. This meant that small boroughs would be joined together to make a single administrative unit, and many mayoralties would disappear.

Richmond was one of the places affected, and in April, 1965, the Borough of Richmond became Richmond upon Thames, incorporating the neighbouring boroughs of Barnes and Twickenham. Old neighbours became members of one family, administratively. Each would retain the flavour, the individuality, which is a feature of towns with a long history.

Inevitably—as so often happens in family life—there were stresses and strains. The centre of local government moved to York

A PROSPECT OF RICHMOND

House, Twickenham, formerly the civic centre for the Borough of Twickenham. The Town Hall at Richmond therefore lost its function. The former Council Chamber is hired out for meetings, and there is pressure from some quarters to demolish the building itself so as to free the site for development. It is not a particularly good example of Victorian architecture, and no longer serves a useful purpose, beyond being available for letting. Its demolition, however, would infuriate many Richmond inhabitants; though, as other locals think, it would be a sensible thing to do.

As in other towns, there has been much demolition in Richmond in the decade since 1960. Two high, gaunt Victorian mansions standing in large gardens on the north side of the Green were pulled down to make way for a development of contemporary houses, designed by a local architect. When they went up there was an outcry, as they were totally out of keeping with the other houses round the famous Green. But, in fact, are the villas on the west side in keeping with the Georgian and early nineteenth-century houses on the east side of the Green, or Maids of Honour Row on the south side? The sight of these villas being built must have given many a Victorian preservationist the vapours. One has to accept contemporary building, like it or not. And this new row of houses got a Civic Award, like it or not.

There was another development alongside Trumpeters' House; a charming pastiche of Georgian-type terrace houses set back in old Palace Yard. The purists grumbled that they weren't the real thing (a fine example of logic!) and the school of contemporary-at-all-costs grumbled because they weren't modern in style.

A change which met with much local approbation was the face-lift given to Paved Court (p. 197). Some of the little shops there had become very shabby, and their interiors dilapidated and vermin-ridden. Harrods, the London group of stores, bought the site at the King Street end of George Street (formerly the Queen's Head public house and then an annexe to Gosling's draper's shop) to build a branch store for one of their subsidiaries, Dickins and Jones. The purchase included the rear of the site, which was the east side of Paved Court. They wished to incorporate this into the new store, though they met with difficulties as one of the owners refused to sell the remainder of his lease. There were further difficulties when there was strong local objection to Paved Court

[184]

being turned into the back of a store. A preservation order was placed on the Court, but permission was given for the shops to be reconditioned, provided they remained as small shops. This was done, and the result is astonishing.

The old façades have been kept or closely reproduced, the interiors intelligently modernised. Most of the shops have been rented to antique dealers whose standards are high, and who attract what used to be called the "carriage trade." Layton's, on the west side of the Court, is an example of what can be done by a discriminating tenant. Rebuilding the inside disclosed old beams and fireplaces; former tattiness has been replaced by elegance and a feeling for period. There is a tiny flower-shop, *Bizzy Lizzy*, on the east side which gives a splash of colour and gaiety to the whole alley, and a charming shop of an unusual kind, *Nota Bene*, can stand comparison with any London or Continental establishment for its display of onyx, alabaster, silver and other prestige objects. Paved Court is now a distinct asset to the Richmond scene.

The town also has a reputation for the high quality specialist shops which have established themselves during the last few years. Houben's, the chartered booksellers in Church Court, are also printsellers and have original engravings; Mark Moore, who runs Richmond Records in Paradise Road, specialises in classical records.

Changes in George Street—the main shopping street of the town—reflect the pattern of practically every town High Street: branches of well-known multiple stores, supermarkets, health food shops. W. H. Smith absorbed Short's wine-house next door when it came on to the market, and transformed itself into a spacious, eye-catching modern store with large book and record departments and dozens of side-lines. The long-established Wright's, once an old-style draper's, had a face-lift, and now displays stock that exhilarates its old customers and surprises their daughters. The equally long-established Kempthorne's became Campbell and Booker's, more Quant-ish than Mary Quant.

Condon's Market, for so many years the hub of fruit and vegetable shopping, has become The Market, with nine or ten stalls of different kinds slotted into the once draughty hall where Mr. Condon set out his counters piled with oranges and apples. Mr. Barber, a minute away from the Market in Sheen Road, still bakes his bread in the old wall-ovens where bread has been made for over a hundred years; the queues outside his shop show how much home-baked bread is appreciated. At the other end of the town, in King Street, Mr. Bun the Baker has reconstituted an old shop—finding eighteenth century beams, and yet older coins and bottle-glass, in the process—and turned it into a modern cake-shop, with a new bow-window to remind you of its venerable beginnings.

There are many more changes in the centre of the town. The old Greyhound Inn and its courtyard, once a post-house (pp. 162 & 163) has been turned into a shop. Side streets which used to have rows of cottages let to artisans at a few shillings a week have been bathroomed and brass-knockered and patio'd into the £10,000 price (b)racket. Most of the old family houses on the roads up the Hill have been divided into flats and flatlets; hundreds of young people live in bed-sitters and congregate in the local discotheques and coffee-shops in the evenings, and buy trendy gear in the many boutiques that have opened up in the last few years. They dazzle the eye and lift the spirits, even when you are not quite sure what their sex happens to be.

But trendiness is not all. One of the most extraordinary transformations in recent years has not been from the past to the present, but from the present to the past. This was the restoration of Asgill House (pp. 197 & 212). The house had various owners in the nineteenth century; at some period a tasteless Victorian addition was built on to the west wing for kitchen quarters. One owner was James Hilditch, a son of "the Richmond Painter," George Hilditch (1803–57), one of the best-known artists of the early nineteenth century.

In the 1940s, the house was occupied by Mr. Henry Ward and Mr. H. Stirling Webb, who bred Siamese cats. After the death of these two gentlemen, the house was empty for about two years. In 1968, the lease was offered for sale by the Crown Commissioners, who administer Crown lands in this area. The house had fallen into such a poor condition that no acceptable offers were made—until Mr. Hauptfuhrer came along.

Fred Hauptfuhrer, an American journalist from Philadelphia working in London, had always been attracted by eighteenth century houses, and he was drawn to Asgill House. Its condition put him off at first, but he kept coming to see it, and in the end he decided to try to do something with it. He had the ambitious idea

The original Theatre on the Green

I

H. Bunbury Del.

II

Richmond Bridge (Watercolour)

III

The old Star and Garter Inn

IV

The Thames at Richmond

v

Richmond, Surrey, after W. G. Reynolds, 1883

VI

Mr. Klanert, Lessee and Manager of the Theatre on the Green, 1817–1829

For the BENEFIT of

MR. KLANERT,

Who will have the honor of presenting (for the first time at this Theatre) an interesting and highly popular Drama, Translated and altered from the French, call'd

THE BROKEN SWORD.

This Piece was produced during the last Season at Covent Garden, and performed near 100 Nights to crowded Audiences with the most universal marks of approbation.

Theatre-Royal, Richmond,

On MONDAY next, SEPTEMBER 22, 1817,

Will be performed (for the first time) a Grand Spectacle, call'd The

Broken Sword:

Or, The VALLEY of the TORRENT.

With New SCENERY, MACHINERY and DECORATIONS.—The Scenes painted by Messrs. Dearlove & Flower— The Machinery invented and executed by Mr. Franklin.

Colonel Rigalio   Mr. BARNARD, (of the Theatre-Royal, Drury-Lane.)
The Baron   Mr. MUSGRAVE,   Claudio (Son to the Baron)   Mr. WEST.
Captain Zavia (a retired Naval Officer)   Mr. SHEPPARD.
Pablo (Gardener to the Baron)   Mr. HUGHES.
Adjoint Mr. CURSON,   Officers Messrs. DEARLOVE, FLOWER, WOOLMER.
Villager Mr. BROWN,   Goatherd Mr. SHAKESPEAR.
Myrtillo (a Dumb Orphan, received and protected by the Baron)   Miss COOKE.
Estevan (a confidential Servant of Myrtillo's late Father)   Mr. KLANERT.
Rosara (Daughter to the Baron)   Miss VIALS.
Stella (a Peasant)   Mrs. KLANERT.
Beatrice   Mrs. JEPHSON,   Jacintha   Mrs. AMBROSE.

IN THE COURSE OF THE PIECE THE FOLLOWING SCENERY, &c.

THE PYRENEAN MOUNTAINS IN THE DISTANCE,

At the Foot of which is a GOATHERD's CABIN and VINEYARD.

THE CASTLE GARDENS,

In which is introduced a DANCE by Mr. BROWN.

The VALLEY of the TORRENT, with a WATER FALL.

FOOT BRIDGE AND PERPENDICULAR ROCK,

ON THE SUMMIT OF WHICH IS A RUIN'D ABBEY.

The Last Scene represents

The Hall of Chivalry.

After the Play will be performed the much admired New Farce of

IS HE JEALOUS?

Belmour   Mr. BARNARD,
John   Mr. WOOLMER,   Robert   Mr. FLOWER.
Mrs. Belmour   Mrs. AMBROSE,
Harriet (her Sister, disguised in Male Attire)   Miss FITZHENRY,
Rose   Mrs. KLANERT.

The Entertainments to conclude with a laughable and highly popular Drama, call'd The

Three & the Deuce!!!

Preceded by an explanatory PROLOGUE, to be Spoken by Mr. KLANERT.

Pertinax Single   Mr. KLANERT!
Peregrine Single   Mr. KLANERT!!
Percival Single   Mr. KLANERT!!!
Mr. Milford Mr. CURSON,   Justice Touchit Mr. AMBROSE,   Mac Floggan Mr. WARD,   Frank Mr. WEST,
Renard Mr. BISHOP,   Waiter Mr. FLOWER,   Pinch Mr. DEARLOVE,
Tippy Mr. BROWN,   Cramp Mr. WOOLMER,   Humphrey Grizzle Mr. SHEPPARD.
Emily   Mrs. AMBROSE,   Phœbe   Miss COOKE,
And Taffline (with the favorite Air of "The SILKEN SASH,")   Mrs. KLANERT.

Tickets and Places may be taken at the Box-Office of the Theatre; and at the Printing Office, Brentford.

Playbill of Mr. Klanert's Benefit

By courtesy of Richmond upon Thames Libraries Committee

Edmund Kean as Richard III at the Theatre on the Green

IX

Plate X

X

e Green

Photograph: Clifford E. Webb

e view from The Terrace

Photograph: Clifford E. Webb

XI

Paved Court

Photograph: Michael Stannard

The Britannia public house in Brewers Lane

Photograph: Michael Sta

Waterloo Place

Church Walk from the Churchyard

Photograph: Michael Star

Eighteenth century houses in Ormond Road

of restoring it to its original condition and living in it. Single-minded devotion to an idea looks a good phrase on paper; carrying out the idea requires dedication, patience, continuing determination —and, of course, money. Mr. Hauptfuhrer was prepared to stake a good deal of his own money on the venture, and the Historic Buildings Council for England, together with the then Ministry of Housing and Local Government, backed him with a grant. He worked with Donald Insall, a Fellow of the Royal Institute of British Architects, and the restoration, begun in 1969, is now complete. The Victorian excrescence was removed, the side-roofs lowered to their original height (as could be observed in old prints), the entire fabric of the house renovated, and the inside repaired and decorated and furnished. Robert Taylor's eighteenth century villa, considered to have been one of his best buildings, now looks as it did when it was erected.

As Twickenham is now part of Richmond upon Thames, the borough has an art gallery, Orleans House. This fine building, situated on the riverside between Richmond and Twickenham, was built in 1710 by one of Wren's chief assistants, John James. The famous Octagon Room was added to the house in 1720. One of the house's most famous residents was Louis-Philippe, Duc d'Orleans.

Most of the original building was demolished in 1926, but the Octagon was left untouched. What remained of the house was bought in 1927 by Mrs. Walter Levy, who married the architect, Basil Ionides. This lady bought an adjoining house, Riverside House, where she lived. Mrs. Ionides was a noted collector of pictures, and when she died in 1962, she bequeathed her paintings to the local authority, on condition that they would build a gallery at Orleans House in which to show this valuable collection. The gallery has been built, and the pictures beautifully hung and lit; it is open to the public. The Octagon has been restored, and should be visited for its rich decoration, in the Roman baroque style.

The local Council are a natural target for articulate citizens who keep an eye on civic activities, and are quick to tell the councillors, via the local press and personal letters, of their sins of omission and commission. The Council, in fact, do a great deal for the town. In 1971 they tidied up the towpath and replaced the old iron benches with simple, well-designed seats which take account of the human anatomy instead of being at cross-purposes with it. More important, they bought Devonshire Lodge, on Petersham Road, in the late '60's, demolished the mansion and laid out the land, thus adding another open space to the Riverside for the enjoyment of the public. The house was of no historic importance, save that it stood on the site of the former Devonshire Cottage (p. 118.)

Northumberland House (p. 210) was demolished in 1970, and there is speculation as to what is going to happen to the site; at the time of writing nothing has been decided. Cardigan House (pp. 144 & 201), which belonged to the British Legion, has been demolished, and a large block of flats built on the site for its member families.

There has been a growing interest in amenity societies, to put forward the views of the inhabitants of the Borough. The Petersham Society was one of the foremost opponents of the proposed development of Rutland Lodge, on Petersham Road. This house (pp. 110 & 111) was sold by its then-owner in 1966. In 1967 a fire destroyed much of the interior but left the façade intact. A developer bought the house in this state, reconditioned the inside to make several flats, and applied for planning permission to erect five houses in the garden. There was immediate protest from the people of Petersham, who said that if planning permission was given for these new houses, it would not be long before others were built in gardens surrounding the Georgian houses in Petersham, and this would wreck the character of the village, which is unique (pp. 103–121). The Council, however, gave planning permission.

Then—shades of the eighteenth century Richmond Vestry, and their sturdy opposition to commercial spoliation! There were soon modern equivalents of the nineteenth century "Indignation meetings", led by the Petersham Society and backed by many Richmond people. The Minister of the appropriate department was approached, an inspector came down to hold a special inquiry, and the Minister over-ruled the Council's planning permission. The developer then amended his application, applying for permission to erect two houses in the garden instead of five, and that is how the matter stands at present.

There was also a public inquiry, initiated by amenity groups, when the owners of the Star and Garter Hotel (pp. 158–160, 181, 203) applied for planning permission to add height to the hotel with an extra floor of rooms. The hotel is on the slope of Richmond Hill, and it was considered that this addition would interfere with the famous view from the Terrace. After the inquiry, planning permission was refused. A later, modified application met with success, and the extension is being built.

The Morshead Hotel (pp. 201 & 202) became the Richmond Gate Hotel, and the new owners applied for permission to add on an extra wing in their enclosed garden at the back. The first application was refused, but the second was accepted, and the extension was built. There was little opposition in the town; it is only a threat to the view from the Terrace which makes Richmond temperatures rise.

Another source of public concern is the use—or change of use—of lands given to the town in former centuries. The Queen's Road Estate, as it is popularly known, is an area of about twenty acres given to the parish of Richmond by George III and Queen Charlotte in 1785, the gift being confirmed by Queen Victoria in 1890. These Charity Lands were given for the purpose of "relief of the aged and poor inhabitants of the parish of Richmond . . . with the object of improving the conditions of life for the said inhabitants". The Trustees of the Charity Lands were to administer the property "and let the houses at the best rent possible", but there was also an implicit obligation to look after the general welfare of the objects of the Charity, especially with regard to housing.

Besides Queen's Road, Cambrian Road, Grove Road and Chisholm Road were within the area of the Charity Lands. Kingsmead Hospital for the aged was built, large houses were erected in Queen's Road, and smaller ones in the side roads.

In the early days, and throughout the Victorian period, the rents helped to keep the poor rate down, but conditions have changed dramatically since then. With the Welfare State, "the poor", as the Victorians knew them, no longer exist; pauperism is practically unknown. But there is a chronic shortage of housing available for people in low income brackets. The Queen's Road Estate is now estimated to be worth between one and two million pounds, if developed. The Trustees of today have to decide if their duty lies in demolishing the large villas, uneconomic from a modern standpoint, and allowing much denser present-day development to go ahead, thus bringing in a vastly greater income for the Charity which they administer. In this way they would be able to give large sums to worthy local causes.

Some of the citizens want a social centre built on the site, with middle-price housing, halls for social activities, and other buildings which would serve the community as a whole. Both points of view have something to be said for them. The debate goes on.

One of the fascinations of the borough is the fact that traces of centuries going right back to Roman times come to the surface from time to time. In Richmond itself, especially near the river, Tudor remains are often found. To return to Asgill House; the Crown Commissioners reserved part of the very large grounds surrounding the house when leasing the villa itself to Mr. Hauptfuhrer. They built a terrace of four houses on this reserved site, fronting Old Palace Lane. While the foundations for the houses were being excavated, workmen came across obstructions which were identified as being of archaeological interest.

Building contractors understandably cannot suspend operations for very long, but information was passed to the proper quarter, and the Department of the Environment sent down a specialist to inspect the site. The Crown Commissioners and the contractors were co-operative, and agreed to a standstill for a limited period. Excavations were begun, and presently parts of ancient walls were uncovered, together with a circular cess-pit, and identified as belonging to the old palace. Once the finds had been measured and photographed and described for the official records, the work on the new houses was resumed.

So Richmond goes on: contemporary houses rising on Tudor remains, modern new roads, and parking-meter plans, and traffic-free precincts being brought up and argued over. The lively Richmond Society is ever-watchful, and its membership is growing; newcomers to the town are as much aware as the old guard of the forces that might destroy the character of the place.

Plus ça change . . . the French have a phrase for it. Essentially, Richmond has not changed its shape, limited as it is by the Park at one end, the line of the river down its side, and the built-up area which reaches into London itself. There is no more room, so what change there is inevitably takes place within the town.

The place still has a magic attraction for visitors, conjuring up the attractive riverside town it has always been. On fine days the crowds come down by train and steamer to walk by the "silver chrystall Streame". The pleasure boats glide by; young men in racing skiffs belonging to numerous clubs pull their oars at the command of a diminutive cox yelling at them above his voluminous club muffler; speed-boats skim over the water like demented arrows.

But the prettiest sight on this reach of the Thames is the yachts. They are best seen from the Terrace. Go up there one fine Sunday morning and watch the graceful flotilla tacking across the river. White sails, blue sails, red sails leaning over and catching the breeze as they turn. There are yacht clubs up-river, too, but nowhere else will you see sails rippling against such a background of islands, meadows, trees, distant spires. If the day is especially clear you can make out the line of Windsor Castle on the horizon; the direction-table will show you where to look.

So we take leave of Richmond, and this book, on the Terrace, where James Thomson loved to walk, and where he enshrined this glorious view for posterity in a matchless phrase in THE SEASONS, when he called it "the matchless Vale of Thames".

CHAPTER SEVENTEEN

Looking at Richmond

MANY of the streets, alleys, courts, and lanes in Richmond go back centuries, and tracing their 'pedigree' is a fascinating and abiding interest. Some of them have been swept into successive widening and improvement schemes (Richmond has a long record of improving herself) but the old names often survive on a row of cottages, a side-turning, or in the busy thoroughfares which are modern, and convenient to the life of today—but which are also part of the ever-present past.

The streets, roads, and lanes have been grouped into areas, so that the stroller in Richmond can take one part at a time, if desired, and perhaps be able to form a picture of what the town was like in the past, in relation to what it is now. It has not been possible to give all the streets, but those with interesting associations have been sought and included, wherever possible.

RICHMOND GREEN

This is one of the most famous greens in England, and perhaps the most beautiful. In a survey taken in 1649, the Green was described as "a piece of level turf of twenty acres, planted with one hundred and thirteen elms, forty-eight of which stand on the west side, and form a hansome walk." The jousting-place of medieval times had become "a special ornament to the town," with the fashionable promenade, the High Walk, a rendezvous for the Quality and the Wits. The Green was not surrounded by houses; the few which were there already indicated that there was beginning a period of building which is considered the high water mark of domestic architecture.

The oldest structure is, of course, the remains of Henry VII's great palace. The original gateway faces the Green; above it are still to be seen Henry VII's arms in stone, much defaced. The fragment of the palace known as 'Old Palace' still incorporates two half-towers which are to be seen, to the left of the gateway, in Wyngeard's north view.

The Old Court House, adjoining the gateway on the other side, is a beautiful early eighteenth-century house with a cottage attached. It is one of a pair of houses shown in *The Prospect of Richmond in Surrey*, 1726, a print published by Overton and Hook. In that map the two houses are shown as flat-fronted, like the Maids of Honour houses farther along. Bow windows have since been added. The one on the Old Court House, done with great skill, was probably added in the late eighteenth century. The second house, Wentworth House, was substantially remodelled in Victorian times.

Maids of Honour Row—or The Maids of Honour, as it was originally named—is an exceedingly elegant set of four houses built in 1723, by command of George I for the accommodation of the ladies of the Court in attendance on the Princess of Wales, as there was no suitable accommodation for them elsewhere in the town. The first Maids of Honour to occupy the houses were Mary Medows, Sophia Howe, Jane Smith, Bridget Cartaret, Mary Howe, and Mary Howard. They were unmarried, but enjoyed the dignity of being addressed as Mrs, that being the custom. Each Maid of Honour received £200 a year, besides board and lodging.

No. 4 Maids of Honour was once the residence of John James Heidegger. Born at Zurich in 1666, Heidegger came to England in 1708, becoming manager of the King's Theatre in the Haymarket, where Italian opera was often performed. In 1745 he engaged the chief scene painter at the theatre, Antonio Jolli, to paint the panels of the entrance hall of No. 4 Maids of Honour Row with views—more or less topographical—in Switzerland, Italy, and China. They are still in a perfect state of preservation, thanks to the care taken of them by the present owner.

The quiet square through the arch is Old Palace Yard, which was once the courtyard of the palace. On the left of this courtyard is the Wardrobe, where the furniture and hangings would have been stored; it was extensively reconstructed in the early eighteenth century but contains some of the original brick-work. The Wardrobe and the Old Palace have been leased by the Crown as private residences. The one-time Privy Garden, at the back of the Wardrobe, has been built on, and similarly leased.

On the south side of Old Palace Yard is the Trumpeters' House, or the Trumpeting House, as it was called in the seventeenth century. It was built on the site of the Middle gate of the palace, and was so called because it had two stone figures of trumpeters, or heralds, standing one on each side of the entrance. As they are apparently wearing early Tudor dress, they presumably date from the beginning of the sixteenth century. The house was built in the early seventeenth century, probably by John Yemens, Wren's successor as Surveyor of Works. It is one of the hansomest houses in Richmond, and has been converted into six spacious flats. The main facade is towards the river, and can be seen from the towing-path, a stately house at the end of the lawn, with a magnificent portico of Tuscan columns, surmounted by a pediment. In the nineteenth century it was known as the Old Palace; Metternich lived there for a time, after he had been forced to flee from Vienna during the upheavals there. Disraeli visited him in 1849, and wrote to his sister.

I have been to Metternich. He lives on Richmond Green in the most charming house in the world, called the Old Palace....I am enchanted with Richmond Green, which, strange to say, I don't recollect ever having visited before, often as I have been to Richmond. I should like you to let my house and live here....It is still and sweet, charming alike in summer and winter.

The name has reverted to Trumpeters' House by the beginning of the present century. During the Second World War it housed a Government department, and began to get delapidated. It has since been renovated, and turned into flats.

The small modern houses in Old Palace Yard were built on the site of a row of tiny cottages and stables which were bombed during the 1939–45 war. They were undisguished little dwellings, but one of them is remembered with affection because it was called Thimble Cottage. The home of a sempstress?

Tudor Lodge and Tudor Place, beyond Maids of Honour Row, formed one house in the late seventeenth century; they are shown as one unit in the drawing by Gasselin. The original house was divided into two houses, with separate doors, early in the nineteenth century. Old Friars was built in the late seventeenth century on foundations of the old Convent of Observant Friars, and added to about fifty years later. The wing joining this house with a smaller house on its south-west side has Venetian windows facing the Green. This addition was probably used as a concert hall: the "Great Room on the Green" mentioned in newspaper advertisements of concerts in the 1720s. Next to Old Friars is Old Palace Place, probably dating from 1700, with a striking façade and a fine front door. Oak House, the next house again, has a plain exterior with a massively supported porch. The staircase in this house is a good example of late eighteenth-century ironwork, and there is a fine plasterwork ceiling in the principle room on the first floor.

Old Palace Terrace, facing the

The Wick, The Terrace,
Richmond Hill

A. F. Kersting.

The Old Court House and Wentworth House, Richmond Green

Kersting.

Interior, Oak House, Richmond Green

Green, is graceful row of Queen Anne houses, once called Powell's Row, after their builder. The name was changed by the Vestry to Old Palace Terrace in 1850. Helen Faucit, who made her début at the Theatre on the Green is said to have often stayed in this Row.

The houses between the Cricketers Public House and Duke Street are Queen Anne or early Georgian. Some of them especially Nos. 11 and 12, possess fine door-cases with the original carved wood cherubs' heads and foilage. No. 3, "Gothic and embattled," conceals behind its façade a very old house with Elizabethan and Jacobean features. No. 1, with its gables and dormer windows, is one of the oldest houses in Richmond. Tradition has it that this was the house of Simon Bardolph, Shakespere's friend, and that the poet often stayed there when he was performing at the palace, and when he visited other friends he had at Isleworth. Simon Bardolph's monument is in the Parish Church.

Madame de la Tour du Pin lived for a time on the Green in 1797–98. She was one of the many émigrés who made their home in Richmond during the French Revolution. A young Englishwoman, born Lucy Dillon, she married a French aristocrat and fled the country with him. She described her house in Richmond for which she paid a rental of £45 a year:

This little house which was a real jewel was only 15 feet wide.

On the ground floor was a hall, a pretty salon with two windows and then a stairway which was hardly visable. The first floor comprised two charming bedrooms, and the floor above, two other rooms for servants. At the end of the hall, on the ground floor, was a nice kitchen which looked out on a miniature garden, with only a path and two flower beds. There were rugs everywhere, and fine English oil-cloth in the passage-ways and upon the staircase. Nothing could have been more attractive, cleaner, and more gracefully furnished than this little house, which could have all been put in a room of medium size. Our house was situated in a remote quarter called "The Green." Hardley anyone ever passed our house.

Little Green. The Little Green is divided from Richmond Green proper by a road. It was originally a piece of waste land and was granted, in 1663, by Charles II, as lord of the manor, to be made into a bowling-green for the use of copyhold tenants of the manor. The custody of the bowling-green was granted to William Drew for twenty-one years at an annual rent of twelve pence, "he having laid the green with good turf at his own expense." At the expiration of this term, the custody of the Little Green could be granted to any person for the benefit of the poor of Richmond. The poor had this benefit until 1765, when George III was allowed to add this land to his Royal Gardens. It still belongs to the Crown, but the public have the right to use it, as they do the Green.

The Public Library faces the Little Green. Richmond was one of the pioneers of the Free Public Library movement in Greater London, and the first building was formally opened in 1881. It has been considerably enlarged since that date.

Richmond Theatre also faces the Little Green (see page 143). the Presbyterian Church of England is near by.

On the north side of the Green, Pembroke Villas stand on the site of Pembroke Lodge, a Queen Anne house, with extensive gardens. It was built for Sir Charles Hedges, Secretary of State under Queen Anne, and was occupied by Sir Matthew Decker during George I's reign. It then passed to Richard, Viscount Fitzwilliam, an eccentric scholar and patron of learning, music, and the arts. He collected pictures, books, and manuscripts, many of them music; and he was an admirer of Handel, and it was through his influence that the Handel festivals were established, the first taking place in Westminster Abbey in 1784. He possessed fourteen volumes of Handel's manuscript sketches and notes, as well as the score of a flute sonata and an opera, *Rinaldo*. Another rarity was a manuscript book called *Queen Elizabeth's Virginal Book*, which contains many music lessons for the Queen's use written by Tallis, Byrd, and other sixteenth-century composers: the oldest one in the book bears the date of 1562.

Lord Fitzwilliam was a friend of George III and his queen, and was frequently their guest at St. James's and Kew; but he disliked ordinary social life, and spent the last twenty years of his life in seclusion in his house on Richmond Green. He died in 1816, and lies buried in the Decker vault in the churchyard. He left his magnificent collections to the University of Cambridge, together with sufficient money to build and endow a museum in which they could be shown. The Fitzwilliam Museum at Cambridge is his monument—a treasure house for student and layman alike.

Pembroke Lodge was rented to various tenants, and was then sold to a builder in the 1850s. He pulled down the house, sold part of the ground to the railway company, who wanted to extend the railway-line to Twickenham, and built Pembroke Villas on the remaining portion of land.

Old Palace Lane continues from The Virginals to the river. The wall on the left is the boundary wall of Garrick Close, built on the site of Garrick Villa which was, in turn, built on the site of the old Theatre. The original lane was often in a rough and muddy state, and a Local Act of Parliament of 1785 included a provision that the lane was to be "well and sufficiently amended and made commodious," as part of the deal George III made with the Vestry for the closing up of Love Lane (page 101).

The Victorian villas at the top of the Lane were built on part of the gardens of The Virginals. The terrace of small Regency houses, farther down, dates from about 1810; though there is a tradition that the Bath stone which faces these houses was left over from the building of Asgill House, fifty years before.

Golden Court, off the south side of the Green, was originally called Channon Row, then Pensioners Alley between 1609 and 1778: the later name probably because the pensioners passed down this passage on their way to the palace. The name was changed to Golden Court in 1903; nobody seems to know why.

Paved Court. Paved Alley appears in the Court Rolls several times between 1694 and 1787, as being "near King Street," After that date it appears as Paved Court. In 1694, the Vestry record states: "Wee present Captain Durrell for want of a water course to his new buildings in the paved alley. If not amended in six weeks we do amerce him 26s/8d."

In 1814, the Vestry ordered that the Surveyor of Highways "do cause a rail to be put at the end of Paved Alley next to the Green to prevent persons on Horse back going that way to the Town and that he do put down posts and turn-stiles where absolutely necessary."

King Street was first called Cross Street, and, in the eighteenth century, Furbelow Street. In the Vestry Minutes for November, 1768, it is recorded that "the street heretobefore called Furbelow Street be from henceforth called King Street"—probably in honour of King George III.

Modernisation and the incursion of trendy shops are causing the street to lose some of its individuality, but the signboard outside the upholstery establishment of M. J. Young is evidence of the continuity of the old type of craftsmanship which fortunately persists, in these old towns, into the present machine age. The business was started in the late nineteenth century by a joiner who was such a fine craftsman in wood that a pair of his hand-turned candlesticks were included in an exhibition. The present represent-atives of the family, the brothers Edward and John Young, remem-ber the donkey engine at the back of the premises, and the apprentices who came to their father's shop to be trained. The shop helps King Street to retain its character: especially since the old pharmacy on the opposite corner, which had been in the Lloyd family for the best part of a century, has been turned into a dwelling house.

Friars Lane marks the boundary line between Richmond Palace and the Convent of the observant Friars established by Henry VII. Many of the houses in the immediate area are built on some foundations of the old friary. There are several small factories tucked away in this corner, including one housed in a converted chapel.

Brewers Lane is one of the oldest streets in Richmond, appearing in the Court Rolls in 1608, and being frequently mentioned during the next two hundred years. The name probably came from the fact of there being several taverns in the Lane. It was once called Magpye Lane, after the ale-house of that name which stood there in the seventeenth century, but it is referred to more often as Brewers Lane.

Duke Street—once "Mr. Duke's Lane," after a wealthy citizen, William Duke, who lived there in the 1620s. The name was changed to Duke Street in 1769. "The Italian Coffee House in Duke's Lane, fronting the Green, in occupation of Mrs. Joyce Baldwin," afterwards the London Coffee House, is mentioned several times in the records of the 1730s and later. It is not quite clear whether this is one that became the Cobwebs public house, or whether it was on the opposite side of the road, where the Gas Company's offices now stand.

The Baptist Chapel in Duke Street was rebuilt in 1963, and is one of the best-known in Surrey.

Parkshot was known as Park Pale Shot in the 1500s. It became Parkshot about the middle of the seventeenth century. A farmstead there called George Farm is mentioned in a lease in 1705. Parkshot and Kew Foot Road appear to have been one highway about 1766, as they are referred to as West Shene Lane. George Eliot lived at No. 8, Parkshot, and wrote *Adam Bede* there. The house was demolished, and Parkshot Rooms built there, now disappears to make room for a county court.

THE HILL

Hill Rise and Hill Street. These roads are so named because they lead to Richmond Hill. They are mentioned in the Court Rolls in 1770 and onward; in a lease referring to the theatre which once stood on the lower part of the Hill, the property is stated to be "situate in a street called the Rise of the Hill." In the middle of the nineteenth century, parts of Hill Street were known by various names; that between Bridge Street and Heron Court was called Royal Terrace, the portion between Heron Court and the Town Hall, Clarence Terrace, and a section between the Vineyard and Lancaster Mews, renumbered in 1895 as 60-74 Hill Rise, was called York Place.

A fine seventeenth-century mansion, where Bishop Duppa lived, stood on the site now occupied by the Royalty Cinema, just past the entrance to Water Lane. The original Maids of Honour Shop was in existence as a baker's and pastry cook's until the 1950s, when the old façade was removed, and the shop rebuilt and modernised. It is said that J. T. Billet, one of the early owners, paid £1000 for the original recipe of the Maids of Honour, a small sweet cheese tartlet which became famous as a Richmond speciality.

Water Lane. This was called Town Lane from 1651 to 1712, when it appears in the Court Rolls as Water Lane. It was also occasionally called Thames Lane. Many of the water men lived here, either in tumble-down hovels or as lodgers in the taverns. The hovels were disparagingly referred to by the townspeople who wanted Richmond Bridge built from the end of Water Lane to the Twickenham Meadows; this would have entailed pulling down most of the buildings in Water Lane.

Red Lion Street, once called Back Lane, is mentioned in the Court Rolls several times between 1696 and 1776. The Red Lyon Inn stood at the corner of Red Lion Street and George Street in the sixteenth century, and remained there for nearly 200 years. It was rebuilt near the place where the present police-station stands, and was demolished in 1909, when the area was being rebuilt.

Lewis Road---named after John Lewis, the Richmond brewer who fought for the rights of the common people to have access to Richmond Park, and won.

Wakefield Road commemorates Thomas Wakefield, vicar of the parish from 1776 to 1806.

Heron Court. This cul-de-sac appears in the Court Rolls from the early eighteenth century until the 1850s as Herring Court. It was built on the site of the old palace mews; at that time a mews was a place where hunting hawks were confined at moulting-time.

Emma, Lady Hamilton, lived there about 1808, at the time she was pressing her claim on the British Government to fulfil Nelson's dying request to "look after Emma." (She did not succeed.) She appears also to have lived for a year or so at a small house in Bridge Street, where Merlin Cleaners now are.

Bridge Street. This was originally Ferry Hill, before the Bridge was built; the ferry was at a place just beyond the present steps down to the tow-path. Tower House, which is such a striking landmark at the Richmond end of the Bridge, is not the eighteenth-century feature that many people think it to be. It was built in 1856 by a Richmond builder called Long.

Ormond Road and Ormond Avenue. The Duke of Ormond owned the land on which these roads were built. Ormond Road was known as Ormond Row in the eighteenth century, the terrace of houses there being built between 1761 and 1778. The tow houses called The Hollies and The Rosery were originally one house, occupied by the artist Thomas Hofland, who painted many pictures of Richmond. Barbara Hofland (page 167) was a well-known writer.

Ormond Road was narrow, and the residents objected to carriages and carts going along it. In 1853, the residents placed a bar across the road to prevent traffic using it. The Vestry objected, in turn, to this high-handed proceeding, and took steps "to do away with the obstruction caused by the Bar now placed across the same." In 1877, a Mr Darley claimed the roadway as his private property (without attempting to substantiate this extraordinary claim) and had a bar put across the road. The Vestry retaliated by posting a notice declaring Ormond Road to be a public highway, and took down the bar. Mr Darley put it up again, declaring that he would follow this custom for two whole days a year. The Vestry's surveyor removed the bar once more, and continued to do so every time Mr Darley erected it. The records do not indicate who got tired first.

The famous eighteenth-century posting-inn, the Dog Inn, later known as the Talbot Hotel, stood at the corner of Ormond Road and Hill Street, where the Odeon Cinema now is.

Lancaster Park and Lancaster Cottages. Lancaster Park was built on the gardens of Lancaster House, in 1889. Miss Ramage, who lived at No. 27 Lancaster Park, achieved immortality by sitting, as a little girl, to Sir John Everett Millais for his famous picture, *Cherry Ripe*. The coloured plate of this picture appeared in a Christmas number of the *Illustrated London News*, and was an enormous success.

Lancaster Cottages were built on the site of the kitchen garden of Ellerker House.

Ellerker Gardens v was built on land belonging to Ellerker House. The large crenellated house on the corner was originally built of red brick in the Gothic style, probably late eighteenth-century. The owner of the house in the 1830s covered the brickwork with cement. the building is now a girls' school.

Friars Stile Road. Monks in the Carthusian Monastery in what is now the Old Deer Park were in the habit of taking a daily constitutional, the route of which was probably across the Green, up Brewers Lane, Church Court, Patten Alley, and Ellerker Gardens, as far as the stile at the top of the Hill, which marked the limit of their walk.

In 1725 there were only two cottages in what is now Friars Stile Road; one of them was known as the Rose Inn, and all around were fields. The Rose Inn became Rose Cottage Hotel, at which Thackeray stayed on his visits to Richmond. It is now the Marlborough Hotel.

Richmond Hill. The road up the Hill appears in the Court Rolls as the Causey, or Causeway, in 1622. The original highway led from Richmond up to what is now the Terrace, down Star and Garter Hill, and into the village of Petersham. The glory of the Hill has always been the wonderful view from the crest, a view which has inspired poets and artists throughout the centuries.

Gentlemen's mansions were built up the Hill from the sixteenth century onward, and there are traces in at least one existing house —the Richmond Gate Hotel—of Elizabethan fabric.

Much of the period architecture on the Hill dates from the eighteenth century. Cardigan House, at the beginning of the Terrace Walk, was built for the Earl of Cardigan in the late eighteenth century. It has a large Venetian window, with an oval window above and a stone relief under the pediment. The old ice-house which belonged to this house has been incorporated in the Terrace Gardens. An eighteenth-century writer, [probably Lady Mary Wortley Montagu,] described the house as standing "so shady that every apartment in it is as cool and gloomy as a grotto. Its pendant gardens are almost in the river, and so thick planted with trees that the sun has no admittance; the river appears very beautiful from it."

Wick House. The original house was built for Sir Joshua Reynolds by Sir William Chambers in 1772, and was occupied by the painter until his death in 1792; he divided his time between London and Richmond. In the Court Rolls for August 1772 there is an item stating that Sir Joshua Reynolds Knight, was erecting brick vaults

to his house on the Hill, and encroaching on the land of the lady of the manor thereby. He had to pay a rent.

The house was altered in the nineteenth century, various Victorian encrustations and a wing being added. These have since been removed. The house was damaged in the Second World War, and has been rebuilt as a residence for the nurses from the Star and Garter Home.

The Wick, at the corner of Nightingale Lane, stands on the site of the old Bull's Head Inn, which was at the top of the Hill on William Hickey's Charity Lands adjoining Sir Joshua Reynold's land. Beresford Chancellor says that the land was leased to Dame Elizabeth St Aubyn for five terms of twenty-one years each (copyhold lands in Richmond could then only be leased for twenty-one years at a time, with power of continuing for periods of the same duration). Dame St Aubyn got the lease for £20 a year, on condition that she should pull down the Inn, and that the mansion she intended to erest would be set back from the road. A new public walk, the Queen's Terrace, had been constructed, and it was proposed to extend the walk to the gates of the Park. The lady of the manor gave an equal part of the land to that taken from the new mansion, which had the dividing-line between it and the Queen's Terrace fenced off with posts, rails, and chains. The mansion was built for

Lady St Aubyn by Robert Mylne in 1775, and it is one of the most elegant eighteenth-century houses in Richmond, with an oval drawing-room which presents a charming bowed window on the river side; this can be seen above the wall as one ascends Nightingale Lane from Petersham Road.

The Star and Garter Home for Disabled Men stands on the site of the second Star and Garter Hotel, which was demolished in 1919. '

Ancaster House, at the other side of the road, adjoins the Park. In 1772, Peregrine, Duke of Ancaster, was granted a piece of waste land by the lady of the manor, Queen Charlotte, outside the gates of the New Park. There was already a house there, owned by Mary Burchell; she surrendered it to the Duke for an annuity of £43 10s. 0sd. He pulled down the house and built a new one of red brick on the site, making gardens and building out-houses.

The house passed to Sir Lionel Darell, a friend of George III. Darell wanted a small piece of extra land on which to build gree-houses, and applied to the Commis-sioners of Crown Lands for it, but there were the usual bureaucratic delays. One day, when the King, riding in the Park, stopped to talk, Darell mentioned, "with due deference", his difficulties. The King asked how much land was required, and when Darell in-dicated the extent, George III got

' See page 160.

down from his horse, picked up a stick, and said: "That is very lillte indeed, Sir Lionel: are you sure it will be enough? Don't stint your-self." He then marked out the line himself, and added: "There, Sir Lionel, that is your ground; it is mine no longer." The proper docu-ments were soon forthcoming after that, and Darell built his green-houses, paying an annual quit-rent for the ground.

The house is now the official residence of the Commandant of the Star and garter Home, and for nursing staff.

Morshead House, now the Rich-mond Gate Hotel, is a beautiful late eighteenth-century house at the corner of The Terrace and Queen's Road. Adjoining it are two much old-er cottages, originally Elizabethan.

Doughty House, a fine mid-eight-eenth-century mansion, acquired its name from Elizabeth Doughty, who lived there, dying in 1826. She was a pious Roman Catholic, and built the Roman Catholic Church of St Elizabeth in the Vineyard. She had property in London, and Doughty Street is named after her family.

Doughty House was completely Victorianised in the late nineteenth century, when a small gallery was built on at the side, to house the pictures collected by Sir Francis Cook, the art connoisseur. The col-lection has now been dispersed, and Doughty House turned into flats.

Downe House, Norfolk House, and Ashburton House were formerly one large house. Richard Brinsley Sheridan lived for a time at Downe House.

In another house near by, known as the Terrace House, Edward Fitzgerald, translator of Omar Khayyám, lived with his mother, in 1849.

No. 3, The Terrace, one of the most famous houses on the Hill, was built in or about 1769, probably by Sir Robert Taylor, the City Architect of the time, and designer of the Mansion House in London. Taylor had studied in Italy, and No. 3, The Terrace is, according to one writer, "a bold and solid version of Pallandianism which contrasts markedly with the more graceful neo-classical forms of the period". It is a lovely example of a small Geogian house, set in a unique situation: the views over the river from that particular spot are superb. Mrs Fitzherbert is said to have been living in this house when she first met George IV, then Prince of Wales. He married her in 1785, the Vicar of Twickenham, the Reverand Robert Burt, performing the ceremony, and they spent their honeymoon at No. 3.

Nightingale Lane descends steeply from the Hill to Petersham Road. It was named after Nightingale Cottage, the home of the daughters of the 2nd Earl of Ashburnham, who had a house at the top of the Hill. The cottage was demolished in 1867. Nightingale Hall, just off the Lane, was a nineteenth-century

house later incorporated into a hotel, the Star and Garter, named after the famous inn which once stood above it.

Queen's Road runs from the fountain, opposite the Star and Garter Home, down to Sheen Road. It was probably named in honour of Queen Victoria, though there was a Queen's Way in the Upper Field of Richmond in 1605. In the early nineteeth century it was called Black Horse Lane, and also Muddy Lane. In 1825 it was a country road with only four houses, pollarded willows, and a pond in which was mirrored a row of weeping willows.

Joseph Ellis, the proprietor of the Star and Garter Inn, proposed to widen Black Horse Lane and make it into a proper road, but tradesmen in the town objected, as they thought visitors would go up the new road straight to the Star and garter, without passing through the town. The Lane was made into a road later in the century.

The Methodist College, 1843 was built on the site of an eighteenth-century mansion in which lived Francis Grose, father of the antiquary. Alexander William Kinglake, the author of *Eothen*, lived at 8, Park Villas West, off Queen's Road.

A public House in Queen's Road, The Lass of Richmond Hill, keeps alive a controversy which generally blows up when inhabitants of the two Richmonds—Richmond in Surrey and Richmond in Yorkshire —happen to meet.

A PROSPECT OF RICHMOND

It is perhaps time to examine the claim that the song, *The Lass of Richmond Hill*, refers to a Yorkshire lady. This claim rests on a tradition that an Irish barrister called McNally was engaged to a Miss Fanny L'Anson of Richmond, Yorkshire, and that he wrote the song in her praise. He may well have celebrated Miss L'Anson's charms in verse, but there is considerable doubt that he wrote the well-known *The Lass of Richmond Hill*.

Controversy over the authorship of the song kept coming up in *Notes and Queries* from time to time during the nineteenth century. An innocent inquiry from a reader would set off a fresh spate of partisan letters, and the same arguments would be repeated again and again. The stand taken by Yorkshire was based on family loyalties, descendants of the McNally-L'Anson union asserting that there was no doubt whatever that Fanny L'Anson was the original Lass. They produced no proof: family tradition was enough for them. Surrey pointed put it was well established that William Upton wrote the words of the song, and James Hook composed the music. There are entries in the Subject Indexes of the British Museum Music Room supporting this. According to the *Public Advertiser* of August 3, 1789, *The Lass of Richmond Hill* was first sung by Mr Incledon at Vauxhall Gardens, "being written by William Upton, author of *A Collection of Songs sung at Vauxhall Gardens*." Upton wrote many of the ballads which were sung at the London pleasure gardens, and Hook composed the music for over two thousand songs sung there; he was organist successively at Marylebone gardens and Vauxhall Gardens.

Several women claimed either to be the heroine of *The Lass of Richmond Hill* or had the claim made for them. A Miss Smith of Richmond in Surrey was convinced that she was the one, and told the local tradesmen so. Lady Sarah Lennox was another candidate, though a stronger one was Hannah Lightfoot, "the fair Quakeress", whose equivocal relationship with George III led to her being expelled from the sect. It is said that a deputation from the Society of Friends presented themselves before the King and informed him of her expulsion. one of them exclaiming: "Now! thee seest what thee hast done!"

Sir Henry Bishop, who collected the national melodies of England, which were published from time to time in the *Illustrated London News* between 1851 and 1855, told one of his associates, Charles Mackay: "The words—I cannot call them poetry—of the Lass of Richmond Hill were written by William Upton, the poet of Vauxhall Gardens."

The evidence seems to come down fairly on the side of the Vauxhall Gardens song-writer, and one can then ask: why should Mr Upton, obviously a highly sophisticated metropolitan, write a song about a girl in far away Yorkshire? Richmond in that county is never called Richmond on the Hill. In ant case, to the frequenters of Vauxhall Gardens, Richmond in Yorkshire would have had no significance, whereas Richmond Hill, on the Thames, would be exactly the place where Londoners would go for an outing.

When all is said and done, however, it is likely that there was, in fact, no original for *The Lass of Richmond Hill*, and that the correspondent in *Notes and Queries* who wrote "It does not appear that the song was intended for any particular person" was probably right. Sir Henry Bishop may not have considered the verses "poetry", but the charming song has a lightness and gaiety which has gained for it a place in the affections of singers and audiences in succeeding generations—far beyond the two Richmonds who claim the "Lass" as their own.

Richmond in Surrey appears—this time without question—in Tom Durfey's *On the Brow of Richmond Hill*, set by Purcell; and also in the same writer's play:

The Richmond Heiress, or
A Woman Once in the Right,
Written by Mr D'Urfey and acted
at the Theatre Royal in Drury
Lane
MDCCXVIII
Scene 1   Richmond Hill

Flowtow's charming little comic opera, *Marta*, is also set in Richmond in Surrey.

RETURNING TO THE
CENTRE OF THE TOWN

George Street—the main street of the town. It was formerly called Great Street, Common Street, High Street, London Street, and Richmond Street, and was re-named George Street in honour of George III, in 1769.

The original Castle Hotel stood at the Quadrant end of George Street.

Paradise Road is a continuation of Red Lion Street. The side of a monastery or a church which faces south used to be called "Paradise", and this name was given to the Row, afterwards Road, which was made on the south side of the parish church about 1716.

The writers Leonard and Virginia Woolf lived for a time at Hogarth House, next to Suffield House, and started the famous Hogarth Press there. Some records state that both houses were once one large country hiuse, divided into two houses in the nineteenth century. It had been sold and divided into two houses in the nineteenth century, and Leonard Woolf tells in the third volume of his autobiography how he and his wife fell in love with Hogarth House and obtained a lease if it in 1915. A year later, they decided to become publishers, taught themselves the rudiments of printing, installed a small printing machine on the dining-room table, and after a month's practice were able to print a 32-page pamphlet.

Paradise Road had a bar-gate across it in the early 1800s and there was another across the end of Mount Ararat Road; these were used to keep private a road to a large house lying back from Sheen Road. This time the Vestry allowed their use, on condition that tenants and owners of houses near by could have keys to unlock the gates.

Church Cour —formerly Church Lane, leading from George Street to the Parish Church. Church Lane is mentioned frequently in the Court Rolls of the Manor of Richmond from 1614 onward.

Church Walk on the north side of the Parish Church, has the charming Church rooms, originally built in 1815 as a residence for the Curate of Richmond.

Church Terrace —probably the Church rowe mentioned in the Court Rolls of 1736–42. The Bethlehem Chapel, built in 1797, is still used as a meeting house. William Huntington, the coal-heaver-preacher who used after his name the initials SS—Sinner Saved —preached here on several occasions. He quoted Scripture, in the pulpit, from Genesis to Relevations,

"with wonderful ease and fluency", rode in his chariot, his postilion wearing purple livery, and married the widow of a Lord Mayor of London.

Patten Alley. In 1754, Ann Patten was admitted tenant of the manor under the will of her late husband, John Patten. In 1762 she surrendered a piece of land in Church shot, leading from Ormond road to the church, and from the church to the Hill. This may be the origin of the name.

Halford Road —named after an old Richmond brewing family prominent in the town throughout the eighteenth century. John Halford, born probably in the 1720s, was licensee of the Castle Hotel, which remained in the family for two generations.

The Vineyard. The orchards and vineyard here belonged to the Carthusian Monastery until the Dissolution which followed Henry VIII's edict and they were built over during the next two hundred years. Next to the Roman Catholic Church of St Elizabeth (1902) is a Congregational Church with a fine porch, built by Vulliamy in 1831. There are three sets of almshouses in the Vineyard. The Michel Almshouses, for ten old men, were founded by Humphrey Michel and his nephew John; they were finished in the early eighteenth century, rebuilt in 1811, and had several more houses added in 1858. The income from Michel's Row, near the roundabout at the junction of

Kew Road and the Quadrant, goes to this Charity.

Duppa's Almshouses are near by. Bishop Brain Duppaa, chaplain to Charles I and tutor to the royal children, retired quietly to his house at Richmond after the King's execution. He lived to see the Restoration, and provided in his will, dated 1661, for almshouses to be erected as a thank-offering for his safety during the dangerous time for Royalists during the Commonwealth. The original almshouses, for ten poor women of the age of fifty upwards, were first built on the Hill, and the almswomen, were each to get, on Christmas Eve, "a fine barn-door fowl and a pound of bacon." They were also allowed £1 15s. 0d. monthly, for their keep. Bishop Duppa took great care to tie up the legal side of the charity, but he could not forsee that the Rev. Mr Comer, the minister of the Parish, and his churchwarden, would manage to keep the Vestry out of office for seventeen years, and so avoid any awkward queations about the income which should have been spent on the almswomen. Local history does not relate how the ten poor women lived during that time.

The almshouses had become dilapidated by the middle of the nineteenth century, and they were removed to their present position in the Vineyard, some of the original stone being used, including the gateway, which bears the inscription: *Deo et Carolo, Votiva Tabula* I will pay the vows which I made to God in my trouble.

Queen Elizabeth's Almshouses were founded by Sir George Wright in 1600 (or 1606, the date given by Lysons and Manning), for eight poor women. They were originally built on the Lower Road, and rebuilt in the Vineyard during the 1760s.

The Hermitage—named after the large eighteenth-century house which is still there. There road is built over some of the former gardens of the house. Duppa's Almshouses stand on part of the orchard which once belonged to the Hermitage.

Mount Ararat Road. Originally called Worple Way, in 1837, this road was a winding lane with hedges; close by were several duckponds surrounded by weeping willows. There was an eighteenth-century house, called Mount Ararat, at the corner of the Vineyard, a farmyard on the site of the present Ely House, and a cottage and yard between Paradise Road and the Vineyard.

Chisholm Road—formerly Chisholm Villas. Here lived Miss Fellowes, hereditary Herb Woman to the royal family, the dignity having been conferred on her by George IV. The duty of the Herb Woman was to strew herbs before the King at his Coronation. The original Miss Fellowes, with six maids, richly dressed in white, performed this duty in style for George IV, she herself wearing, in addition, a scarlet mantle trimmed with gold lace.

—probably named after Dynevor House, a mansion which stood at the top of Mount Ararat Road. Lieutenant General Sir Bernard Freyberg, V.C., D.S.O., was born at No. 8 in 1889.

named after Rebecca Houblon, who, with her sister, founded the almshouses bearing her name in 1757, She was the descendant of a Huguenot family which fled to this country in the mid-sixteenth century. Her father, Sir John Houblon, became Lord Mayor of London in 1696, and was one of the founders of the Bank of England, and its first governor.

Audley Road—named after Miss Braddon's famous novel, *Lady Audley's Secret*.

Returning again to the town, a good starting-point for a further stroll is   a miniature street-circus with radiating streets. In the seventeenth and eighteenth centuries, this part of Richmond was known as World's End. (World's End is a common term in country districts, and is usually given to the farthest house or field from the village centre.) The Bear Inn was the beginning of the town; the pound and the Town Gate were situated here.

The square in its present form was built in the 1870s. Henry Rydon, a member of the Richmond Vestry, took a lease of the buildings then standing at the corner of Duke Street and George Street. They included Tolley's saddler's shop, a blacksmith's forge, a print-shop, a tobacconist's, a number of small wooden sheds used as shops of various kinds, and an old drill-shed of the local Volunteer Corps. They were all dilapidated, and Rydon had them pulled down, building a row of good shops in their places. He also widened this end of Kew Road.

Dome Buildings were reconstructed from a Baptist Chapel and later used as a Mechanics' Institute, and still later, a public baths.

The original name of this road was Marshgate, which appears in the Court Rolls from 1603 onward. The land in the vicinity was of a swampy nature; there is an item in the Court Rolls for 1656 which refers to a piece of land near Marshgate:

We do find [it] to be full of bogs and founderous places whereby the cattle feeding and depasturing upon the Common and thereon indangered and sometimes destroyed by sinking into those springy places out of which they cannot at some times be gotten forth but are thereby destroyed.

They go on the petition the lord of the manor "to inclose it to the best advantage of the Parish." The name survives in Marshgate House, No. 36, Sheen road. In an auction sale catalogue of 1857, the road is shown as Marsh road. It is probable that the name was changed to Sheen Road about the end of the nineteenth century, in order to preserve the old name of Richmond.

Lichfield Court was built on the site of Lichfield House, a Victorian mansion standing in its own grounds. This was the home for many years of Miss M. E. Braddon, the novelist, John Maxwell, her publisher, invested in a great deal of property in the King's Road district, and named several roads after characters in Miss Braddon's novels.

The Houblon Almshouses were built by Rebecca and Susanna Houblon in 1757–58, for nine poor women. Hickey's Almshouses, for men and women. also stand in Sheen Road; a chapel divided the men's from the women's quarters.

King's Road. This road may be named after King's College, Cambridge, the patron of the living of Richmond; or it may have been so named as a suitable balance for near-by Queen's Road. In 1868, the site of King's Road was still all fields. There were a few small houses, and one large mansion, Abercorn, built about 1866, contining a fine entrance hall and staircase. Ex-King Manoel and his mother, the ex-Queen Amélie, lived here for a time when they came to England after the revolution in Portugal in 1911.

King's Farm Avenue perpetuates the name of a farm of about 80 acres belonging to George III which stood on the site of this road. "Farmer George" used to ride over from his palace at Kew to supervise the work at the farm.

Lower Richmond Road is the continuation of Lower Mortlake Road. In a house near the present Gas Works, known as Shakespere Cottage, lived an old lady, Nrs Elizabeth Evans, who died there i. 1914, at the age of eighty-four. She was a Crimean heroine, having accompanied her husband to the Crimean War, remaining there for two years. Mrs Evans was one of the three women who were permitted to go with the army on the march to Alma, and she was also present with the camp-followers at Inkerman, and helped to tend the wounded there.

Gainsborough Road——named after the painter. Thomas Gainsborough (1727–88). He often stayed at Kew. Two of his best-known portraits are "Little Miss Haverfield," of the Kew family of haverfields, and of Elizabeth, the lovely Duchess of Devonshire, a famous eighteenth-century beauty.

Evelyn Gardens and Evelyn Road, off Kew Road—probably named to commemorate John Evelyn, who visited Richmond many times, and mentions the town in his Diaries.

Kew Foot Road, or Kew foot-road, as it is sometimes written in the records, is on the other side of the by-pass leading into Kew Road. Its chief interest is Richmond Hospital, which incorporates the home of James Thomson, the poet, who lived at what was then Rosedale House from 1736 until his death in 1748. The house was then a simple cottage; behind it was his garden, and in front he looked out at the Thames and the wooded landscape beyond. Thomson is buried in the Parish Church, where there is a brass tablet to his memory. After his death the cottage was sold, in 1749, to George Ross, a friend of the poet, who spent £9000 on enlarging and improving it, in memory of Thomson. Ross called it Rossdale House, which became Rosedale House in time.

The property later came into the possession of Francis Boscawen, the widow of Admiral Boscawen, who was an admirer of Thomson's and preserved all the relics of the poet she could collect. On her death in 1805, the house was bought by the 6th Earl of Shaftesbury, who lived there and re-named it Shaftesbury House. After his death, and that of his wife, the Thomson relics were removed to the Shaftesbury seat in Dorset, where they still may be. The house reverted to its name of Rosedale House, and was made part of the Royal Hospital in the latter part of the nineteenth century. The entrance hall is part of James Thomson's original cottage.

Petersham Road forks away from Hill Rise at the beginning of Richmond Hill. It was originally known as the Lower Causey or Causeway, to distinguish it from the Causeway, Richmond Hill's former name. It then became known as the Lower Road, untill the name was officially changed to Petersham Road in 1893.

Compass Hill, which runs from Petersham Road to the beginning of the Hill, is named after the inn, the Compasses, now demolished. In the Court Rolls for 1737 it is recorded that William Toms was fined 4s. per annum for building and enclosing a bench outside the Compasses, the fine to continue until the bench was removed.

There are a number of old houses on Petersham Road. Northumberland House* was built in 1766 for George Colmann the Elder, dramatist and stage manager. He called it Bath House after his patron, the Earl of Bath, and lived there until his death in 1794. David Garrick and Oliver Goldsmith often visited Colman there. It was later called Cambourne House. In 1857, the house was let to the Duchess of Orleans. Eleanor, Dowager Duchess of Northumberland lived there from 1873 to 1879, and changed the name to Northumberland House. It has been the headquarters of the Richmond Club since 1884.

Bingham House Hotel was formerley two small houses, built about the middle of the eighteenth century on the site of a small riverside tavern, the Blue Anchor. In 1821, Lady Anne Bingham leased the land and houses, and built the present house.

Ivy Hall Hotel was known as Mr Hobart's house in the late eighteenth century; this was the Hon. Henry Hobart, a prominent member of the Vestry. The Duke of Clarence is said to have lived here with Mrs Jordan, 1789–90, while his own house in the Vineyard was being restored after a fire.

*now demolished

The four houses which comprise Paragon Row, in Petersham Road, are very probably late eighteenth century. No. 1 was the home for some years of Edith Emma Cooper and Katherine Harris Bradley, two poets who wrote jointly under the name of "Michael Field." Miss Cooper died here in 1913, and Miss Bradley in 1914.

The British Legion Poppy Factory, which makes all the poppies that are sold during the Remembrance period every November, is in Petersham Road.

THE RIVERSIDE

Cholmondeley Walk, which stretches along the riverside from the end of Old Palace Lane to Water Lane, is called after George, the 3rd Earl of Cholmondeley. It has always been a favourite place for strolling. John Evans recommended it wholeheartedly to the readers of his Handbook in 1824:

The Promenade, on a summer evening, along Cholmondeley Walk, and in view of the Bridge, with a band of music playing on the water, imparts an animation to the whole range of its rustic scenery. Gentlemen and ladies, beaux and belles, cross each other in every direction. Indeed Fashion exhibit themselves with every possible attraction. A fine female face, beaming softness and intelligence, never fails to command admiration. He went on to conjure up a scene which epitomised Richmond on a fine summer's day. The pleasure steamers from London, "stately as swans," appeared every two hours or so, and the passengers disembarked at the pier below the Bridge, the Fashion and Beauty from the capital mingling with the local

Quality walking on the Promenade. Not all the visitors were of the "remarkably refined character" which he so admired. There were pickings to be had at Richmond—at the Assembly Rooms, the houses of entertainment, the Coffee Rooms and gaming establishments. Many a pickpocket, confidence trickster and women-of-the-town prinked out in fashionable clothes stepped jauntily off the London steamer, ready to mix business with pleasure. So it had always been in this riverside resort, as in other places where holiday crowds gathered; there were frequent warnings in the London newspapers against such "miscreants."

The steamers still come from London during the summer season, and though the beaux and belles dress differently, and a trail of transistors has replaced the bands of music playing on the water, there is still animation and a sense of anticipation and enjoyment as the passengers disembark at the piers.

Until the mid-eighteenth century there was no public right of way along the riverside. Private gardens, and quays belonging to the villas on the banks, reached to the water's edge, with spaces here and there—as at Water Lane—for a ferry. A small strip of river front, known as Waterside, connected Friars Lane with Water Lane, and in 1780 a barge-walk was constructed as far as the grounds of Buccleuch House. Here permission was refused for the continuation of the walk, and it was not until the 1880s, when the grounds of Buccleuch House and Lansdowne House were acquired by the town, that this towing-path was connected with a promenade which had been made on embankments shoring up the river banks from Petersham to Richmond.

There are a number of fine houses facing the river. Asgill House, at the end of Old Palace Lane, was built by Sir Robert Taylor in 1758 for Sir Charles Asgill. It is of buff-coloured stone, and has an unusual frontage-dictated by the ground plan, the house having been built on some of the foundations of the old palace, which probably included a turret. There are extensive gardens behind a high wall which runs along Old Palace Lane. The interior of the house is notable for its staircase and plasterwork. The beautiful octagonal room on the first floor was decorated by Andrea Casali.

Sir Charles Asgill was a wealthy banker. Starting as a clerk in a banking-house in Lombard Street, "he rose progressively by merit, and soon after marrying an amiable woman with a fortune of £25,000, joined his name to the firm."

The riverside elevation of Trumpeters' House, already described, is next seen at the end of its long lawn (Page 186).

An ancient copper-beech tree with a barrel-shaped trunk on the towpath is the landmark for Queensberry Mansions, a large block of attractive flats which have been built on the site of the second Queensberry House that stood in these grounds. The entrance to the flats is in Friars Lane but they can best be seen in their garden setting from the towing-path. They stand on ground of some local historic significance. George, 2nd Earl of Cholmondeley, built the first house in 1708, on some of the foundations of the old palace. The house was sold in 1780 to the 4th Duke of Queensberry, notorious in the early decades of the nineteenth century as "Old Q"—a decrepit roué, a man of pleasure who is said to have sat on the balcony of his Piccadilly house ogling pretty passers-by "with the only eye available for this purpose, a messenger standing by a saddled horse in readiness to pursue any young female who took his fancy." True or not, this legendary tit-bit illustrates the image his contempories had of Old Q. "The key to the infirmities of his character," says Garnett, seems to be that, like Charles II, he had an excess of common-sense unassociated with any ideal or patriotic aspiration which would have pointed out a befitting employment of his vast wealth and remarkable abilities. The consequent course of selfish dissipation, relieved only by charities which, although magnificent, imposed no trouble upon the benefactor, gradually wore down an originally buoyant nature until the spirited youth became the sated voluptuary.

The saddest comment on Old Q comes in Wilberforces's account of an occasion when he came to Richmond to dine with the Duke. The views from the villa were delightful and the river looked glorious that day; but the Duke of Queensberry gazed at it with indifference. "What is there to make so much of in the Thames?" he asked. "I am quite weary of it; there it goes, flow, flow, flow, always the same."

Old Q had other sides to his complex character. His letters to George Selwyn bring out his common sense and an unexpected, unselfish kindness and loyalty. He was a connoisseur: he filled his house with good paintings, tapestries, and furniture. Horace Walpole wrote to Mary Berry in 1790 that the Duke "had frequent company' and 'music of an evening. I intend to go," and mentioned that the Prince of Wales (afterwards George IV) and Mrs Fitzherbert were dining at Queensberry House. Such lavish and constant hospitality meant quite considerable business for the local tradesmen. Old Q was well liked in the town; not only did he spend a great deal of money in the shops but he gave generously towards local charities. It was therefore a great pity that he should have fallen out with Richmond. He enclosed a strip of land (now the towing-path) to add to his grounds; the reason why he wanted it is not quite clear, but the way he took it, without a by-your-leave, roused local resentment. It is possible that it did not occur to him that the common land belonged to the parish: he may have looked on it as waste land and there for the taking. If he had not acted so highhandedly, some compromisee might have been made. As it was, when the Vestry protested the Duke flew into a passion—but did not return the strip of land.

The Vestry were in a difficulty. The Duke of Queensberry was a benefactor to Richmond, and they did not wish to antagonise him. At the same time, the land he had unlawfully taken as common land belonging to the town, and the Vestry's duty was to the inhabitants. As the Duke would not give way, there was no course open but to institute proceedings against him. The Vestry won the lawsuit, and the Duke of Queensberry left Richmond and never returned to it. He bequethed his house there to a young lady of Italian extraction on the distaff side, of whom he believed himself to be the father (his friend, George Selwyn, thought

A PROSPECT OF RICHMOND

he was the father). In the event, the young lady did very well out of the connection. She married Lord Yarmouth (who recieved £200,000) ultimately became the Marchioness of Hertford, inherited another fortune from George Selwyn, and "for excellent reasons always resided in Paris." Queensberry House, long unoccupied, was pulled down in 1829. Sir William Dundas built another house near the site with materials taken from the old one—this was the house described by Baroness Orczy as the Richmond home of the Scarlet Pimpernel.[1] It was demolished in the 1930s, and the present block of flats erected.

Cholmondeley Lodge and Cholmondeley House, now separate houses, were originally parts of an eighteenth-century mansion.

St Helena's Terrace—a row of early nineteenth-century houses, approached by private steps, above boat-houses which still bear the names of old Richmond families of boat-builders and watermen. The Terrace records Napoleon's banishment.

Lansdowne Alcoves. This is the best preserved of the three grottos in the Thames Valley; the other two were Pope's Grotto at Twicken-

ham and Garrisk's Grotto at Hampton, Samuel Johnson, in his *Lives of the Poets,* describes a grotto as a subterraneous passage to a garden on the other side of the road, adding that "Pope's excavation was requisite as an entrance to his garden, and, as some men try to be proud of their defects, he extracted an ornament from an inconvenience, and vanity produced a grotto where necessity enforced a passage"—the reference being to the outlandish decoration of shells and other "fossil bodies" with which Pope adorned his underground passage.

The Lansdowne Grotto connected Buccleuch House with the riverside, and has well-preserved Roman marbles built into the walls. **Glover's Ait,** the biggest island in the river here, and one which gives such distinction to the view from the Terrace, was presented to the town at the turn of the twentieth century by Sir Max waechter.

Mears Walk—named, in 1935, after Alderman Joseph T. Mears, who presented the strip of land for the improvement of the towing-path. The Mears family have been local watermen for generations.

[1] With a novelist's licence, however, as this house did not exist at the time of the French Revolution.

APPENDIX A

Richmonds Overseas

There are towns called Richmond in several parts of the world: in Cape Province, Natal, New South Wales, Queensland, South Australia, Tasmania New Zealand, the Fiji Islands, Ontario, Quebec, Jamaica; and over twenty in the United States of America. Many of them were named by men who had emigrated from either Richmond, Yorkshire, or Richmond, Surrey. For instance, Canon Smith, an Anglican minister, established a small mission in Alberta, Canada, and called a near-by hill Richmond Hill because it reminded him of the famous hill in his home town, Richmond in Surrey. William Snow, who named a new settlement near Nelson, South Island, New Zealand, after Richmond, in Surrey, went a step further and called the public houses there the Star and Garter, and other inn names after those in the Surrey town.

Richmond, Virginia, was given its name in the 1730s by William Byrd, a wealthy young Virginian planter who had been sent to England for his education and returned home to become a leader in the young Colony. He possessed "brilliant talents, culture, and a captivating personality," and he was ambitious for Virginia. In 1733, when he wanted some of his property surveyed, he asked four or five of his friends to make up a party to travel into the wilderness. "In the evenings, while the servants prepared dinner, the gentlemen would sit round the camp-fire and talk of their experiences and their dreams for the future. Colonel Byrd and his friend, Peter Jones, who owned lands along the Appomattox River, had a dream in common. They wished to build cities—one on the James [River] and the other at the falls of the Appomattox. . . . 'Thus we did not build castles only, but also Citys in the Air.' "

Byrd built his city on the James River, and called it Richmond, "because the red hills rising from the river reminded him of Richmond on the Thames, near London, where he had spent many happy days while studying in England." The formation of the river must have reminded him of the Thames at Richmond, too. It loops and curves near the city in a way that is extraordinarily reminiscent of Richmond in Surrey, with several islands patterning the water, the largest reminding one irresistibly of Glover's Ait, which is such a feature in the view from Richmond Hill.

[215]

APPENDIX B

The Old Shots related to Modern Streets

The approximate boundaries of the Shots were on the sites of the following modern streets:

Long Common or Heath Shot—Friars Stile Road to the top of Richmond Hill, Queen's Road, Park Road.

May Bush or Red Conduit Shot—Ellerker Gardens, Richmond Hill, Friars Stile Road, Mount Ararat Road.

West Bancroft Shot—Ellerker Gardens, Richmond Hill, Vineyard, Onslow Road.

East Bancroft Shot—Onslow Road, Vineyard, Mount Ararat Road, Ellerker Gardens.

Long Downs Shot—Queen's Road, Mount Ararat Road, Marchmont Road, King's Road.

Church Conduit Shot—Vineyard, Hill Rise, George Street, Sheen Road, King's Road, Marchmont Road.

Marsh Furze Shot—Queen's Road, Sheen Road, King's Road, Marchmont Road.

Upper and Lower Dunstable Shots—between Sheen Road and Lower Mortlake Road, Manor Road, Quadrant.

Lower Shot—triangle between Kew Road, Lower Mortlake Road, and Pagoda Avenue.

Park Shot or Park Pale Shot—Duke Street, Quadrant, Kew Road, and Kew Foot Road to Kew Gardens.

Bank Shot—Kew Road, Broomfield Road, Mortlake Road, Sandycombe Road, Lower Mortlake Road, Pagoda Avenue.

Sources

Sources include

State Papers, 1232–1772.
Court Rolls, 1603–1792.
Vestry Records.
Parish Registers.
Annual Register.
Notes and Queries.
Richmond Notes.
Richmond and Twickenham Times.
Thames Valley Times.
Richmond Herald.
Surrey Comet.

Stow's *Annales.*
Gentleman's Magazine.
London Magazine.
General Advertiser
and other journals
of the eighteenth and
nineteenth centuries.

Books consulted include

MANNING, O., and BRAY, W., *History etc. of Surrey* (1804–14).
HERVEY, JOHN, BARON: *Memoirs of Reign of George II.*
HAWKINS, LAETITIA-MATILDA: *Anecdotes*, etc. (1822).
PAPENDIEK, MRS C. L. H.: *Court and Private Life in the Time of Queen Charlotte.*
WALPOLE, HORACE, FOURTH EARL OF ORFORD: *Correspondence*, 1788–1796.
BURNEY, FANNY: *Diary and Letters.*
HOFLAND, B.: *Richmond and Its Surrounding Scenery* (1832).
EVANS, JOHN: *Richmond and its Vicinity* (1825).
STRICKLAND, AGNES: *Lives of the Queens of England.*
WILLIAMS, FOLKESTONE: *Domestic Memoirs of the Royal Family, and of the Court of England, Chiefly at Shene and Richmond* (1863).
CRISP, R.: *Richmond and its Inhabitants from the Olden Time* (1866).
CHANCELLOR, E. BERESFORD: *History and Antiquities of Richmond, Kew, Petersham, Ham, etc.* (1894).
GARRETT, R.: *Richmond on the Thames* (1896).
GASCOYNE, S. T.: *Recollections of Richmond* (1898).
BURT, C.: *The Richmond Vestry* (1890).
CUNDALL, H. M.: *Bygone Richmond* (1925).
COLLENETTE, C. L.: *A History of Richmond Park* (1937).
WARREN, C. D.: *History of St. Peter's Church, Petersham* (1938).
SALUSBURY-JONES, G. T.: *Street Life in Mediaeval England* (1939).
SALZMAN, L. F.: *English Life in the Middle Ages* (1926).
TREVELYAN, G. M.: *English Social History* (1946).

[217]

Index

Index

Church Rooms, 206
Church Terrace, 206
Church Walk, 206
Cibber, Theophilus, 136
Clarence Terrace, 198
Clarke, Mary Anne, 113
Cleves Road, 112
Cobwebs, The (formerly Coffee House Tavern), 162, 198
Cockdell, Thomas, 68, 71
Comer, Rev. William, 78, 207
Common Street (now George Street), 205
Compass Hill, 161, 210
Compasses Inn, 161, 210
Compton, Sir Spencer, 78
Condon's Market (now The Market), 185
Congregational Church, 206
Court Rolls, 66, 76
Cowper, William, 103
Cricket, 96, 153
Cricketers Inn (formerly the Crickett Players), 162
Cross, Charles Frederick, 178

Darell, Sir Lionel, 202
Dee, Dr John, 52–53, 57
Devonshire Lodge (previously Devonshire Cottage), 118, 188
Dickens, Charles, 111, 121, 159
Dimbleby, Richard, 182
Dog Inn, 161, 200
Doggett's Coat and Badge, 146
Dome Buildings, 208
Doughty House, 202
Douglas, Catherine, Duchess of Queensberry, 108–110
Douglas, William, 4th Duke of Queensberry ("Old Q"), 212–213
Douglas House, 108, 117
Downe House, 112, 202–203
Drainage, 68–69
Duck, Stephen, 83
Ducking, 68
Duke Street (formerly Duke's Lane), 47, 198
Duppa, Bishop Brian, 62, 198, 207
Duppa's Almshouses, 207
Durfey, Thomas, 205
Dutch House, Kew, 97
Dynevor Road, 208
Dysart, Elizabeth, Countess of—see Murray, Elizabeth
Dysart, Lionel, 4th Earl of—see Murray, Lionel
Dysart, William, 1st Earl of—see Murray, William

Edward the Confessor, 1
Edward I, 3

Edward II, 4
Edward III, 5–6, 7–9
Edward IV, 23–24
Edward V, 25
Edward VI, 39, 41, 52
Eleanor of Castile, 3
Elizabeth of York (queen of Henry VII), 25, 31, 32
Elizabeth, Princess (daughter of George III), 131
Elizabeth Tudor, 40, 41, 43, 44–46, 49–57, 95
Ellerker Gardens, 200
Ellerker House, 200
Ellis, Sir John Whittaker, 173, 174, 175
Ellis, Joseph, 159, 203
Elm Lodge, 111
Evans, Mrs Elizabeth, 209
Evans, Dr John, 137, 159, 164–166, 211
Evelyn Gardens and Road, 209

Faucit, Harriet, 140–142
Faucit, Helen, 140–142, 195
Feathers Inn (formerly the Golden Hinde), 161
Ferdinand II of Aragon, 31, 32, 33, 34
Ferries, 147, 212
Ferry Hill (now Bridge Street), 147, 149
"Field, Michael" (E. E. Cooper and K. H. Bradley), 211
Finucane, Wing Commander Paddy, 182
Fishing, 154–155
Fitzgerald, Edward, 195
Fitzherbert, Mrs M., 203
Fitzwilliam, Richard, 7th Viscount Fitzwilliam, 196
Foster, Sir Michael, 129
Frederick Augustus, Duke of York, 113
Frederick George, Prince of Wales (later George II), 74, 75, 77, 80
Frederick Louis, Prince of Wales, 81–83
Friars Lane, 197
Friars Stile Road, 200
Friends of Richmond Theatre, 144
Fuller, Thomas, 89–90
Fulsham, Benedict de, 5

Gainsborough, Thomas, 99, 209
Gainsborough Road, 209
Garrick, David, 137
Garrick Close (on site of Garrick Villa), 196
Gay, John, 109
George I, 74, 77, 126
George II, 77–78, 80, 82, 83, 109, 126, 127. See also Frederick George, Prince of Wales
George III, 88–90, 97, 98, 100–101, 130–131, 202, 209. See also George Frederick, Prince of Wales
George IV, 99, 203

Index